# ECHOES OF EAGLES

Charles Woolley

*First to the Front: The Aerial Adventures of 1st Lt. Waldo Heinrichs and the 95th Aero Squadron 1917–1918*

*The Hat in the Ring Gang: The Combat History of the 94th Aero Squadron in World War I*

*The Kaiser's Army in Color: Uniforms of the Imperial German Army as Illustrated by Carl Becker 1890–1910*

*Uniforms & Equipment of the Imperial German Army 1910–1918, A Study in Period Photographs* (Two Volumes)

*German Uniforms, Insignia & Equipment 1918–1923*


Bill Crawford

*Border Radio: Quacks, Yodelers, Pitchmen, Psychics and Other Amazing Broadcasters of the American Airwaves*
(with Gene Fowler)

*Stevie Ray Vaughan: Caught in the Crossfire*
(with Joe Nick Patoski)

*Cerealizing America: The Unsweetened Story of American Breakfast Cereal* (with Scott Bruce)

*Rock Stars Do the Dumbest Things* (with Margaret Moser)

*Movie Stars Do the Dumbest Things* (with Margaret Moser)

*Democrats Do the Dumbest Things*

*Republicans Do the Dumbest Things*

*Austin: An Illustrated History* (with David Humphrey)

*Texas Death Row: Executions in the Modern Era*

(with the SunRiver Cartel)

# ECHOES OF EAGLES

## A Son's Search for His Father and the Legacy of America's First Fighter Pilots

### CHARLES WOOLLEY

#### WITH BILL CRAWFORD

DUTTON

DUTTON
Published by Penguin Group (USA) Inc.
375 Hudson Street, New York, New York 10014, U.S.A.
Penguin Books Ltd, Registered Offices: 80 Strand, London WC2R 0RL, England
Penguin Books Australia Ltd, 250 Camberwell Road, Camberwell, Victoria 3124, Australia
Penguin Books Canada Ltd, 10 Alcorn Avenue, Toronto, Ontario, Canada M4V 3B2
Penguin Books (NZ) Ltd, Cnr Rosedale and Airborne Roads, Albany, Auckland 1310, New Zealand

Published by Dutton, a member of Penguin Group (USA) Inc.

First printing, November 2003
1 3 5 7 9 10 8 6 4 2

⑤ REGISTERED TRADEMARK—MARCA REGISTRADA

Library of Congress Cataloging-in-Publication Data

Woolley, Charles.
Echoes of eagles : a son's search for his father and the legacy of America's
first fighter pilots / Charles Woolley with Bill Crawford.
p.   cm.
ISBN 0-525-94757-4 (alk. paper)
1. Woolley, Charles H., d. 1962. 2. Fighter pilots—United States—Biography. 3. World War,
1914–1918—Aerial operations, American. 4. World War, 1914–1918—Campaigns—France.
I. Crawford, Bill, 1955– II. Title.
D606.W65 2003
940.4'4973—dc21          2003006461

Printed in the United States of America
Set in Caslon 224 Book
Designed by Leonard Telesca

This book is printed on acid-free paper. ∞

*To all fighter pilots, present and future*
*—may they fly in peace.*

# Contents

# ECHOES OF
# EAGLES

# CHAPTER 1

# In the Beginning

For the last forty years, I have been researching this story, the story of the young eagles, the men from Harvard, Yale, Princeton, Andover, and Groton who took to the skies over France in 1918 and became the first American fighter pilots. First Lieutenant Charles H. Woolley, United States Army Air Service, my father, a Boston boy who left the Massachusetts Institute of Technology to answer the call of duty, was one of these men.

Although I did not know it at the time, my research actually began when I was a twelve-year-old boy. I was unnerved, confused, and concerned by the Japanese attack at Pearl Harbor that December Sunday. Impending war had relocated our family. It had moved my father, my mother, and me from our home in suburban Boston to Washington, D.C. It had brought Dad, then a Reserve Major, back into the military. It was the world he loved: "fifty mission crush" visored hats; "pinks and greens," as the officers' uniforms were called; new aircraft to fly; and cryptic orders that would soon send him on missions around the globe.

The world of war brought a constant stream of visitors to the city of Washington and our home. Most of them were my father's old comrades from the Great War, seeking new commissions in the Army Air Corps and the opportunity to serve the cause. Many of these men were to become the leaders of America's "greatest generation," as Tom Brokaw was later to call them. They were men with straight backs, easy smiles, refined tastes, and sharp wits, who at the cocktail hour made us all laugh with their unending stories as they sipped their martinis, dry, very dry, with an olive.

Many of our guests had served in 1918 with Dad in the 95th Aero Squadron, United States Air Service, the first American-trained fighter squadron ever to see combat. There was Sumner Sewall, the recently elected Governor of Maine, a jovial bear of a man whom I knew from our summers in Maine; Harold Buckley, a fast-living Hollywood screenwriter and the author of a highly amusing history of the 95th; Jimmy Knowles, a fearless ace who had attained a top position in the pharmaceutical business; and Ted Curtis, General Ted Curtis, who was soon to be sent to England to create and help build the United States Eighth Air Force, the mightiest air force in the history of the world.

Others were with them in spirit: Quentin Roosevelt, the youngest son of Teddy, who put action into his father's bellicose words; Hamilton Coolidge, a classmate of Quentin's at Groton and Harvard, who could quote the poetry of Tennyson as well as he could un-jam a Vickers machine gun; Dick Blodgett from Williams College and West Newton, Massachusetts; "Big Bill" Taylor, one of the prep school boys who sailed overseas with the Andover Ambulance Unit; and Waldo Heinrichs, the missionary's son who disapproved of the binges prompted by good times as well as bad on the front.

The man who impressed me the most was Colonel Harold B. Willis, a six-foot-two-inch, barrel-chested man who before being commissioned in the U.S. Army Air Corps sported the French-tailored uniform of the American Field Service, a corps of volunteer ambulance drivers with whom he served in 1916 and again in 1940. Flamboyant in his light-blue French beret and full white moustache, Willis took extra time to talk with me as I stood self-consciously among those heroes in our living room. He told me stories about his service with the famous Lafayette Escadrille, the French fighter squadron manned by American volunteer pilots. The stories he told were always light, but laced with adventure. He told me about chasing German Rumpler two-seat observation planes that flew so high he could never quite reach them and nearly froze in the attempt; he told me about his special Spad equipped with an aerial camera with which he would dash behind enemy lines, snap pictures of some important subject, and then streak home with enemy Fokkers spraying hot lead in pursuit. He told me about the Spad in which he was shot down: "A real beauty, fast and steady as a rock. I painted a large green "W" on the upper wings so all would know where Willis was in a scrap." He was the first family friend to welcome me into the inner world of aerial warriors.

On one visit Willis casually said to me, "I'm going to send you a German Mauser rifle I picked up on a battlefield in France when I was an ambulance driver."

I was ecstatic! A Mauser! An actual German military rifle! To feel it, to hold it, to own it was the most exciting experience imaginable. To me, a rather lonely only child in the world of wartime Washington, the idea of holding a Mauser was as thrilling as wandering through my newly found favorite place, the Smithsonian Institution. When I first arrived in Washington, I fell in love, love at first sight, after my first visit to the Smithsonian. It was open every day, free of charge, and easy for a boy to get to, a pleasant ride for me on the "Friendship Heights" trolley car. I would lose myself for hours in the redbrick arts and sciences building known as "The Castle," staring at the vast exhibits of firearms, the large glass cases filled with full-figured mannequins wearing complete uniforms from the Civil War, the Spanish-American War, and best of all, the Great War, and the aviation building with its World War I fighter aircraft, the Spad XIII and the German Fokker D VII. These inanimate objects, so unfamiliar at first, became my companions, unforgotten companions who have been with me ever since. My grandmother's treasure-packed attic in Winchester, Massachusetts, paled by comparison to my newly discovered attic, the nation's attic. I had found a place where I felt I really belonged.

But to actually own a Mauser, to actually feel it! Mauser barrels were a beautiful blue color, the action finished silver bright, the sculptured stock a handsome honey brown. After Willis made his offer, I pestered my father almost every day, asking him when the gun would arrive.

"Where the hell is that damn gun?" Dad asked Willis several times over the next few months. Finally a large long package arrived by Railway Express, addressed to me. The Mauser! With trembling fingers I ripped apart the string and brown paper and there was revealed not a Mauser—but a rusted, Revolutionary War–era muzzle-loading musket. My hero had forgotten that he had given the German gun away years before. I was heartbroken, but I didn't give up. Some time later I was able to trade a rusty sword for a vintage Mauser with a broken stock. I was thrilled with the Mauser, but even more thrilled when Dad presented me at Christmas a brightly wrapped package that contained an original unbroken stock. My father wanted to reinforce my interest in things military. There was indeed a Santa Claus that year!

It is strange that at that time of my life, the war in the air never seemed as exciting or heroic as the war on the ground. Sure, I bought model airplanes and sent them flying across my bedroom on strings to battle German aircraft in imaginary dogfights. Before moving to Washington, I had spent many Saturday mornings in Dad's second-floor study, sitting with him at his oak desk, tracing the outlines of the various aircraft he had encountered in the Great War.

"That's an excellent Nieuport," he enthused over my crude rendering. "Now the Fokker, you see, had a much longer profile, like this." Spads, Albatroses, Sopwith Camels, I learned to draw them all, and learned which planes were the fastest, and which could climb the highest.

But I was more interested in the Mauser. Bullet-riddled helmets, rifles, bayonets—that is what I thought war souvenirs should be. Dad's souvenirs from the war were the type collected by an aviator, not a mud-spattered infantryman. Aviators' souvenirs were apt to be less war-like—decorated vases formed from empty shell casings, brass cigarette lighters shaped like French helmets, matchbox covers made from German belt buckles, a Luger pistol and a bone-handled folding knife.

One spring day in 1942, at Bolling Field near Washington, I took my place in the rear seat of an Army Air Corps AT6 airplane with Dad at the controls. My presence was covered by regulations. As a military dependent, I was entitled to one thirty-minute flight each year. I was thrilled. It was rare enough for me to spend thirty minutes with Dad, much less to fly with him!

His ground crew zipped me into a fleece-lined flying suit and strapped me into the rear cockpit of the AT6, a general purpose and advanced training aircraft. As we took off, I felt a rush in my stomach. As we banked steeply over the Capitol, I looked down at the tall white tower of the Washington Monument and began to understand for the first time my father's thrill in flight.

I recalled the insignia of the 95th Squadron he had once drawn for me. A defiant kicking mule. Airborne over Washington with Major Charles Woolley at the controls, I felt as if it were 1918. I felt that kicking mule. I felt Dad's flying skills, his reliability, his strength. I trusted him and knew he would bring us through the hard war days ahead. In those few moments, I felt that I was more than his son. I was his friend. His flying companion. An honorary member of the 95th Aero Squadron, United States Air Service. Diminutive to be sure, but strong, resourceful, and noble like the others. A young eagle.

It was not until after Dad died in 1962 that I was drawn once again into his extraordinary world. I began to seriously examine his papers, his logbooks, photo albums, and library. I was working in the financial services industry, but spent all my spare time scouring attics, barns, out-of-print bookstores, and antique shops, searching for antique cars, boats, old photographs, military curios, and books. My mother claimed that I had inherited the collecting bug from her father, who loved all old things and became an antiques dealer and antiquarian bookseller in his later life, with a shop on Charles Street, antiques row in Boston. My fascination with military history only grew stronger over the years. Before I became interested in World War I aviation, I joined the Company of Military Historians in 1955, and in the late 1960s became a frequent visitor to J. S. Canner, a large out-of-print bookseller in Boston.

"What do you think of this?" I asked Ray McGuire, who managed the bookstore's military department. Ray, an adventurer who had served with the French Foreign Legion in Indochina, had become a good friend. He carefully opened the book I had brought, *Up and At 'Em* by Lieutenant Colonel Harold E. Hartney, and read the inscription on the title page: "For Up and At 'Em Charlie Woolley (Major, U.S. Air Corps) a gallant officer of the 95th Aero Squadron in our outfit—one of the gang that made this book possible and got for me so much unearned satisfaction. With warmest regards and best wishes. Harold E. Hartney, Washington, DC, November 28, 1941."

I could tell Ray was impressed. He held the book gingerly, turning the pages carefully, skimming the story of the 95th Squadron and the other squadrons of the First Pursuit Group that Hartney had commanded. As he read, he seemed to be transported to the skies above the muddy flying fields of France, sitting in the cramped cockpit of a Spad, pushing the stick forward into a dive on the tail of a Fokker D VII, the exhaust pouring out of the straight pipes of the Hispano-Suiza eight-cylinder engine, waiting to squeeze the trigger of his Vickers machine guns and send his adversary to earth in a flaming wreck of wood, wire, and linen.

"Your father actually flew with the 95th Aero Squadron?"

"Sure," I answered with a shrug.

Ray shook his head, "Imagine flying and fighting in those Nieuports and Spads! They were nothing but motorized kites. Those guys invented aerial combat. They fought by their wits and improvised as they went along!"

I shared with Ray more of Dad's books: Harold Buckley's *Squadron 95*, Norman Archibald's *Heaven High, Hell Deep*, and *Riders in the Sky*, a full-length epic poem by Leighton Brewer of the 13th Aero Squadron. I showed him some of my father's war letters to my grandmother and his large, folded 1917 passport. We studied his brevet, a wallet-sized document bound in blue leather and imprinted *Pilote-Aviateur, Fédération Aéronautique Internationale—France*. Inside was his photo, stamped with an imprint of the Aéro-Club de France and his brevet number, 9,163. He was the 9,163rd licensed pilot in the history of French aviation.

We pored over other items, including his identity card issued by the American Expeditionary Forces, with two photographs signed by "Chas H. Woolley, 1st Lieut. A.S.S.C.U.S.R., Aviator." Always Chas, never Charles. Then came the photo albums that contained sepia-toned photographs of his first days in France driving an ambulance with the American Field Service, his flight training at Tours and Issoudun, his move to the front with the 95th, the first American fighter squadron, and later his time as Flight Commander with the 49th Aero Squadron, the "Wolf Pack." Ray's enthusiasm for the subject was infectious. The more details I uncovered relating to the military career of Charles H. Woolley, the more I wanted to learn.

I began searching out old squadron logs, combat reports, and personnel reports that were available in the U.S. Archives. I located a fifty-year-old 95th Squadron address book that, despite its age, yielded some names and contacts that were still valid. I began to write and to phone every lead, asking each if he or his family would be willing to share their war letters, diaries, photo albums, snapshots and reminiscences about that time, the dawn of American combat aviation. Being able to use the name of Woolley opened many doors. When asked what I planned to do with this information, I promptly answered, "Why, write a book, of course." True, I had never written a book, but I knew that I would do it someday and that I would learn a lot more about my father and his fascinating cronies in the process.

Traveling with my wife, Nancy, whose transcription skills proved to be invaluable, we covered the New England area and interviewed my dad's closest surviving friends. We visited Sumner Sewall's family in Maine and Ted Curtis, a six-victory ace and a vice president of Eastman Kodak, who had a summer place near the Sewalls. We met with Jimmy Knowles in Boston, where his son headed Massachusetts General Hospital. We found Bill Casgrain, one of the early casualties of the 95th, alive and well at his summer home in New Hampshire.

A name I had heard mentioned in those Washington gatherings of old eagles was Waldo Heinrichs. When doing some of my preliminary searching for veterans of the 95th, I discovered that Waldo had been a professor at Middlebury College after the war. The college, located in the town of the same name, was twenty-five miles from my wife's family home in Rochester, Vermont. The phone book indeed listed a Waldo Heinrichs in Middlebury, and with the triumphant feeling of a successful treasure hunter, I dialed the number. A woman answered. I quickly introduced myself and explained my reason for calling. The woman who had answered was Waldo's widow, Dotty, and she explained that he had died in 1954. She was willing to help, but explained that she only had a few photos and two diaries he had faithfully kept during his experiences in France. She willingly agreed to a visit the next time I was in Vermont. A date was set.

During our visit, she showed me the photos, and then out came the two small diaries, treasured reminders of the thirty-five years she had spent with a man she deeply loved. As I read through some of the small, neatly written lines, I realized that I was holding one of the most accurate and detailed records ever made of an American flyer's experience in World War I. I could not help but notice that there were some missing pages that had been neatly removed. Had they been removed by Waldo, or by his wife, who was so often mentioned on the other pages? What had they described? Sexual exploits, lapses in devotion to her, lapses in courage, spiritual floundering? A mystery that was not to be solved.

As I continued my search for squadron members, I visited with Walt Avery in a New Jersey suburb outside of New York City. In Washington, D.C., I met Johnny Mitchell, a wonderful, warm guy, and later, in the same city, the son of Carl Menckhoff, the German thirty-nine-victory ace that Avery had shot down in his first fight. All the flyers were eager to help. All were products of America's finest prep schools and colleges, among the best educated, most adventurous, most idealistic, and most patriotic men of their generation. Most regarded duty and honor as more than mere words. They understood that education and social position brought with them social responsibility, a responsibility that would lead them to be among the first Americans to give their lives overseas in defense of democracy. All supplied me with additional names and contacts that expanded our research network. With Nancy taking copious notes, my eyes and my heart opened to the story as it unfolded.

As word of my research spread, other scholars offered their kind assistance. In 1969, Royal Frey, at that time the head of the Air Force Museum at Wright-Patterson Air Force Base in Ohio, invited me to the fiftieth and last meeting of the Archie Club, an organization of First World War air combat veterans that my father helped found. At the meeting in Boston I met Eddie Rickenbacker, America's ace of aces, Doug Campbell, the first American-trained ace, "Sheep" Alexander, a highly decorated bomber pilot, and many others with remarkable stories to tell. They had all known "Chas," as they called my father, and welcomed me to their ranks.

My investigations led me to write and publish articles on the subject of military aviation. I became a member of *Cross and Cockade*, the Society of World War I Aero Historians, which published a quarterly journal, and in 1976, I became one of its editors. I continued to search for more diaries, letters, photos, and official reports, finding treasure troves at the Smithsonian, the United States Archives, the Library of Congress, and at the Musée de l'Air in Paris.

I found that I was the first to study the 95th in any depth, and one of the first to uncover the story of these aviators as men rather than as statistics or as unblemished heroes. I felt duty-bound to write the story, the *real* story, of a group of young men, with all their real strengths and real weaknesses. These men forged on the anvil of experience the first links of aerial combat knowledge that bind the F-16 pilots of today to the pilots of the Great War, who soared in the flimsy wood and canvas aircraft of 1918.

Now my research is complete, or as complete as I can make it. One can never completely detail a life, much less a group of lives tossed about by a world at war. The eyewitnesses, the aviators I interviewed, are all gone. I am more than seventy years old myself. The airfields now lie under apartment complexes and industrial sites. Even the aircraft, except for the few in museums, have long ago turned to dust. Writing this history has enabled me to appreciate and know my father and the men he led in combat.

Though it has been forty years since "The Colonel," as he was known in his later years, died in his beloved Maine home, he is as alive with me today as he was sixty years ago, when our spirits met in the cockpit of that AT6 as we cut a path together across the American sky.

# CHAPTER 2

# Some Family History

On September 9, 1894, as Minnie Lunger Woolley gazed at Charles Hildreth Woolley, her newborn son and first child, she was confident that he was born at the appropriate time to enter a world of stability and unlimited promise. The telephone had just come into her home on White Street in East Boston, Massachusetts. Soon electric bulbs would replace the gaslights in her bedroom where she sat cradling her son, and in the baby's room as well. Maroon, green, scarlet, and yellow trolley cars rolled beneath a web of electric lines that crisscrossed the city of Boston, so much faster, cleaner, and more reliable than the horse-drawn trolleys. Charles, her husband, had recently purchased the most up-to-date equipment for their flourishing family-owned business, a large laundry in East Boston. Garments and fashions were changing; new clothing styles required more professional attention than just the flatiron on the stove. Business was booming.

Good things were occurring all over the United States. Grover Cleveland was President and the country under his leadership enjoyed economic prosperity. Americans were confident, comfortable, enjoying all the best that life had to offer. In just fifteen years, Boston's population had grown from 250,000 to more than 450,000. The city could not compare in size with New York or Chicago, but the economy was strong and Boston's per-capita income was higher than that in most emerging commercial centers. Boston financiers had a large role in funding the great railroads, the engine of the American economy, and proper Bostonians were teaching New Yorkers how to manage and finance their burgeoning business trusts.

The Woolleys were a comfortable, well-established family of Boston's upper middle class. My grandfather, Charles Ambrose Woolley, was a successful and respected businessman, a devoted husband, who liked nothing better than returning from his office on Condor Street to his home on White's Hill above Boston Harbor and settling in with Minnie, whom he adored. Prior to their marriage, she had been a teacher and was artistically and, in a gentle way, socially more inclined than her husband. In their young married life, she had urged her husband to participate more actively in the sophisticated life of the city—to attend art exhibitions and concerts of the Boston Symphony Orchestra and to dine at the Ritz, the Parker House, or the Hotel Vendome. But after giving birth to Charles, then a daughter who died at age six, and then another son, James, born eleven years after Charles, Minnie was content to confine her life to overseeing the society of her household—her cook, her maid, her husband, and her two unruly boys.

"Charles," she scolded on more than one occasion, "a tricycle is not meant to be ridden through the halls of this house!"

East Boston was a mercantile community perched on the edge of the sea. In many ways, the Woolley family and the entire community of East Boston moved with the tides of the Atlantic Ocean; dry goods, groceries, and even mail crossed Boston Harbor bringing the necessities to this satellite of the main city. Minnie and her boys often took the ferry to Boston to visit the State House Tower, Faneuil Hall, or even, on one occasion, to watch the elephants of the Ringling Brothers' Circus parade down Boylston Street.

The family home stood just a few blocks above Boston Harbor and the Mystic River. Constructed for his family by Donald McKay, a master clipper ship designer and builder, the interior of the house had the feeling of a ship. And well it should. There had been no finer or faster craft in the world than McKay's *Flying*

*Cloud*, which in 1851 crossed from Canton, China, to Boston in eighty-nine days, a record.

Ship's carpenters, barrel makers, sailmakers, cordwainers, and caulkers swarmed over East Boston's shores in the mid-nineteenth century, many of them employed at McKay's shipyard at the bottom of White's Hill, just a few blocks from his home. When modern and more economical steamships began to replace the clippers, McKay's fortunes declined. In the 1870s, he sold his home to James Woolley, my great-grandfather.

James was also a man of the sea. He owned and operated the Commercial Tow Boat Company and knew McKay from their business dealings in the harbor. He owned, in addition to a towboat business, the Boston Submarine Dredging Company, operating from East Boston. The Woolleys' gigantic steam dredge *Goliath*, a monster of the age, did much of the work dredging the Charles River, turning what was once a foul-smelling marsh into today's fashionable Back Bay.

My grandfather was proud of his family's martial history. He boasted of his uncle, who had served in the Federal Navy during the Civil War with Admiral Farragut, and who had witnessed the epic battle between the U.S.S. *Kearsage* and the Confederate raider C.S. *Alabama* off the coast of France. On more than one occasion, Grandfather stood with my father in front of an oil portrait of another ancestor, painted by the great English portraitist, Sir Joshua Reynolds. The subject's proud brown eyes, his firm mouth, his hair cut in bangs in the style of the late eighteenth century, and his dark-blue sea captain's uniform with its shining brass buttons intrigued the young Woolley.

Grandfather explained to Dad, who later passed the story on to me:

> Sir Joshua Reynolds, the famous English artist, painted that portrait of the first Charles Woolley to come to the United States. He left his home in Newcastle-upon-Tyne, England, seeking more important commands, and sailed for America shortly after the Revolutionary War. He first settled in Newport, Rhode Island, then was given command of a ship out of Bos-

ton. He moved to the city in 1790, where he met and married Susannah Bentley in 1796. Her father, Joshua Bentley, was a dedicated American patriot and a friend of the engraver and silversmith Paul Revere. On the night of April 18, 1775, he and another boatman had rowed Revere across the Charles River to Charlestown, maintaining silence by muffling their oars with their wives petticoats. Once on shore, Revere leapt on his horse and rode to Concord to warn the Minutemen with his famous cry, 'The British are coming!' Later, Joshua Bentley served as a commissioned officer in the Massachusetts forces of the Continental Army against the British.

Then there was Captain Zachariah Hildreth, whose name you bear, who was born in Groton, Massachusetts, in 1754. In his twenties he commanded an infantry unit in the Revolutionary War.

I suspect my father delighted in the romantic images of the sea captains, patriots, and warriors who were his ancestors. They were the family heroes: men in uniform, commanders of ships, and leaders of men.

Throughout his East Boston boyhood, the sea and ships fascinated him. He sat at the edge of the harbor with his friends, throwing stones at the gulls, watching the multi-masted coastal schooners ghosting into the harbor. He and his friends were absorbed by the sight of enormous oceangoing freighters unloading mysterious and exotic cargoes from Shanghai, Bombay, Liverpool, and other ports from around the world, and muscled "bully-boy" stevedores moving the crates through the tendrils of fog.

After leaving elementary school, my father daily rode one of the numerous ferries plying the harbor, then hopped a trolley to take him to his studies at Mechanical Arts High School. There he studied drafting, mechanical design, mathematics, and other subjects of a more technical nature. He also studied Latin, literature, and modern languages, mandatory subjects for any well-educated boy in 1910. He was a good student with a flair for foreign languages.

Outside the classroom, he absorbed even more. He became

fascinated with internal-combustion engines, the noisy, gasoline-fed mechanical beasts that were revolutionizing transportation and industry. The horse was no longer the preferred and fashionable means of transportation for the more prominent citizens of Boston. The Woolleys and their friends putt-putted through the city streets in Wintons, Maxwells, Reos, and the steam-driven Stanley, manufactured in Newton, Massachusetts, all terrifying the horses that continued to haul local freight for decades to come. Charles felt that the days of the horse were numbered. The internal-combustion engine was here to stay.

The ships that most caught Dad's boyhood interest were the gravity-defying ships of the air. He stood among the crowd of 30,000 fashionably dressed aviation enthusiasts clad in boaters and wide-brimmed straw hats at the annual Harvard Air Meet held at Squantum on a flat field next to the waters of Boston Harbor. There he craned his neck skyward to watch Claude Grahame-White, Thomas Sopwith, and Charles Hamilton sporting jackets, ties, puttees, goggles, and plaid plus fours, with their caps turned backward as they navigated the Wrights' biplane, Glenn Curtiss's latest design, and flying machines of wood, wire, and canvas through the air. Flying thrilled young Charles more than auto, bicycle, or boat racing, the mechanical sports of his age.

Not only my dad, but a whole generation of young men and women could see themselves flying into the modern world alongside trendsetters like Eleanora Sears, who had set Boston society on its ear when she took to the air in men's clothes. They learned quickly and only too well the dangers of early aviation when Harriet Quimby, the first American woman licensed to fly, crashed to her death at the Harvard-Boston Air Meet at Squantum in 1912.

My grandparents moved from East Boston to the suburb of Winchester, a pleasant town on the Boston & Maine Railroad line, nine easy miles from the city, at about the same time Dad entered the Massachusetts Institute of Technology. He joined a fraternity and moved into its house on Commonwealth Avenue. A photograph of the time shows him standing with members of his fraternity, a confident young man in a vested suit, high starched collar, striped tie, watch chain and fob, and a cigarette casually held in his hand.

At MIT, he majored in Course XI, Sanitary Engineering, no doubt under the influence of a father who approved of his son's interest in things mechanical and wanted him to take over the family laundry business. According to the MIT catalog of 1914, Course XI was described as "essentially one of Civil Engineering," designed for students with an interest in public health. In addition to regular civil engineering classes such as surveying and plotting, quantitative analysis, and topographical drawing, my father took courses in organic chemistry, general bacteriology, and water supply and wastes disposal.

However, he found this course of study less than thrilling. He excelled in languages—French and German, and had a passion for literature and architecture. He was also more intrigued by economic theory than industrial water analysis.

No wonder. The world seemed to be exploding. In 1916, the Mexican revolutionary Pancho Villa attacked a United States army post in Arizona, killing twenty-six American soldiers on American soil. General John J. "Black Jack" Pershing led a force of 15,000, including eight Curtiss JN-3 "Jenny" airplanes, into the mountainous deserts of northern Mexico to search out the terrorists. It was the first time that airplanes were used by the American army, but that air power was not enough to capture the outlaw bandit.

Most Bostonians skimmed over the news that Gavrilo Princip, a young Bosnian nationalist, had shot Archduke Franz Ferdinand of Austria and his wife, the Duchess of Hohenberg, in the streets of Sarajevo on June 28, 1914, after the Archduke's chauffeur made a wrong turn. The rest of the world took notice of the event. The assassin's bullet had pitched all of Europe into a war that no nation seemed to want.

During the summer of 1914, most were convinced that the war would be over quickly. Either Allied forces or the Central powers would doubtless achieve a fast victory. Most, however, were amazed as the struggle bogged down into a long siege of trench warfare marked by pointless, tragic infantry assaults and massive artillery barrages.

By the end of 1914, the opposing sides faced each other from established defensive positions along a line of battle that ran for

450 miles from Nieuport on the coast of Belgium through Flanders and western France to the mountainous Swiss border. It was called the Western Front to distinguish it from other war zones that had erupted in Russia, the Balkans, Italy, and the Middle East.

In the age before radio or television, the only way those interested could follow the progress of the war was through the printed news reports that were filtered through a tightly censored press. It was a time for new terms: the front lines; the trenches; No Man's Land; "over the top."

American press coverage of the war was a laundry list of German barbarisms: the invasion of neutral Belgium; the burning of the great medieval library of Louvin; attacks by German submarines, or "U-boats," on unarmed neutral merchant ships. There were even unsubstantiated and false rumors that German troops were bayoneting Belgian babies, rendering French corpses into soap, and crucifying Canadian prisoners.

My father and his contemporaries, many of whom had personal and professional contacts with England and France, felt no moral dilemma in choosing sides. The Germans appeared to be power-mad militarists, launching a war that threatened the entire civilized world.

From a technological standpoint, the war was intriguing for young, mechanically inclined men. The machine gun, trench telephone communications, the dreadnought class of battleships, poison gas, long-range artillery—it was a war of innovation as each side sought a breakthrough in weaponry that would give them a winning technology on the battlefield. Advances in aircraft design and performance were astonishing, as France's Louis Breguet, England's Thomas Sopwith, and Holland's Anthony Fokker led the world's most brilliant aviation engineers to transform within a few years what had been hobbyist vehicles of sport into birds of war. The morale of the combatant countries fell as conditions at the front became appalling and casualties in the ground war mounted. To bolster public morale, propaganda ministers and the press promoted aviators as special heroes of the war, the knights of the air, daring combatants who fought in the skies over France.

The promotion was effective. The more eager and adventurous young Americans could not wait for the United States to enter the war, so they volunteered to serve under the flags of Britain, France, and Italy.

Many volunteered for service as non-combatant ambulance drivers. Their firsthand accounts of driving at the front were published in Leslie Buswell's *Ambulance No. 10*, William Stevenson's *At the Front in a Flivver*, as well as in the pages of *Atlantic Monthly*, *Collier's*, *Munsey's*, and other leading magazines. Teddy Roosevelt wrote the foreword to "With the American Ambulance in France," an article that appeared in the September 15, 1915 issue of *Outlook* magazine and was written by James McConnell, who later flew for France with the Lafayette Escadrille:

> Every young man just leaving college . . . ought to feel it incumbent on him at this time either to try to render assistance to those who are battling for the right [thing] on behalf of Belgium, or else to try to fit himself to help his own country if in the future she is attacked as wantonly as Belgium has been attacked . . .

Rebuffed in his efforts to lead a fighting force to France—a force akin to the Rough Riders he had recruited and led twenty years earlier in Cuba—Roosevelt talked, wrote, and did whatever possible to promote the war effort. He helped lead a private effort to train Americans for the military, an effort that became known as the "Plattsburgh Idea," after the location of the summer training camps in Plattsburgh, New York. The facilities at Plattsburgh went back to the War of 1812. In 1915, General Leonard Wood conceived the "Plattsburgh Idea" as a way to maintain a reserve of trained civilians to draw upon in case of a military emergency. The "Idea" was voluntary summer training lasting four weeks, the cost of which was borne by the students. The course appealed primarily to professional and business men, and was intended to provide a small but influential cadre with basic military skills and enthusiasm for the military service. Other military training programs sprang up on college campuses throughout the country. Three thousand uniformed members of the Harvard

Student Regiment were cheered as they marched down Boston's Columbus Avenue on May 27, 1916 as part of a "preparedness" parade. Some Americans did talk cynically about the war. They said it was no wonder J. P. Morgan and other financiers were in support. After all, they were supporting the British with profitable lines of credit. But the cynics and pacifists were in a minority. Teddy Roosevelt's youngest son, Quentin, a Harvard student, described the feeling of many college students when he wrote to his father in the winter of 1917, "We are a pretty sordid lot, aren't we, to want to sit looking on while England and France fight our battles."

As the war progressed, most Americans came to support the Allied cause. On May 17, 1915, a German U-boat sank the British passenger liner *Lusitania*. Among the 1,198 civilian passengers killed were 128 American men, women, and children. On January 31, 1917, the Germans declared unrestricted submarine warfare on all ships, including American ships. The next month, the United States severed diplomatic relations with Germany. On March 1, 1917, the American press published a chilling telegram from Germany's Foreign Minister Alfred Zimmermann to the German minister in Mexico that American and British intelligence agents had intercepted and decoded. In the telegram, Zimmermann authorized the minister to push the Mexicans for a declaration of war against the United States. In return, Zimmermann promised that Germany would support the return of the "lost territory in Texas, New Mexico, and Arizona" to the Republic of Mexico. When the contents of the infamous Zimmermann telegram were published in March 1917, it was no longer a question of whether or not America would enter the war. The only question was when.

My father did not want to wait for America's formal declaration of war before he joined the Allied effort. The idea of volunteering to drive an ambulance intrigued him. At the war's outbreak, the Ambulance Service had replaced the horse-drawn carts that hauled most of the wounded from the battlefield with an *ambulance*, the French word for hospital. The word *ambulance* by 1917 had come to refer to the vehicles that were increasingly used to transport the wounded, one of the technological innovations of the Great War.

American drivers and American cars, in the form of Henry Ford's Model Ts, were particularly well suited for ambulance work. Volunteering for an American-led ambulance service was a way of helping the Allied cause without serving under a foreign flag. The American Red Cross organized one volunteer group, but the organization that attracted Dad's attention was the American Ambulance Field Service, founded by A. Piatt Andrew, and which was later to become known as the American Field Service, or AFS.

In 1914, after a distinguished career in education, finance, and politics, Piatt Andrew had traveled to Europe to see how he could support the war effort. He used his personal connections to secure a job driving an ambulance for the American Hospital in Paris, a private institution established and supported by American expatriates. Fed up with the inefficiency of the British and French ambulance services, Andrew decided to build his own organization. He succeeded in creating an organization of young American volunteers for the French army to drive Model T Fords outfitted with specially designed ambulance bodies.

In the spring of 1917, my father attended a lecture by actor and ambulance service veteran Leslie Buswell. He watched a recruiting film, *Our American Boys in the European War,* produced by the French government for viewing in the United States.

I have watched the film, which is almost as moving today as it must have been more than eighty years ago when my father first saw it. Its flickering black-and-white images depict smiling American boys in French uniforms hand-cranking their Model T Fords in the falling snow, climbing onto the canvas-covered driver's seats, and bouncing over the shell-pocked muddy roads of a ruined French village. The film shows clean-cut college boys bandaging muddied, grizzled French soldiers, carrying them on their backs, laughing as they carefully place the wounded in the rear of an ambulance; American and French youths smiling and watching soldiers sing bits from *Carmen* while performing on a makeshift stage. Americans smile sheepishly as French officers kiss them on the cheek, commending their bravery. Yankees and

Frenchmen celebrate an outdoor mass, their ambulances forming a background for the altar.

Charles Woolley decided to enlist for a six-month tour of service with the AFS. As he filled out the application papers, he found that he met all the qualifications. He was over eighteen and an American citizen born to parents who were native to the United States. He even knew how to drive and repair automobiles, something that was highly recommended but not required.

Dad had no problem soliciting six letters of recommendation from local prominent citizens, but he was a bit anxious when he submitted his completed application. The AFS was so popular and screened its applicants so carefully that it accepted only about four out of every ten young men who applied.

A few days after turning in his paperwork, my father got the news that he had been accepted! He was going to France! He would have to drop out of MIT before his graduation, but that was acceptable.

My grandfather, with mixed emotions, agreed to help with the initial expenses. The grand total was $350: $170 for passage to France, $90 for a uniform and equipment, and $90 for six months of incidental expenses. Not a king's ransom, but in those days, a considerable sum. Today, that would be over $2,000. Dad purchased a steamship ticket for an April sailing, then exchanged the rest of the money for American Express Company checks, as suggested by the AFS literature.

As his departure date drew near, he traveled to New York. There he picked up the passport that would allow him passage to the war zone in Europe. The passport, which I have today, is an oversized, folded, single sheet of well-worn vellum with heavy creases, bearing stamps of the Consulat Général de France in New York and the U.S. State Department. In red ink appears the notice, "This passport expires Sept. 29, 1917 unless previously renewed," the date that marked the end of his six-month enlistment in the AFS. The reason for travel to France is listed simply as "Hospital Work."

The document provides a description of my father written in a flourishing hand: "Age: 22 years, Height: 5 feet 11 inches, Forehead: low, Eyes: brown, Nose: short, Mouth: small, Chin: round,

Hair: brown-wavy, Complexion: sallow, Face: oval." The passport photo tells a more vivid story. It shows an attractive young man with a frank, open face, a strong full neck, and powerful sloping shoulders in a well-tailored dark suit, starched collar, and neatly knotted tie.

Armed with his passport, his American Express Company checks, a few dollars in cash, and a small steamer trunk, he boarded the S.S. *Chicago* and sailed for France.

# CHAPTER 3

# *Uniforms Without Rank*

"**M**y health is fine," my father wrote home to my grandmother from the waters of the Atlantic in early April 1917. "My courage good."

The "old *Chicago,*" as my father described it, "was a sort of glorified freighter capable of a speed under forced draft of about thirteen knots . . . deeply laden and steady as a church." He roomed with two other American Ambulance Field Service volunteers, in his words, "splendid fellows." Some of the "boys" on board had signed up to drive ambulances with the Norton-Hartjes unit of the American Red Cross Volunteer Ambulance Corps, led by Piatt Andrew's former partners. "The personnel of the latter organization," my father noted proudly, "is not nearly as good as that of the American Ambulance."

The boys on board the S.S. *Chicago* enjoyed clear spring weather, accompanied by a cool wind. They spent most of their time on deck playing shuffleboard, or reading books from the ship's well-stocked library. In the evening, they enjoyed the concerts of La Société des Instruments Anciens, a French quintet returning home, played bridge, or joined the other volunteers in the smoking room.

As the *Chicago* steamed through the submarine zone for two days and two nights of the five-day voyage from Halifax, all on board looked anxiously over the ocean swells for signs of a U-boat attack, pointing at unusual waves and wondering how the wake of a torpedo actually looked. They speculated about life at the front, about the lethal new weapon, gas, and about the food—horsemeat or worse. They joked with each other about why they had volunteered in the first place, and always responded, "Damifino."

One of the passengers was a Frenchman from Los Angeles, a bank cashier who had been conscripted in the French army at the start of the war. He had fought in the trenches, rising to the rank of sergeant, and was returning to France after spending time in Los Angeles on furlough. He offered an informal class in French, which gave the volunteers their first opportunity to learn the military words and phrases needed at the front. Serving under a French officer, dealing with French troops, and serving as part of the French required words like *blessés*, the wounded; *grands blessés*, the seriously wounded; *brancardier*, stretcher-bearer; *éclat*, shell-fragments; *essence*, gasoline; *mitrailleuse*, machine gun; several all-purpose curses, and the phrase *C'est la guerre*, "That's war," a phrase used by soldiers and civilians alike to explain any situation.

On April 25, 1917, the *Chicago* sailed up the reddish waters of the Gironde to Bordeaux, docked in the colorless dawn, and disgorged its cargo of war supplies, Model T Ford chassis, and gentlemen volunteers.

The American boys, slightly disheveled in a mixture of flannel shirts, civilian suits, and various caps, assembled on the crowded wharf. They were marched, out of step, through the city streets, which were stacked with the essentials of war packed in enormous boxes and crates covered with waterproof tarpaulins. They were halted at the railroad station. Several took chairs at a nearby small café and sat checking their passports, fingering the unfamiliar French francs and nervously smoking cigarettes while waiting for the train that would take them to Paris and *la guerre*.

"The quaint French villages were scattered on all sides," Dad wrote in a letter home describing his rail journey. "Soldiers on leave were everywhere, women working in the fields, military motor trucks, aeroplanes, all in a constantly changing bewildering succession. . . ." As the train crossed the Seine, they glimpsed the towers of Notre Dame emerging above the mists of the river.

Enchantment turned to business at the Paris railroad station Gare d'Austerlitz, which handled the rail traffic from the south and west of France. A khaki-uniformed man met the volunteers and bundled them and their baggage into the rear of several Model T ambulances. They were whizzed to the neighborhood of Passy along the banks of the Seine and deposited in front of the AFS headquarters at 21 Rue de Raynouard, a 300-year-old château known by the ambulance drivers as "Twenty-One."

Dad was awed by the place. "The entrance hall is of white marble and there are wonderful marble pillars supporting columns in many of the downstairs rooms," he wrote. "Hardwood floors everywhere . . . secret passages to the Seine abound behind mirrors and in unexpected corners. . . ." He warmed himself briefly at the two huge stoves on the stone staircase leading to the "cave," as the dining hall was called. He gulped a meal of hot milk, coffee, sugar, and bread from a big tin mess kit, and placed his few belongings on an empty bunk in the basement. He walked down to a subterranean passage, filled a waiting tin cup, and sipped from a pool of reddish spring water, *Les Eaux de Passy*, which visitors had enjoyed since the seventeenth century. Wandering out to the terrace, he gazed across to the Seine and spied the slim gray lines of the Eiffel Tower. Paris.

The next morning, Piatt Andrew—"Doc," as he was called— welcomed the new volunteers as they sat on the lawn of the château, overlooking five acres of parkland that sloped gradually down to the banks of the Seine from the hill of Passy. "Doc" Andrew stood up in a spotless, sharply creased British-style uniform and spoke with the crisp manner of the Ivy League economics professor he had once been.

He explained that for the next six months the boys would wear the uniform of the American Field Service with the grenade insignia of the French military automobile service, but no other insignia of military rank. For all intents and purposes, they would be treated like French foot soldiers, better know as *poilus*— literally, the hairy ones.

Andrew described the glorious history of 21 Rue de Raynouard.

Rousseau had written part of his *Le Devin du Village* in the long gallery of the château. Benjamin Franklin had often walked through its grounds when he lived in Paris from 1777 to 1785. Balzac had lived across the street, and Bartholdi, sculptor of the Statue of Liberty, had been a frequent visitor. Andrew recommended that every volunteer visit the half-scale model of Lady Liberty located nearby.

Piatt warned the boys to steer clear of the evils of wine and women, and concluded his remarks with what he hoped was a stirring evocation of "the quenchless spirit and unfaltering will" of the French people. "You, who are here, will realize, as the days go by, that you are not merely here to serve France, but that in a much more real sense, you are here to serve your own country . . . *Tous et tout pour la France*," Andrew said, quoting the motto of the American Field Service. "Everyone and all for France. We all feel it. We all mean it. It is forever ours."

After the introductory lecture, Dad rushed to various French government offices to collect his *Permis de Séjour*, his *Permis de Conduire*, and the other documents he would need.

Back at "Twenty-One," he approached the front of "Old 74," the Model T on which head instructor Bobby Gouch first tested the volunteers. Like all AFS vehicles, the Model T light chassis had been shipped from the U.S., the body specially built at a Paris workshop from matched boarding of tough mahogany. Despite his connections, Andrew was forced to pay the Ford Motor Company full price for the vehicles and for the spare parts to keep them running. Because of the chassis' short wheelbase, the wooden bodies projected far beyond the rear wheels, giving the ambulances an odd, unbalanced look—in the words of one driver, like an "overfed june bug."

The Model Ts could accommodate three stretcher cases or five sitting cases, and in extreme instances, even seven or eight sitting cases. *Blessés* were grateful for the relatively smooth ride of the *petites voitures*. Other military vehicles of the time had solid rubber tires and heavy, coil-type springs that made for rough riding on anything but paved roads. These "little machines" had a high ground clearance that enabled them to pass over rutted and mountainous roads and wallow through muddy plains.

Though smaller than the ambulances used by the French and the British, the Model T more than made up for its lack of size with its durability and its simplicity of design. The "Tin Lizzie" was an auto built from interchangeable parts. It featured a four-cylinder engine cast in a single block; the cylinder head was bolted to the block to cover the valves, the oil pan attached to the underside. The engine design made the valves and upper cylinders accessible for easy service. The Model T had no oil pump, no water pump, and no fuel pump. Many times, drivers had to climb long, steep hills in reverse to keep gas flowing from the gas tank to the gravity-fed carburetor. Despite its idiosyncrasies, this "flivver" was a masterpiece of engineering efficiency. Total cost for the chassis, shipping, and building of the customized body was $1,600.

To pass his driver's test, Dad first had to start "Old 74." He bent down and gripped the handle of the crank below the radiator. He was careful not to wrap his thumb around the metal shaft, knowing a backfire could spin the crank backward and snap a thumb in a second. He spun the crank, the engine fired, and he climbed onto the driver's seat, grabbed the throttle—one of the two levers just below the steering wheel—and set the engine speed. Grabbing the other lever, he set the spark, advancing or retarding it depending on the speed of the engine. Two pedals operated by his left foot controlled the shifting of gears, while his right foot was used on the brake pedal. Brakes wore out quickly, as did the driver's shoes, after endless hours of pedal-jamming on the rutted muddy roads of the battlefields.

He passed his test, as he knew he would, receiving a French army driver's license. Next came a complete medical examination and the painful inoculation against typhoid. As others predicted, this laid him low for a few days, but he went on being measured for his uniform and shopping for necessities for duty at the front. Those first days of May 1917 were busy ones at "Twenty-One," but there was still time for sight-seeing, shopping in the well-filled market stalls of Passy, riding the Metro for fifteen centimes, taking in a cinema, snapping photos, and mingling with the crowds at the Place du Trocadero.

Everywhere he went, there were American flags hanging out

of the windows. All the talk was of America and the Americans who had just entered the war. "An army of millions," the Americans had promised the Allies, but in the spring of 1917, my father was one of the few Americans who actually were headed toward the front. And he was working for the French army, not the American.

"Paris," my father wrote. "She is wonderful and always beautiful."

Over five o'clock tea in the salon of "Twenty-One," he talked with other new recruits and *permissionaires* ambulance drivers on leave who knew what was happening at the front. There were no ranks in the ambulance corps. Everyone served on a first-name basis. The volunteers could talk with perfect frankness.

Suddenly, he was forced to make a difficult choice. The day before, Andrew had announced the formation of a new branch of the service: transportation of supplies, under the supervision of the ambulance service. These supplies, mostly ammunition, would be driven up to the lines in *camions*, or trucks, five-ton Whites and Pierce-Arrows. Some thirty men from Cornell University had already volunteered for the new service. There was a need for twenty-five more.

Dad waited for his posting. Currently, there were too few ambulances for drivers, and it would be two or three weeks before he could get to the front. It was his introduction to the balance needed in modern war. This was a war of tonnage, and to many it was more important to get the tonnage of French shells to the front than to haul the victims of German shells away from the front.

My father was torn. He had volunteered to bring wounded men from battle, not transport armaments to battle.

But a spot opened up; a driver was going on leave from SSU 9, one of the ambulance units at the front, and Dad decided to take the posting until the other driver returned. He hoped for a transfer later to Salonika, which was described as a more dangerous and difficult front. The night of his decision he wrote his mother that he prayed he would show up well in the "splendid company that I am about to find myself."

The newly assigned drivers left Paris by train on May 9, 1917, headed for the front. Seven hours and forty-five minutes later, they disembarked, took their places in the back of an ambulance, and rode out to their quarters in the village of Vandœvre, near Nancy, about ten miles from the front. Upon arrival, they found the unit *en repos*—not on active duty—a rather common occurrence for the ambulance units on the quieter fronts.

Like other units, SSU 9 was under the command of a French officer of the Automobile Service, in this case a Lieutenant Ostheimer, and two Americans with the rank of *Sous*-Lieutenant. The French also provided one small truck, a touring car, a sergeant, a corporal, and two enlisted chauffeurs. The Americans provided two American mechanics, twenty-two ambulances, one repair truck, a touring car, and spare parts. One of the two Americans with officer rank in SSU 9 was the *Commandant adjoint*, Walter "Jep" Jepson. A University of Nevada man from the town of Sparks, Nevada, Jep had served with the unit at Bar-le-Duc and Verdun in 1916. He had steered his flivver through the chaos of towns and landscapes devastated by heavy explosives. Driving back and forth from the *poste de secours* at night without headlights to avoid German artillery, he had endured fists banging against the side of the ambulance and the cries of *"Doucement!"* ("Slow down!"). Worse than the cries was the silence, which all too often meant that the wounded had died.

Jep's sous-chef, or assistant, was George Cogswell, a Harvard man from Cambridge, Massachusetts, who was serving his second six-month tour of duty with the AFS. Jep and Cogswell were highly thought of by the group of forty American volunteer drivers under their somewhat loose control. They did not demand strict military discipline, but were not lenient with the fellows when they erred.

A photo from one of my father's albums shows the exterior of his quarters in an "old, old house" where he and two others shared a room on the third floor. He explained in a letter to my grandfather that one-third of the room was shelves, one-third was covered in straw, and the other third was lined with three beds. "These my roommates and I occupy. The beds are made with an iron frame in the shape of an ellipse, with a canvas laced in to lie on, and the whole business is set on legs. These beds fold up very small and are carried in the cars when we are on the move."

Life at SSU 9, while *en repos*, was quite pleasant; breakfast, available before nine, consisted of bread, toasted, *confiture*, or jam, and black coffee, sweetened, to be consumed while standing. Work began at nine, which consisted of automotive maintenance, greasing twenty-odd fittings on the vehicle, checking the oil and water, testing the commutator that sent the current to the coils, washing the vehicles and repainting them. Five-man crews were assigned to work as a team, but in the Woolley crew, one was such a poor painter that the others refused to let him paint. Another was a fair letterer who practiced his skills going from car to car, which further reduced the crew to three.

Mealtime was a highlight for the boys. Dad wrote:

> Lunch is served at 11:30, and consists of soup (very good), meat (usually liver) and vegetables, fresh and well-cooked, bread, jam and coffee, with cheese thrown in. At noon we generally go into the garden to have our coffee (a very beautiful place). Dinner is the same as lunch and is most welcome when the time comes. We have a fine cook and the grub is very good. Places at the table are reserved by staking out a claim, which means sticking your knife in the table in front of the place where you want to sit.

In this letter to my grandfather, Dad asked him to send the largest folding knife he could find, adding that knives were used for many purposes; eating was only one of them. My grandfather complied with this request, and as a very small boy I recall being shown the large, bone-handled jackknife during a lecture given on "things to be careful of. . . ."

In general, conditions were better than Andrew had outlined in that first lecture at "Twenty-One." They were not being served the standard French army fare of canned beef or horse meat (called *singe*, or "monkey meat"); raw red wine known as *pinard*, which was often referred to in the most uncomplimentary terms; and round loaves of bread a foot in diameter and usually two weeks old, as revealed by a baking date stamped on the bottom. One driver who had sampled the bread described it as "often brittle, like a piece of wood, and about as palatable as soft pine."

The drivers learned to respect the *poilus*, with their thick moustaches, faded "horizon blue" uniforms and their fatalistic sense of humor. They spoke of their wounds *"Ça pique, mon vieux, mais ça ne fait rien—allez!"* ("That stings, my friend, but it is nothing—go!"), and they joked as they filled out their wound tag *"Oui, c'est une guerre de papier. Donnez-moi une cigarette."* ("Yes it is a war of paper. Give me a cigarette.") After almost three years of war in the most ghastly of conditions, the silence of the French infantrymen was their most eloquent expression. Their unrelenting resolve was their most powerful weapon.

When not on duty, the volunteers walked the pleasant rural lanes, played a vague sort of football, and staged boxing matches with enormously oversized gloves. Souvenir hunting for shell casings and brass fuses from the German 77 mm guns was another popular pastime. They gave their finds to French soldiers at a nearby camp, who were more than happy to craft them into vases, letter openers, and cigarette lighters in exchange for a few francs or some good American tobacco.

In one of his last letters from SSU 9, written in mid-May, Dad complained that there was little news to write about, but he hoped that a move would take place in a week or so. Poor weather had stopped the German air raids over Nancy. He and the others in his unit had found a wonderful pool for swimming. Fed by a natural spring, it was constantly at a temperature of eighty degrees and, therefore, a pleasure to use. They had good shower baths, but he was running low on soap. "A dozen cakes of that precious stuff over here would surely be appreciated," he wrote his mother.

The Americans attended a party given by one of the French soldiers connected to the unit to celebrate his own promotion to sergeant. There was a fine dinner of soup, roast beef, french-fried potatoes, asparagus with hard-boiled eggs and sauce, lettuce salad, bread and butter, fancy crackers, coffee, St. Julien cheese, common *pinard* wines, and then champagne! After dinner, there were toasts and singing in English and in French. Out of courtesy to a regiment of French Zouaves who were billeted nearby and had to be in their quarters by 8:30 P.M., the party ended early and SSU 9 went back to their quarters "to talk it over." My father recalled the party jokingly, "Oh, the horrors of war."

The greatest horror the men in SSU 9 experienced was the horror of inactivity. The most common gripe among the ambulance drivers was that there was too little to do. One volunteer called it "the dullest monotony imaginable." Another complained, "I'll go crazy if we don't get out of this soon. . . ."

Orders came on June 15 for SSU 9 to join the 11th Division of French infantry in the region of Pont-à-Mousson. Rumors said that the Germans were about to launch an offensive in that area and an attack could happen at any time. Action at last! The drivers checked their cars, reviewed their assignments, and received warm encouragement from "Jep."

Like most divisions of the French army, the 11th included three infantry regiments and an artillery regiment, each with its own stretcher-bearers and doctors who gave hasty dressings at first-aid stations close to the first lines. The 11th Division, in addition to the regimental doctors and bearers, had its own corps of surgeons, doctors, attendants, and stretcher-bearers called the G.B.D. (*Groupe des Brancardiers Divisionaire*) who maintained at least one dressing station, or *poste de secours*, where reexaminations were made and, if necessary, further treatment given. Additionally, the division maintained a sorting station, or triage, assigning cases according to their nature and gravity to particular hospitals in the rear. Where road conditions allowed, the AFS ambulances would transport the wounded to the G.B.D. *postes*. Under heavy shelling, stretcher-bearers brought out the wounded on stretchers slung on light two-wheeled frames, or carried them out by hand. The ambulances then transported the wounded to the triage and again, from there, to the base or evacuation hospitals.

On the night of July 1 came an unfamiliar sound. It reminded one of water swishing through gravel. Gas shells! Hand-cranked warning sirens wailed, and empty cannon-shell casings that were hung like bells rang out the alert for one of the war's greatest horrors: a gas attack! For the first time, the men of SSU 9 unpacked their crude gas masks. The masks were constructed from canvas and chemically impregnated gauze, and protected the men's vision and eyes with isinglass lenses near the top. They pulled the masks over their heads, fixing them in place with elastic straps, and rushed out to their Model Ts.

Cranking up their Fords, they headed for the front lines. Driving forward in total darkness, they struggled to follow shell-pocked roads marked with the sign *Eteignez les lumières blanches* ("no lights allowed"). As he drove, my father strained to see through the isinglass eyepieces of his gas mask to discern a broken wagon wheel, a shell hole, or a rock wall strewn across the road by an errant artillery shell that might wreck his ambulance and mean death for the stranded wounded gagging in the trenches.

Great clouds of a creamy, yellowish vapor stretched along the lines near Beaumont for a mile or more, pushed slowly forward by the wind, oozing into every crevice of the French lines. When the Germans first used gas in 1915, the world had been shocked. By the spring of 1917, gas was in the arsenal of all the combatants.

The drivers of SSU 9 hauled the French *poilus*, gagging with blistered lungs and scalded eyes to the nearest medical facility. Although the French did have gas masks, they were often not donned in time to prevent poisoning. Each ambulance that pulled up at the doors of an evacuation hospital brought with it a peculiar and ghastly odor, the odor of blood, poison gas, sweat, and filthy surgical dressings.

Twenty-four hours after the first warning, the evil fumes had dissipated; the four hundred gassed and wounded were being treated, and the men of SSU 9 had proved their mettle. They were later to be cited by General Vuillemot in the 11th Divisional Order of 22nd July, 1917.

A few days after the gas attack, Jepson went on leave to Paris. There he enlisted in the American Air Service and was never again seen in an A.F.S. uniform. Cogswell took over as leader of SSU 9 and quickly began to be concerned about the lack of activity and the plummet in morale, morals, and attitudes among his charges. He dismissed one man for drunkenness, but requested that headquarters in Paris not give him a dishonorable discharge; two others had problems with wine and women and were dismissed with venereal diseases. Another, described as "a corking good fellow with no mechanical sense, incapable of driving a Ford," frankly declared to any that would listen, "anything mechanical bored [me] to extinction." "Such a man," Cogswell said, "should be left to his own hobby, writing and poetry," and he promptly sent him, too, back to Paris.

Rumors abounded that with the United States in the war, the Field Service was breaking up and would be absorbed into the U.S. Army. Dad knew that he did not wish to become an ambulance driver in the American army. He wanted to fly. He, like Jepson and many others, felt the time had come to find a more productive way to serve his country. After three months of service, he took his first week's leave. Once in Paris, he decided it was time to quit the ambulance service. Now he would enlist in the United States Army Air Service. Yes, flying was his goal.

## CHAPTER 4

# Fledglings Gather

**W**hen the United States Congress declared war on Germany on April 6, 1917, the Air Service of the American Army was little more than a patriotic ideal. In 1903, bicycle shop owners Wilbur and Orville Wright had made the world's first successful demonstration of a heavier-than-air flying machine at Kitty Hawk, North Carolina. In the years that followed, the U.S. military had done little with the odd-looking, delicate flying machine. Until 1911, the air arm of the U.S. Army Signal Corps consisted of one "Wright Flyer" aircraft. In 1913, the House Committee on Military Affairs organized the Aviation Section Signal Corps, and in Texas City, Texas, the First Aero Squadron was formed.

Three years later, in March 1916, ten pilots and eight underpowered Curtiss JN-3 "Jenny" aircraft of the First Aero Squadron accompanied General Pershing to northern Mexico to hunt for the bandit and revolutionary leader Pancho Villa. The high winds, fierce storms, and rugged mountainous terrain took its toll, leaving the Army with only two flyable aircraft. To many doubting Army observers this was proof that the airplane had failed as a tool for observation and reconnaissance. The prospects for aerial bombardment seemed equally dim. One cynical commentator said that an aerial bomb was less hazardous to someone on the ground than "a falling aeroplane, or even a falling aviator."

While American efforts to develop a practical military air arm had not substantially progressed, the Europeans, with more than two years of war under their belts, had made gigantic strides by 1916 in the advancement of military flying techniques and aircraft. At the war's outbreak, European combatants had flown Blériots, Farmans, and Taube aircraft over the lines to observe troop movements and locate targets for the artillery. During the waning months of 1914, pilots ignored each other, or even waved at one another as they carried out their aerial duties. But by 1915, they began shooting at enemy aircraft with carbines and pistols, even going so far as to throw bricks and metal darts to deny the skies to the opposition. The gunfire was laughably inaccurate and casualties were light.

The next step was to mount a machine gun on the aircraft to be operated by the observer in the rear seat. A fine idea, if the plane was a two-seater, but what about the *chasse*, or pursuit plane, with only the pilot to operate the gun? It had to fire forward and clear the arc of the spinning propeller. Early in 1915, Roland Garros, a Frenchman, came up with a solution to the problem of how to shoot a machine gun attached to his aircraft through, not around, the propeller blades. The solution: protect the rear of the propeller with metal, V-shaped wedges, so that the machine-gun bullets would be deflected and not shear off the wooden propeller. The steel deflectors were not always effective, but this crude device made Garros the first *chasse* pilot to successfully and regularly shoot down enemy aircraft. He quickly became the world's most successful fighter pilot, but when engine failure eventually brought him down behind German lines, his device was no longer a secret.

As the air war progressed, engineers on both sides synchronized the machine gun so that the bullets would miss the propeller blades as they passed through. By the end of 1915, there were aircraft specifically designed for observation and artillery spotting, others for rudimentary bombing, and finally, with the machine-gun problem solved, there were the elite, swift-pursuit— or *chasse*—single-seaters, designed to shoot down the enemy.

The Europeans quickly discovered that there was propaganda value in publicizing their aerial victories. In June 1916, French military leaders began to publicly acknowledge their "aces," pilots such as Georges Guynemer, Jean Chaput, and René Dorme, who had shot down five or more enemy aircraft. The German military upped the ante by requiring that *their* aces, such as Max Immelmann, Oswald Boelcke, and Manfred von Richthofen—the "ace" of aces—shoot down ten enemy aircraft. Each country's highest awards were presented to their flyers with great publicity and ceremony—the *Légion d'Honneur* by France, the *Pour le Mérite*, popularly known as the "Blue Max," by Germany, and the Victoria Cross by England. As opposed to the stalemated ground war, in which brave attacks by enormous forces consistently ended in mass slaughter and further stalemate, the air war provided governments with the opportunity to single out and reward one individual for continuing bravery and success at arms. It seemed like knighthood. A knighthood of the air.

Just prior to the United States's entry into the war, the U.S. Army Aviation Section, Signal Corps, sent five officers to Europe, one as an observer, one to the office of the military attaché, and three to be flying students. Major William "Billy" Mitchell, a trained aviator and air power visionary, was the observer. Captain C. G. Chipman was the attaché in London. One of the flying students was Lieutenant Davenport Johnson, a West Point graduate and also a trained pilot. Their mission was to study French aviation training techniques. At that time the Aviation Section, Signal Corps, totaled sixty-five officers, about 1,100 men and 200 training-type airplanes. Of these two hundred planes, none was considered fit for war service, nor were any currently being built, nor had there been plans to build any. That is until America entered the war.

With the declaration of war, enthusiasm for aerial development swept through Washington. Politicians and military leaders seemed to feel that American industrial skills could provide just the boost to the air war that would help achieve a quick Allied victory. In the spring of 1917, the U.S. War Department put forth an ambitious plan to build 22,625 airplanes and twice as many aircraft engines by the spring of 1918. Congress supported the effort and voted to spend $640 million for military aviation— the highest amount ever appropriated for a single military purpose. Army recruiters asked young Americans to "put the Yankee punch into the war by building an army of the air, regiments and brigades of winged cavalry on gas-driven flying horses." It was a rather overblown appeal, but it worked and thousands eagerly lined up to enlist.

High-sounding rhetoric was one thing. Actually putting an air service, or any type of service, in the field was quite another. Mitchell and the others on his staff concluded that the first American volunteers for the Air Service would be trained at French fields, with available French planes, and by French veteran instructors. A further contract with the French known as "The Agreement of August 30, 1917" was prepared and signed by the French Air Ministry and General "Black Jack" Pershing, the Commander-in-Chief of the American Expeditionary Forces, or A.E.F., as the overseas American force was called. Provisions of the contract were that the French would deliver to the Air Service in France 5,000 airplanes and 8,500 engines by June 1, 1918. For America's part, it agreed to furnish by November 1, 1917, specified tools and materials necessary for the fulfillment of the French part of the deal. The contract also provided that the airplanes and engines from the French would be delivered by February 1, 1918, even if the United States should not meet their terms of the agreement.

Even setting up recruitment offices proved to be a challenge for the unprepared American military, then considered to rank a lowly nineteenth among military organizations in the world. One of the first American recruiters who landed in France spoke no French, got lost trying to find the city of Nancy, and had to return to Paris. Another enlistment officer arrived at the town of Soissons and proceeded to enjoy the local fruits of the vine until he literally got "dead drunk." The official cause of death was listed as "heart failure." As the first American officer to die in service in France, he was buried with full military honors.

In Paris, my father managed to find a sober recruiting officer and enlisted immediately in the United States Army Air Service. The American Field Service volunteer was soon to become an Air Service volunteer. With his application approved and his physical passed, he had taken the first step to become a flyer. He was now a Cadet, a private, in the Air Service Signal Corps, United States Army Reserve. He would be trained by the French in French flying schools, and upon graduation would be granted a commission in the United States Army. Most important, he would fly.

Woolley was one of hundreds of volunteers then overseas to enlist. They came from the various ambulance services as well as from service in the French and British military forces. One was Sumner Sewall, a dark-haired Westminster Preparatory School graduate, who had left Yale in the middle of his freshman year to drive an ambulance with SSU 8 of the AFS. Sewall was descended from an old Maine family of shipbuilders and merchants. What today is the Bath Iron Works, builders of fast Frigate Class warships for the United States Navy, had its more humble beginnings as the Sewall Shipyard, where six-masted schooners and clipper ships were built on the banks of the Kennebec River in Bath, Maine. Sumner's departure from SSU 8, a unit that had performed tremendous service at Verdun, and his subsequent entry into the Air Service and schooling at Tours coincided with the same movements of my father. Sewall was an athletic, handsome young man with a fine moustache, devilish sense of humor, and infectious chuckle. He and my father took an instant liking for one another and shared the many triumphs and tragedies of learning to fly.

Another volunteer who later became a close friend of my father's was Ted Curtis. Edward Peck Curtis hailed from Rochester, New York, had graduated in 1914 from St. George's School in Newport, Rhode Island, and had attended Williams College before volunteering for the AFS. Ted, rather small in stature, was an intense, serious guy who would never miss a good fight or frolic. Awarded the *Croix de Guerre with Star* for bravery with SSU 15 in August 1917, his citation noted "the degree of his coolness in saving the life of a French soldier who was drowning" and exceptional service at Verdun.

Joe Eastman, from Pleasanton, California, and Stanford University, served with SSU 14. Camion drivers Dick Blodgett, from West Newton, Massachusetts, and Williams College; Bill Taylor from New York City and Phillips Academy, Andover; and Harold Buckley from Agawam, Massachusetts, and Andover, left their ammunition trucks and also came to Paris to enlist. They had spent several months together in *Transport de Matériel 526* delivering ammunition in support of the French offensive at Chemin des Dames. Taylor, the youngest at nineteen, served as the *sous-chef* of the section, designated as TMU 526. Far from a glorious victory, the offensive at Chemin des Dames was one of the most costly defeats ever suffered by the French army. French soldiers, the *poilus*, were so incensed by the slaughter that they mutinied, took over towns, and forced a change in the leadership of the French military, a fact that was kept from the public for the duration of the war. Buckley wrote of his experience as a camion driver:

> The sight of old, tired men, as old as our fathers, covered with mud and carrying a pack of heavy equipment, dragging themselves along the roads to and from the trenches, was too much for us, and practically all of us have changed . . . from the field service to something else where we can feel that we are doing all we can.

Delayed by the usual red tape and physical examinations, the ambulance and camion drivers would meet at the Crillon Bar, swap stories, both amorous and adventurous, and contemplate the challenge ahead. They had experienced the presence of aircraft in the air, both enemy and Allied; they talked with other Americans who were flying with the British, or the French Lafayette Flying Corps, and they were sure they had a feel for things to come. Among the group of old flying pros to be seen at the Crillon were Raoul Lufbery, a leading American ace, Bill Thaw, Bobby Soubiron, Norman Hall, John Huffer, and "Pete" Peterson, veterans of the famous Lafayette Escadrille, the French fighter squadron that only allowed Americans at the controls of the famed Spad VII pursuit ships. Together they constituted a very small and very exclusive club: Uncle Sam's first winged warriors.

Finally, the waiting was over. Orders had arrived for them to report to the *Ecole d'Aviation Militaire*, a primary training center operated by the French near the city of Tours in the Vouvray wine country. Traveling by third-class rail, they passed enormous stores of ammunition and equipment hidden from enemy aerial view by vast camouflage nets, and waited respectfully for trains filled with wounded English to be transferred from field hospitals by rail to the Channel for evacuation. Finally the Cadets arrived at Tours, and then traveled to the airfield located on Route Nationale No. 10, which ran from Paris to Bayonne. They marched through the school's main gate, over which hung a large winged propeller and the legend *Ecole Tours Aviation Militaire*.

The school was a self-contained town of eight large hangars and many one-story structures, which housed the infirmary, director's office, chief pilot's office, guard post, prison, meteorological office, canteen, officers' club, soldiers' barracks, and four workshops. The flying fields stretched away into the distance, the edges dotted with airplanes, mostly Caudron G3s and twin-engine G4s.

The American Cadets were privates, ordinary soldiers, and as such were issued the usual uniform and equipment of an American enlisted man, as well as the flying equipment of a French aviator: wool-lined breeches, leather coats, fiber and leather crash helmets, knitted wool helmets, sweaters, gloves, and goggles. The most important item issued was the *Carnet d'Emploi du Temps*, the official logbook in which they would record their progress as they struggled to earn their Aéro Club de France brevet, the first significant marker on the road to becoming full-fledged military pilots.

Sanitary conditions in the barracks were minimal. On their first night, bedbugs made sleeping impossible for the Cadets. The following morning, they stripped the beds and treated them with a bizarre solution of creosol, an expectorant used in the treatment of bronchitis, and gasoline. After that, they could get some sleep.

They were introduced to the staff of the school: four captains— one of whom was the school commander, Capitaine de Villepin— three lieutenants, four *sous*-lieutenants, and a number of non-commissioned officer instructors. All were French. The fascinated Cadets toured the runways and hangars inspecting the aircraft in which they would soon take to the air. The Caudron G3, first designed by the French Caudron brothers in 1914, was an ungainly-looking craft that seated the pilot in the rear and the

pupil in the front of a bucket-shaped fuselage. The G3 was powered by a fixed radial eight-cylinder Anzani engine. It had a top
speed of about seventy miles per hour, a ceiling of 9,500 feet, and
could remain airborne for three and a half hours without refueling. Although only four years old, the Caudron was considered
a museum piece by many. But the Caudron's robust construction and controls made it forgiving for clumsy students. It could
withstand rough landings. Most important for the students, the
Caudron was simple to fly. It was more than adequate for basic
training.

At Tours, those who had enlisted in the U.S. Air Service in
France bunked with the other volunteers who had joined the Air
Service in the States. These volunteers had graduated from
ground schools located at Cornell University, MIT, and other colleges throughout the United States. In many respects these ground
schools were little more than selection sites for the untrained flying Cadets. They wore their uncomfortable, newly issued, rough
wool uniforms as they sat through rudimentary classes on aero-
dynamics, the principles of navigation, and aircraft and engine
design.

The training at Tours under French instructors and in French
aircraft, like all military aviation training at the time, was a survival test. The Cadet's motto was: "Those who do not die can fly."
In 1917, there were no computerized flight simulators, no detailed manuals. In fact, the only manual the American Cadets
received was an eight-page booklet entitled *Flying School of
Tours—Instructions of the American Pupils.*

My father read the booklet, which noted quaintly that in-
terpreters wearing white arm badges would be available to the
trainees. He was lucky. He spoke some French. Many of the other
Cadets would go through their preliminary pilot training in a language that they barely understood.

The manual set forth the daily timetable:

| | |
|---|---|
| Morning Call | 4 o'clock, A.M. |
| Morning Work | 4h.30 |

| Lunch | 10h.30 |
| Rest | from 12 heures until 4:30 P.M. |
| Dinner | 4:30 P.M. |
| Conference | 5:15 P.M. until 6:00 P.M. |
| Afternoon Work | from 6:00 P.M. until night |

It would appear that no breakfast was served.

At first glance, it seemed to be a light schedule, with flying scheduled for the morning and the evening when atmospheric conditions were calmest and safest for the novice pilots.

The manual was rather cryptic with respect to the actual act of flying an aircraft. Included in the fourteen General Rules were the following:

The machine when rolling on the ground must not go faster than a man walking.

Every machine must leave or land in a straight line facing the wind.

Never pull on the lever when climbing nor when leaving the ground.

The 'Caudron' aeroplane is in flying position when its struts are vertical.

In case of any slight or severe accident, everybody must remain in place. It is formally forbidden to run to the spot of the accident. Only the qualified people for aid go to the machine. These people are: the instructor and the mechanic who are the nearest to the place where the accident occurred.

No mention was made of any medical personnel being qualified to give aid.

For those Cadets who felt nervous or edgy about flying, the manual suggested, "Every indisposed pupil or any pupil who does not feel confident must immediately advise his instructor of it."

Even though they sat just a few feet from one another, verbal communication between *moniteur* (instructor) and Cadet was impossible in the air. There were no intercoms or radios in the training aircraft, and the roar of the Caudron's engine drowned out even shouted commands. The manual outlined the following communication basics:

> When flying the pilot instructor communicates with the pupil in the following manner:

> A short slap on the right shoulder means: 'turn to the right.'
> A short slap on the left shoulder means: 'turn to the left.'
> A pull on the exterior side of the coat while turning means: 'redress the machine and put yourself in normal flying position.'
> A knock on the helmet means: 'let go all commands and turn around so as to look at the instructor.'
> A light pressure in the middle of the back means that the machine climbs too much so push slightly on the stick.
> A pull backwards on the coat means that the machine is too inclined forward so pull slightly on the stick.

This was the extent of the printed flight-training material that the American Cadets were given before they learned, hands on, how to fly.

Studying the *Carnet*, or logbook, of *Soldat* Woolley, Charles H., I found that for the first three days at Tours, he was in *repos* and that on Sunday, August 26, 1917, he finally took his place in the front seat of the Caudron G3. Puzzled, he looked at the wires that led from the control stick to the wings and from the foot pedals to the rudder.

At a signal from the instructor, the mechanic spun the propeller. The engine fired and began to idle. With the instructor in command, the aircraft moved out on the runway. Careful not to touch the controls, my father felt the first rush of air as *Moniteur* Vallois, sitting behind him, guided the aircraft aloft. He was in the air for the first time in his life; he was flying!

"First flight practice, passenger with *moniteur*, duration 10 minutes, altitude 900 feet," he later recorded in his logbook. I have tried to imagine how he felt during that first flight. I cannot believe he felt as secure with his *moniteur* as I felt with Major Woolley, flying in that AT6 over Washington more than twenty-five years later.

The French *moniteurs* were a special breed. They had to be excellent flyers and keen judges of character as well as skillful teachers. With each training flight a *moniteur* risked not only the life of his student but his own.

My father flew as much as the weather would allow, which in the warm clear September of 1917 was quite often. In a letter to my grandmother he noted:

> For the first two flights we were passengers only, going up with the *moniteur* and occupying the front seat of the machine. The control in a directional sense is in a rudder operated by a foot bar, the foot bar being advanced on the side in which you desire to turn. The depth and lateral balance are governed by a stick coming up through the floor of the machine and free to move forward and backward and at the same time to the right or left. Pushing on the stick causes the machine to dip or dive, allowing the stick to come back toward one causes the machine to mount, placing the stick to the right or left causes the machine to drop the right or left wing and bank to the right or left. Thus we have control of the machine in the three senses, and all combinations of positions are possible.

The stick and rudder controls in the Cadet's front seat were very short so that the *moniteur* could take over control of the aircraft at any time, even from a Cadet who was clinging in panic to the controls. My father made his third flight with his hands gently on the stick and his feet just resting on the rudder bar, feeling the manner in which the *moniteur* made corrections and how the controls were handled to obtain certain results. On his fourth trip, he was allowed to take control of the aircraft in the air, the *moniteur* tapping his shoulder to direct the flight and correct his mistakes.

After ten ten-minute flights, he moved on to machines powered by the more powerful ten-cylinder Anzani engine. He sat in the seat behind the *moniteur* and flew with a full-length control column and rudder bar, connected by heavy rubber elastics to the *moniteur*'s controls so that the experienced pilot could take over the aircraft at any moment. My father learned quickly and easily to take the Caudron off the ground, and with the assistance and guidance of the *moniteur*, commenced acquiring the hardest skill—landings. According to Dad, landing was "the most difficult part of aviation."

Early on the morning of September 23, the Cadets rode in a French army truck three or four miles until they reached the broad, three-mile-long practice field that followed the river at St. Avertin. There, Woolley made fourteen landings in the space of an hour under the guidance of his *moniteur. "Bon vol!"* "Good flight," the *moniteur* enthused. After only two of these circuits of landing on the training field, he had advanced to the solo class.

As the summer of 1917 turned to fall, the Cadet's life was ruled by the weather.

The speed of his training was also determined by the longevity of the available aircraft. Due to the frequency of accidents, aircraft were in short supply. On just one day, for example, one Cadet made a pancake landing, smashing his wings, struts, and landing gear. Another caught a wire fence with the undercarriage of his Caudron; the aircraft turned over, catapulting him twenty feet out of his seat. A third Cadet smashed up his aircraft in a cornfield. The pilots usually survived, but the tired old Caudron G3s did not. On one day alone, eleven machines were wrecked. When the American students had arrived at Tours, there were fifty G3s in service. Four months later, there were but twelve.

Too many young pilots wound up wearing a "wooden kimono." During the war, twice as many American pilots died in training as in combat. A few days before my father had arrived at Tours, the Cadets there heard the shrieking crash of splintering wood and then silence. They rushed onto the field and saw a young American's body trapped in a mangled mass of wires and wood. The American, George Manley, who was part of a U.S. Naval detachment in training, had collided with another pilot at takeoff. After Manley's burial, a fellow Cadet composed a long letter of condolence to the aviator's parents beginning with the words "My dear unknown Friends," and ending with, "Our country owes its gratitude to you for the sacrifice of your boy, who paid 'the last full measure of devotion.' "

Among the American ground school Cadets sent to Tours was Waldo Heinrichs. Born in Ongole, India, to a German-American Baptist missionary, he was raised and educated in a Baptist school near Boston and graduated from Denison University, where he had excelled in sports. After college, he found employment with the YMCA in Hawaii, and from there, he enlisted in the Aviation Service.

Waldo Heinrichs, with his Baptist upbringing, noted with disapproval in his diary that many spent their spare time pursuing the fairer sex, and not always in the most tasteful manner. "They speak of the prices of various women they see as they would of goods in a store," Heinrichs complained. Even crossing the Atlantic, Heinrichs had felt out of place. His diary describes his early reaction to the men on shipboard and their swearing, gambling, and drinking. He felt in this environment "ashamed to be in touch with anything religious. I must swim against, not with, the general stream of negligence of religion, profanity and immorality."

Heinrichs recorded in his diary that one evening some French women from Tours drove out to the training field and stopped on the road outside. "A mob soon collected, mostly Americans, and took all sorts of liberties with them but not going the limit." French soldiers in shirtsleeves came out from the field "and the harlots flew in a hurry."

Finally, in October, my father walked out onto the *piste central*, the main field, ready for his first "hop," or solo flight. "This is made in a 60 H.P. Gnome powered Caudron, and is rather disconcerting after driving Anzani's," my father wrote. "With the Gnome motors we are not permitted to touch the throttle but must stop the motor for our glide or descent by breaking the contact."

The Gnome rotary engine had other idiosyncrasies. The engine was lubricated with castor oil, the only oil of the time that could withstand the engine's high operating temperatures. Castor oil mixed with the gasoline and air in the crankcase and was drawn into the combustion chamber. A fine mist of gasoline exhaust and burned castor oil lubricant would fly back as the motor spun around its fixed crankshaft. Inhaling the exhaust caused many students to endure bouts of incontinence. Worse than dealing with castor oil, my father had to watch out for the Gnome's tendency to catch fire. The engine had no carburetor. Raw gasoline was fed directly into the cylinders. When turning over a cold motor, un-ignited gasoline accumulated in the engine cowling before the motor started. This accumulated gasoline had a tendency to ignite when the engine began to fire. When the plane was airborne, and the pilot had to reduce speed for a landing, the spark, or ignition, had to be continuously turned off and on via a "blip switch" attached to the stick. Unburned fuel continued to feed to those cylinders—and collect in the cowling. Any chance spark could ignite the pool of gasoline, and although the flames were usually snuffed out by the wind, the greatest horror of all pilots was to have the flames ignite the heavily doped canvas and wooden body of the aircraft, burning the trapped pilot alive.

On that special bright October day, Woolley climbed into the Caudron selected by his *moniteur* and strapped himself in. A mechanic started the motor, which roared up to full speed, while two ground crewmen held the aircraft in place. At a signal given by the instructor, the crew let go, and the plane began to taxi along the ground. "I think that my heart was going about three-hundred beats faster than the motor, which was turning at 1,200," my father confessed.

As the Caudron gained speed, Dad pulled back on the stick and he was airborne, soloing for the first time, in complete control of his aircraft. He flew straight ahead for a quarter mile at a maximum altitude of fifty or sixty feet. Fifteen seconds later, as he descended, the ground seemed to come up too fast. He hit, bounced, hit more softly, and rolled to a stop. He smiled to himself. *Bon vol! Bon vol!*

In the air, my father learned to cope with many things; the unsettling motion caused by the propeller wake from the plane ahead of him, the bumps from unstable air, and the tendency of a rotary engine to force the airplane to bank to the left. He learned not to rise too fast, to level off, and to steady the plane before landing. He attended lectures on map reading and cross-country flying. He watched flying demonstrations as instructors took the Caudrons up, cut the motors, sideslipped, stalled, nose-dived, and performed the fluttering "falling leaf" maneuvers. He took longer flights in sixty- and then eighty-horsepower Gnome rotary-engine G3s. He continued to practice landings and learned how to perform spirals, the first of the many acrobatic techniques he would need as a fighter pilot.

He finally set out on his *petit voyage*, a triangular journey of 120 miles with two prescribed stops. As instructed, he climbed to 3,000 feet, his Caudron ascending easily. There, he checked his chart, barograph, compass, and altimeter. With the motor turning at about 1,175 rpm, he soon passed through the scattered clouds floating at 1,800 to 2,000 feet. All went well until he arrived over the field where the first landing was to take place. As he wrote my grandmother, "Here I mistook the direction of the T, or wind marker, and tried twice to land with the wind before I noticed my mistake and landed as I should against it." After changing a spark plug, or *bougie*, he started again on his second leg. This time he had a fair wind, flew at 3,600 feet and serenely sailed along checking off all the reference points on the map and "having a glorious time."

After a fine landing, he took off again and completed the third leg of the triangular journey. Sumner Sewall, who was at the same point in his training, was particularly eloquent about flying through clouds on his *petit voyage*.

> It is a queer, yet not unpleasant feeling, to sail along over the clouds, which form a sort of floor and roll over and over like waves or clouds of smoke. Clouds always cause terrible bumps which throw you around like a piece of paper, and if you go above the clouds, you will probably lose your way, as you can only get an occasional view of the earth through the holes in the clouds. And if you go into a cloud, you are simply a damn fool as there is absolutely no way of telling whether you are sailing upside down or with your

wings vertical. The first thing impressed on a green pilot is to keep clear of clouds.

Waldo Heinrichs had less luck than Woolley or Sumner Sewall
when he took his small journey:

> Started at 9 AM after the fog lifted for Vendome on
> my *petit voyage*. Mists made the way a little uncer-
> tain. Two plugs bad when I landed at Vendome—good
> landing. Met Goodman, the Chief Erecting Mechanic
> at Vendome, who came up on the train from Paris
> with me. Started back well and just before I got to
> Mounare, five and a half miles from Tours, 3 cylinders
> went bad—good landing. Tried to fix them and got
> away, but had to land again—heavily and bent an axle
> and broke one flying wire. Telephoned for a mechanic
> and while they were coming, I had breakfast in a little
> hotel in Mounare which cost 3 francs. Mechanic tested
> my motor and found five sparkplugs bad. Went up,
> circled once and found more were bad. Good landing.
> Fixed, landed at Tours. Rested a few minutes, ate a lit-
> tle chocolate, grapes and water and started on my tri-
> angle. Flew for Pontlevoy at 1,500 feet over Vouvray,
> Amboise, and Mountrichard. Lost my way absolutely
> and started off toward Blois. Good landing and asked
> of a French First Lieutenant (Legion of Honor) the
> way to Pontlevoy and started off well. Circled over a
> town like Pontlevoy and picked out a landing field
> which looked good, but very narrow, bounded by a
> railway, ditches and bushes, all dangerous. Wind drift
> was too far left and blew me into a ditch with my right
> wheel. Two feet more and I would have been safe.
> But wheel caught, landing gear smashed and I went
> up on my nose. Belt held me—unhurt. Crowds quickly
> gathered, soldiers, children, old men, women. Got ma-
> chine up straight, removed chart, barograph, tools,
> compass, altimeters and reported at Gendarmerie Na-
> tionale where the Brigadier's daughter spoke English.
> Had shave and slept at the Hotel de Lion d'Or in a big
> old French bed.

The following day the remains of the machine were loaded onto a trailer and returned to the aerodrome, where Heinrichs' *moniteur* brought him a new machine that tested well on the ground, but began to miss in the air. He could not get the plane above 1,000 feet, at which level he flew to the field at Châteaudun, where he installed three new plugs, got thirty liters of gas, and finally completed another *petit voyage*. When he flew his triangle, it was punctuated with more bad plugs and a broken valve, which meant replacing the entire cylinder.

The last test Woolley had to pass was the *hauteur*, the altitude test. He climbed into a Caudron G3 with an eighty-horsepower Gnome engine, and climbed to 1,800 feet in ten minutes, then more slowly to a height of 8,700 feet. He was careful not to stall the engine by climbing too steeply in the thin air. Once he gained his altitude, he kept the Loire River on his left and followed it for ten or fifteen miles, passing over the towns of St. Avertin, Vouvray, and Amboise. "I stayed up until the ink on my barograph or altitude registering apparatus gave out, which was after I had been 1 hr. and 10 min above 9,000 feet," he later wrote. "So my test counted." He returned to Tours and landed. After about two hours in the air at 9,000 feet he was cold, tired, and had a splitting headache, but he didn't care. He had passed the test.

Heinrichs had a tricky time passing his altitude test, which he carefully noted in his diary:

> Was called from sleep at 1:30 PM to go on my altitude test. Put on one extra pair of socks, and usual uniform, one extra sweater, vest, muffler, and a knitted helmet. Had 'Gnome 80 hp' for the test. Climbed to 1,800 feet fast (about 10 minutes) then to 5,000 slower, all the time circling above the field. At 5,500 feet my engine stalled on too steep a climb due to decreased pressure on the gasoline and my failing to feed more air. Nearly ruined me by dropping fully 350-400 feet, then I caught it out of a wing slip and got up to 7,200 feet at which height I had been told to fly. I flew inland, keeping the Loire on left, crossed

about 10 or 15 miles down, still keeping it on left, flew over Tours, St. Avertin, Vouvray, Amboise where I crossed again and came back. After 2 hours in the air I dropped to 1,800 feet, took one circle then another at 1,000 feet. Was very deaf when I landed, and tired too.

Sumner Sewall was surprised when he was asked to take the altitude test in the same machine that he had used for his *petit voyage*:

I drew a good plane and by struggling for 45 minutes, I at last reached 6,500 feet, where I literally froze for an hour. But beautiful was no word for it. There were miles and miles of wonderful cloudbanks just below me that looked exactly like pictures of the ice floes in the Arctic. There were many holes, thank God, through which I could look every now and then at sunny Southern France, the warmth of which I never appreciated until that moment. Then, too, and to my disgust after an hour, I shut down my engine and took a dive through a hole in the clouds only to find that I was off my map, but again, luck was with me as I just happened to see in the distance a building that looked like a hangar and which turned out to be the place I was looking for. I sure will never again try to make an altitude test with a machine like that, but I have the satisfaction of being the first American to have done so. I really feel so darn much at home in one of these planes that I can't understand why I could not drive one the first minute I ever sat in one. Every movement comes absolutely automatic, just like riding a bicycle. In fact, once you get into the air you can balance your plane by slowing your engine so that you can fly for five minutes at a time without touching the controls. When you get it, I believe it's easier than driving a car.

Sewall, like my father, was a natural pilot.

Many years later, Ted Curtis, in an interview, told me that one of his *moniteurs* in the early stages of his training had said he, Curtis, was gifted with a sense of "feel" in the air, a sort of innate ability to keep his machine on an even keel without effort, and that, consequently, with practice, he would be a good flier. Curtis admitted to me that flying had come easily, and that he quickly was making landings without any assistance. He described his first sensation as "a mild surprise at the lack of any startling impression." To Ted flying was natural and easy and provided a sense of exhilaration. He was entering a sport that was irresistible. In his early training at Tours, fear was never in his mind as he watched all the machines in the air, landing and taking off with never a more serious mishap than a bad landing with a few broken wires.

Glancing up from his *Carnet*, or logbook, to which he was referring for details from fifty years before, he was reminded of one particularly memorable flight:

> I made the last flight of the day just at sunset, a real French sunset, with the great banks of clouds which we never seemed to produce here at home, clouds so thick it looked as if one could walk on their mountainous sides. From a height of 900 feet I could see the city of Tours lying below, the course of the river Loire glowing and shining in the sunlight, with all the country for miles around laid out in squares like a chessboard, with great white châteaux sprinkled here and there for the pieces; not a very war-like scene, but quite as impressive as any battle front.

On October 22, 1917, with all tests completed, my father was awarded the metal wreath and wings insignia of a French aviator, plus a pocket-size, blue-leather-bound folder, his brevet. It was brevet number 9163; only that number of men had ever earned the right to fly in France. He was a *Pilote-Aviateur* licensed by the *Fédération Aéronautique International-France*. Opening the folder, more than eighty years later, I can appreciate the profound pleasure my father must have felt to have completed his preliminary training and been awarded his brevet.

He had passed the first major hurdle in his effort to become a fighter pilot. He was ready for whatever came next. He must have reflected soberly, however, on the uncertainties of his newly chosen career when he marched in a funeral service for France's greatest flyer, their leading ace and most popular hero, Capitaine Georges Marie Ludovic Jules Guynemer. After surviving thirty-one months of aerial fighting, which had entailed eighty-nine combats resulting in fifty-three confirmed kills, Guynemer had been shot down. His body was never found. Some say that the Germans buried him; some say his body and his Spad were pulverized by a French artillery barrage in the area where he fell. The French schoolchildren believed he flew so high into the heavens that he could never return. The memorial service ended with a single Spad flying low over the field, where it dropped a commemorative wreath in honor of the Allies' greatest airman.

# CHAPTER 5

# *Honing Their Skills*

Issoudun had been planned as the advanced training school for the pilots of the American Expeditionary Force, but when my father arrived in early November 1917, it was little more than a vast, barren construction site. The American army's most advanced, most sophisticated fighter training school, which eventually consisted of a staff of more than sixty flight instructors, 800 mechanics, forty-five hangars, hundreds of aircraft, and barracks for hundreds of Cadets, was then little more than a sea of mud.

Captain James E. Miller was the officer in charge of getting Issoudun, potentially the world's largest flight-training facility, up and running. Jim Miller was, in every sense, one of the unsung early leaders in American military aviation. Born in 1883, he graduated from Yale University in the class of 1904, excelling in athletics as stroke on the Yale eight and as a varsity guard on the football team. Upon graduation he entered the world of finance, rapidly advancing on Wall Street. In 1915, he participated in the Reserve Officer's program at Plattsburgh, and was then instrumental in organizing the First Aeroplane Company within the New York National Guard, later to become the First Aero Squadron. Early in his military career, Miller qualified as a pilot and an instructor, and became one of only seven military aviators to complete what was then considered an arduous hundred-mile test. In 1917, given the charge to "organize, build and start" the American Flying School at Issoudun, he was allowed sixty days to commence flying from the dismal swamp that was to hold the vast complex of hangars, barracks, engine facilities, and landing fields.

Other Cadets had preceded my father to the muddy fields of Issoudun. Many of them had traveled across the Atlantic with Waldo Heinrichs aboard the R.M.S. *Ordina*. Douglas Campbell, Harvard, Class of 1917 and the son of a well-known astronomer from San Jose, California, had left school before graduation, enlisted in the Aviation Section, Signal Corps, on May 18, 1917, and was immediately detailed to the School of Military Aeronautics at MIT. When he learned that he had been selected for an experimental training program that eliminated preliminary training at Tours, he was thrilled. His excitement turned to disappointment when he was confronted with the conditions at Issoudun.

First Lieutenant Hobey Baker had dazzled fans at the Princeton-Yale football game in 1916, when he led a formation of U.S. Army Signal Corps Curtiss JN-3 "Jennys" in a halftime display of aerial acrobatics. The blond-haired Baker was one of America's most famous amateur athletes. He had led the Princeton football team and revolutionized the collegiate game of ice hockey with his speed and agility, punctuated by his modest sportsmanship. On his own, before the war, he had learned how to fly at Mineola Field on Long Island while working full-time on Wall Street. Now, in 1917, he was at war in Europe directing work on the soggy fields of France, striving to help build an American Air Service and the best air-training facility in the world.

Nineteen-year-old Quentin Roosevelt, the youngest son of the former president, Theodore Roosevelt, had attended Groton School and Harvard. According to his brother Kermit, who had also served as an officer in France, Quentin had a "bent for mechanics which was not inherited." He liked nothing better than to buy broken-down motorcycles for sixteen dollars, or ramshackle autos for twenty-five dollars, fix them up, and drive them until they broke down again. He was naturally attracted to flying and signed up for the Reserve Officer's training program at Plattsburgh. It was not an easy program for the young Roosevelt, who had suffered a terrible injury while hunting out west in the summer of 1915. He had been thrown from his horse, cruelly twisting his back when he hit the ground, causing an injury from which he never fully recovered. At Plattsburgh and later in France, he endured considerable pain in the hope that he would one day be able to play an active role in the war.

Quentin's best friend at Groton and Harvard had been Hamilton Coolidge of Brookline, Massachusetts. Almost two years older than Quentin, Coolidge was not an outstanding student and took seven years to graduate from Groton's six-year program. However, he proved himself to be one of Groton's most popular and talented athletes, described by a contemporary as "a nearly perfect physical specimen . . . a magnificent figure of a man." Like his friend Quentin, Coolidge attended the Plattsburgh officer's training program, and had a love of machines. From his own pocket he paid the tuition to attend the Curtiss Flying School in Buffalo, New York, where he earned his pilot's license from the Aero Club of America.

Hangars and barracks at Issoudun were in various stages of completion, and the airfields were seas of mud. Construction sawdust covered the floors of the crowded, dark, cold, muddy barracks. Each held ninety Cadets sleeping in double-decker wooden frame bunks, on mattresses supported by canvas slings. Clothes and baggage were piled everywhere. The area for bathing was a four-by-six-foot enclosure attached to the end of the barracks. Water was heated over a wood stove; baths were only sponge baths. Sanitary facilities were primitive.

For the first weeks of their "training," the Cadets did no flying. They helped the enlisted men frame up the hangars and barracks and dig latrines. They slogged through the mud shoulder to shoulder with the *mécaniciens,* as the French called the airframe riggers and engine mechanics. A former auto racer named Eddie Rickenbacker, then a sergeant, was the chief engineering officer at the base, supported by Sergeants Roosevelt and Coolidge.

The American enlisted men had been assigned to specific squadrons that existed on paper long before there were pilots or planes. The 95th Aero Squadron, for example, had been formed in the summer of 1917 at Kelly Field, Texas. At the end of September, their Army basic training finished, the enlisted men began the long journey to the front. Upon arrival in France, the enlisted men were separated into seven detachments and then assigned to various engine or airframe factories to learn their basic trade firsthand. After the completion of this training, they joined the unhappy Cadets in the mire and confusion of Issoudun.

Waldo Heinrichs arrived at Issoudun in November. Heinrichs and the other earlier graduates of Tours had been sent for advanced training to the school at Avord while waiting for Issoudun to be constructed. Avord was home for more than 900 French aviation students and the only advanced training facility open to the first American graduates of Tours. The Americans referred, not so lovingly, to Avord as the "Cess-Pool of all Creation." The town's red light district was even less lovingly called "Syph City," based on the prevalence of venereal diseases suffered by its inhabitants. Waldo reported that at the school he had encountered rats, fleas, and bedbugs, which distracted him and his fellow students from their lessons. The hostility of the French, at and near the base, toward the Americans was blamed on the behavior of the First Aero Squadron and a U.S. Army regiment of engineers. They were the first from the United States assigned to the area and were so rowdy and undisciplined that the French populace reportedly almost would have preferred German occupation.

By mid-November, enough of the facility was finished for training at Issoudun to commence. Initially there was no flying in racy Nieuports. Penguins were the first training vehicles at Issoudun, as they were at Avord, much to the disappointment of all. Penguins, also called *rouleurs*, or rollers, were Blériot monoplanes with the wings clipped so short they could not leave the ground. Steering the Penguin with foot pedals connected to its rudder simulated the control of the Nieuport, the fast fighter aircraft that the students would eventually be flying. The Nieuport, which had a wing surface of twenty-three square meters, had a tendency to swing left or right when landing or taking off. If this was not anticipated by the proper rudder control, the plane would spin around in a *cheval de bois*, or ground loop, and end up flipped on its back or forward on its nose. Penguin training was intended to teach the proper touch to avoid such disasters.

The goal was to maneuver the Penguin to travel in a straight line. This was not an easy task. The first time pilots got behind the controls, the plane went around in circles, rolled over, or smashed into one obstacle or another. These antics highly amused the waiting students, but became a little less funny when their own turn came.

In one of our conversations, Doug Campbell described working with the Penguins. In his words, the *rouleurs* were:

> much more touchy than a regular airplane. The first day of class they decided to let me smash up the first, so I got in, had the motor started, received last instructions and set off. The other students and the French pilots expected to see me spin around and do everything else incorrectly, and were looking forward to a good laugh and maybe an exciting accident. To their great, and my even greater, surprise, I found the rudder work easy, and the elevator manipulation nearly so and ran the fool thing in almost a straight line. I then tried it faster, which went well, too. When I stopped, I was informed that I had *roulé comme un as*, 'rolled like an ace.'

After the ten required days of the *rouleurs*, Woolley had managed to steer his Penguin in a straight line and then moved on to the twenty-three-meter, dual-controlled, Le Rhone eighty-horsepower-engine Nieuports. The challenge of flying a "real" plane was his at last. The *moniteur* sat in front, my father in the rear, where the controls were attached to those in the front by elastic cords. As at Tours, if he made a false move, the instructor could immediately take control and return to the proper line of flight. The Cadets took "circuits" or "hops," which consisted of three landings along a straight line of flight, or *ligne de vol*, down the length of the huge airfield. They were allowed three circuits in the morning and three in the afternoon, totaling a little over thirty minutes of time in the air.

This was the period when flying techniques were finely tuned. Remember: keep a light touch on the controls; be careful not to stall during climbs and turns; be alert to what is happening around you. You and your aircraft should become one.

When the *moniteur* felt my father was ready, he gave him the controls. Dad immediately felt the pressure of the rudder bar on his foot, and the stick became responsive to his touch. Every sense was involved, and also that new sense, that sixth sense called "air sense." Air sense was the automatic ability to feel whether or not the machine was in the proper position. Was it climbing, losing altitude, turning? Was it truly going where you wanted?

The dual sessions with the *moniteur* seemed to pass quickly, and the next step was for him to solo. He had flown well and had been encouraged by his instructors; now it was up to him to further develop that sixth sense. Finally, it was his turn. He climbed into the cockpit of the Nieuport, adjusted and buckled his seat belt, checked the sparse instrumentation panel, and wiggled the "joystick" and rudder bar. Everything was in order. He advanced the throttle to the proper power setting, the ground crew released the plane, which had no brakes, and he was airborne.

Doug Campbell described to me his feeling of flying a Nieuport:

> As soon as you got into the machine, every worry you ever had—and we all had some—simply vanished. When you opened the throttle, and the tremendous power set you in motion, you couldn't think of anything else. While you are ripping along the ground, you had to be alert so as not to swing sideways or get your tail too high and turn over. Then when you were in the air, the panorama of this beautiful world, which looked better every time you went up, unfolded itself under you and gave you a thrill of delight which would last for a long time. Coming down seemed more like one's preconceived notion of flying, the motor silent, you were simply floating down. You didn't have much time to enjoy that part of it, for you were busy picking out that landing field, judging your height and distance, keeping the nose straight into the wind and later leveling off before the ground hit you, keeping the wheels just off the ground while you lowered the

tail and made the angle of incidence greater and greater as you lost speed, until you couldn't stay in the air any longer. You then touched the ground as lightly as a feather—sometimes.

As I listened to Campbell, I could not help but compare these feelings to those I have had when departing on an extended coastal cruise in our family sailboat. With no more worries of business, your concentration is on matters that are not earthborn cares. You focus on setting your course, trimming your ship, and watching for dangers in your path. It is the same, only the medium is different—one the endless sky, the other the endless ocean.

Woolley circled the field in his Nieuport 23, cut the motor at 2,000 feet and glided onto the landing field, aiming his aircraft to land as close as possible to the marker. He did not land absolutely smoothly, but he was within a few hundred feet of the "T" that marked his landing site and the wind direction. He shared a grin with the French pilot, his instructor.

A new American training system was being put into place. This new system was intended to speed up the training as conducted in the French method. Now, in the new system, there were two or three runs in the Penguins, while practicing landings in the twenty-three-meter Nieuports; three or four solo flights in the smaller, trickier, and faster eighteen-meter planes; then five or six flights in the fifteen-meters before starting the thrilling spiral class. The French *moniteurs* argued for the return of the familiar French system, to no avail. In early January, a second new American system was established. Students, both Cadets and Reserve Officers, were divided into close to twenty-five sections of ten men each. Each section worked on one phase of flying until all were proficient. Spirals, altitude tests, petit voyages, acrobatics, and solos in fast, high-powered fifteen-meter Nieuports were taught, and advancement was made when the entire section was ready. The reorganization was popular with the Cadets, because the "Loots," those pilot trainees who had received their commission stateside, could no longer pull rank and jump ahead of the Cadets who were waiting their turn to fly.

After the twenty-three-meter, Woolley found the Nieuport eighteen-meter a fast, nimble machine due to the smaller wing surface. Each one had slightly different flight characteristics. Some engines ran roughly; some frames tended to twist and bend. Tail-skids, which were used to dig into the ground and brake the aircraft at landing, often snapped off on airfields frozen solid by the fiercely cold winter. As trainers, these planes had been abused and repaired numerous times; the engines had been over-worked and, due to the continuous airframe repairing, the fine adjustments to assure level flight had been lost; and no two ships were alike when airborne.

Many students suffered crashes and injuries, some fatal. Ham Coolidge hit a small tree with a wing tip and demolished his ma-chine, but escaped unharmed. Heinrichs was flying a machine with an ill-fitting gas cap. Upon landing, gas spewed up into his face, the aircraft bounded and went into a *cheval de bois*, break-ing a wing. Waldo was more than a little miffed when he found that the *moniteur* bringing the machine from the hangar to the practice field had experienced the same ill-fitting gas cap prob-lem, but no *cheval de bois*. One student, while taking off, nearly collided with another. He banked to the left, gave his rudder a kick to the left, and turned into a spin. The Nieuport's nose hit the ground. The sickening crash was followed by moans of "Oh, Christ, Oh, Christ!" Cadets ran to the wreck and pulled him out. He was badly shaken and bruised, his legs sprained, but nothing was broken and he had no serious injuries. It was just another day in the life of a flying Cadet.

Curtis told a story about one of his more exciting training flights. He had been at 15,000 feet above a thick cloud cover that lay at 3,000 feet. When the time came to return, he cut his motor and headed for terra firma. Breaking through the clouds he saw that he was miles from the field. Leaning forward, he flipped the ignition switch to the "ON" position for power, but the motor wouldn't start. Again he tried the switch. Silence. He fussed with every control and gas connection he could find as the air whooshed around him, losing altitude every second. At 1,000 feet, Ted real-ized the damn thing just wasn't going to run. He desperately looked around for a place to land and saw nothing but swamps and forests. Then, hooray! A little field just to the left. He tried to hit the field, but he misjudged his speed and the distance badly; he was headed directly for the forest, going at nearly a hundred miles per hour! Seconds before he was going to crash, Ted pulled violently back on the stick, ducked his head, and sailed through six or seven trees, leaving wings, wheels, and elevators in his wake, finally coming to earth with nothing but a motor and a fuselage. Ted shook himself gently to see if everything was functioning and then tried to climb out of the wreckage, only to find that one wing had collapsed over his head. By the time he had extricated himself, a small crowd had gathered at the crash site. Laughing, he told me about an old Frenchman in the crowd who asked, "What did they do with his remains?" Curtis told him that he was the pilot, but the Frenchman remained unconvinced. Later, Curtis discovered the cause of his engine trouble: a dirty distributor plate. "It is all in the game . . ." he wrote to his parents. "I expect to go through a lot more such accidents before I go home . . . it will be a relief to finish this trying training and to feel that I am really of some use to the U.S.A. instead of smashing their expensive play-things."

Two American Cadets collided in mid-air, fell over a thousand feet, and were killed instantly. A funeral service with full military honors was held two days later. A Ford tractor pulling the two flag-draped coffins on a wheeled caisson was followed by pallbearers, thirty Cadets and more than fifty flying officers. The graveside services were somber and impressive, although strangely, there was no squad of infantrymen firing the farewell volley over the departed. All knew there would be more funerals, many more. The only thing not known was who would be the next to die.

Those pilots who survived an accident with little more than damaged pride inevitably had to face the razzing of their fellow students. There was heavy competition as to who was the best, who was going to survive the rigors of *chasse* training, who was going to graduate to fly a swift pursuit ship and fight the hated Huns. The *mauvais pilote*, the pilot who just did not have those special ingredients—fast reflexes, ability to shoot accurately and "air sense"—was sent to the bombardment or the observation schools, duties that were no less important, but somehow, did not have quite the same degree of glamour.

To meet the criterion for shooting straight and accurately, target practice was a large part of the training program. The men rode on French Renault or English Dennis trucks the six miles to the gunnery range to shoot swivel-mounted drum-fed Lewis machine guns at targets waving on ten-foot-long boards some seventy-five yards distant. Not to waste ammunition, they were taught to shoot in short bursts of five shots, and to assist their aim, every third or fourth round would be a tracer leaving a smoke trail indicating the line of fire. A Marine Gunnery Sergeant taught them how to dismantle, clean, and reassemble the guns while blindfolded, and how to clear jams and stoppages. They practiced distance estimation, squinting through ring sights at silhouettes of German aircraft to simulate what could be seen from 75, 150, 300, 370, and 600 feet. They trained on the British Vickers guns of the type they would encounter on their planes. With shotguns they fired at the elusive clay pigeons, and when walking along the frozen roads in the countryside, they fired their government-issued .45s at rabbits, crows, and even clods of dirt in the frosty fields.

Training was not only deadly, but also sometimes dull. To keep entertained, the Cadets sang along with Oscar Gude, who played his homemade ukulele. They watched movies at the YMCA hut, attended minstrel shows, boxing and wrestling matches, and yawned through lectures on discipline, obedience, health, map reading, and machine-gun maintenance. When they were paid, they gambled with dice and cards. Cadet Gude won 3,500 francs shooting craps with the galloping dominoes.

Morale was high when flying was possible, even though some of this flying seemed to be mismanaged. Officers sometimes forgot to have transport trucks available for travel to the flying fields. The drivers sometimes got lost on their way to the field selected for flying that day, wandering through the maze of muddy, unmarked tracks that crisscrossed the enormous, burgeoning base. Often they arrived late, causing the loss of valuable flying time. And after arriving at the fields, there was always more waiting.

Morale also sank when pay records were lost, vouchers were

misrouted, commissions were mired in the sea of paperwork that flowed from Washington, and the unexplained hours, even days, of inactivity mounted. At one point, Roosevelt and Heinrichs went to headquarters to complain formally about not being paid or assigned to active duty.

The harsh winter weather was also a concern. Each day was much like the last—frozen and mud-coated. Thanksgiving and Christmas came and went, highlighted by elaborate meals of turkey with all the trimmings, candy from the Red Cross, and packages from home bearing socks, more candy, shredded wheat, cigarettes, chocolate, sweaters, handkerchiefs, inflatable pillows, and the inevitable fruitcakes.

Some lucky Cadets enjoyed breaks from the drudgery when prominent local families invited them for social visits. Military courtesy and courtesies in general were still alive and well in wartime France. Miller, as the Commandant of Issoudun, was invited to visit the château of a General Exelmans. Cord Meyer, Ham Coolidge, and Doug Campbell accompanied him, and together they traveled the thirty miles from Issoudun to the fifteenth-century château, which had been modernized with elegant taste. The General's grandfather had been one of Napoleon's *maréchals*, a cavalryman commanding the elite horse grenadiers. Many souvenirs of his service remained in the château, including an epaulet worn by "the great" Napoleon at Waterloo. The General and his wife provided them a sumptuous meal, with many hors d'oeuvres, three meat courses, and four different wines, including a wonderful Burgundy and a fine champagne. Campbell described their sensible method of drinking:

> They give you small amounts of different kinds of wines that they have stored in their cellar for fifty years and drink it just as one would eat a particularly rare dish.

Joining the group at the luncheon were four very attractive young ladies, one of whom made a great impression on Ham. The Americans' comfort with the French language was adequate for the occasion and improved with the wine. Before departing they discovered a landing field near the château and bets were taken that Ham would have a *panne de château* (a motor failure that occurred at a most opportune time and place) on his next cross-country flight.

By the end of the year, the aviators' lot had begun to brighten. Commissions finally arrived and the advanced group was sent to Field Number 5, St. Valentine's, about eleven miles from the main camp at Issoudun, for the final phase of *chasse* training. They moved to the St. Valentine barracks, where German prisoners of war served as waiters and chefs.

Spins, or *vrilles*, were the first tests at the new airfield; then came altitude tests at 13,000 feet, cross-country flights, acrobatics, and formation flying. Aerial combat with camera guns completed the agenda.

The mastery of evasive maneuvers was essential: Controlled spins could mean the difference between life and death in a fight with a member of the German Imperial Flying Service. Practicing spins, my father took off into the wind, flying away from the field. He climbed to 3,300 feet and turned, now with the wind, toward the field. When he was over the assigned landing spot, he reduced the throttle and banked over to the left until the stick touched his knee. This placed him on his wingtip in a vertical bank. In this position, he pulled back on the stick and began using his elevators, which in the banked position had become a rudder to enter a spiral. At a height of 1,650 feet he reversed the entire process and came out of the spin. His Nieuport quickly began to dive, in response to a neutral stick, elevator, and rudder position. To stop the dive, Woolley pulled back on the stick ever so gradually, so as not to strain the wings and flying wires, and resumed level flight.

Ted Curtis described his reactions to the spin that he began by performing a loop:

> The sensation is more or less like falling off a cliff in a bad dream. You rear up in the air, go over on your back [performing a loop] and then start spinning round in a dive. To come out, you straighten your rudder, move the stick back to the center and push it

slightly forward until you come out in a straight dive. Then you can pull back on the stick [and] put on power again, only for a while it seems as if the earth is still spinning around below.

In December 1917, Europe was experiencing one of the coldest winters in memory. Dressed in two suits of woolen underwear, heavy woolen trousers and shirts, several sweaters, a fur-lined "teddy bear" flying suit and leather, and fleece-lined gauntlets, my father undertook another dreaded altitude test. He flew in an open cockpit for fifteen minutes in the bitter sub-zero chill at 12,000 feet, then spiraled to the right for 3,000 feet, then to the left for 3,300 feet, recovered from the spirals, landed, and wondered how long it would take to get any feeling back into his seemingly frozen extremities.

Next came cross-country flights. Despite the cold, sailing the eighty miles in fifty minutes over woods, winding rivers, châteaux, and little villages seemed like a lark. Landing in time for lunch, refueling and flying back to St. Valentine was a pleasurable part of the program.

Then came acrobatics. In machines specially strengthened to withstand the strains of clumsy mishandling, the group took to the air. Once aloft, they began to practice loops, *renversements* (changing direction in a twisting loop), and stalls—in fact, any maneuver that could be used when fighting for their lives in the air.

Formation flying was a welcome break from the isolation of the previous training. They practiced in groups of three, four, and five, forming "vees," stacked echelons in line, and a variety of formations that would be useful for their mutual protection. Formation flying was not easy. Sometimes they flew too close to one another or too far away; sometimes one would get separated and be unable to catch up; sometimes the wrong pilot would fall into the wrong place, or even into the wrong formation. Confusion would reign for a while, but they gradually caught on.

They practiced reconnaissance flights, mapping canals and sites of military significance near the airfield. It is not easy to draw a map while struggling to lock the control stick between your knees and keep a temperamental machine in a straight line of flight.

Mock air battles were fought, shooting camera guns shaped like Lewis machine guns and armed with twelve exposures of 2" x 2" film. When developed, each frame included preprinted circles that showed a "kill" if one had been made. The forty minutes spent in these simulated combats were the closest they would come to the real thing. If Dad was "the attacker," he would hang under his opponent's tail, imaging streams of tracers flying into the cockpit. As "the attacked," he flew low, spun, and turned to dodge the camera, hoping to turn the tables and fix himself on the tail of his "enemy." On the occasions when his opponent could not locate him, he, now alone, had the chance to perform any and all acrobatics he wished.

While our heroes were struggling for mastery of the air, a group of earthbound Air Service officers were struggling to organize things on the ground. In mid-January, Major Burt M. Atkinson, A.S.S.C., Captain Philip J. Roosevelt, A.S.S.C. (a cousin to Quentin), and Captain John G. Rankin, A.S.S.C., were assigned to duty with the First Pursuit Organization and Training Center. These officers were the brains and nerve center of the First Pursuit Group. This small group was the American answer to the vast German Luftstreitkrafte, with its units from Dunkirk to the Swiss border, a force with four years of combat experience and a star-studded cadre of killer fighter pilots. Three officers, six sergeants, one clerk, a civilian, no pilots, and no aircraft was all there was in America's war chest to fight against the most formidable air weapon ever forged in the brief history of aviation.

Instead of the desired quick results, the First Pursuit organization experienced a month of confusion and delays. The organization traveled to Villeneuve-les-Vertus, a French airfield, to plan and establish facilities for the first American pursuit squadrons. The French promised to build barracks for the Americans, then proceeded to use the newly built barracks for themselves. Major Raoul Lufbery told the First Pursuit planning officers that there was plenty of room for an American squadron at the airfield where he was once based with the Lafayette Escadrille. There wasn't. A French liaison officer announced that plans had been made to supply the Americans with thirty-six Nieuports, but also reported that "where and when these planes will come is still undecided." The Air Service had an airfield under construction. They had a squadron of trained flyers and mechanics. The only thing they did not have was aircraft.

On February 13, 1918, the now-trained pilots, unaware of the continuing bureaucratic entanglements, saw Special Order No. 45 pinned to the wooden wall of the headquarters office at Issoudun: "The following named First Lieutenants ASSC, USR, are hereby relieved from duty with Headquarters Detachment and assigned to the 95th Aero Squadron for duty." My father anxiously scanned the list of names: Blodgett, Buckley, Casgrain, Curtis, Fisher, Heinrichs, McLanahan, Sewall, Eastman. There at the end of the list was Woolley, C.H. He had made the cut.

Two days later, with trunks packed, mess bills paid, flying equipment returned to the supply officer, and the transfer checklist completed, the 95th Aero Squadron was ready.

# CHAPTER 6

# First to the Front

At six A.M. on February 16, 1918, the members of the 95th Aero Squadron, America's first pursuit squadron, formed up by the headquarters building, Third Aviation Center, Issoudun. Even at that early hour the Army band led the way, playing a lively Sousa air. Slightly teary-eyed Red Cross nurses and YMCA girls waved handkerchiefs and cheered the eighteen young aviators, three ground officers, and 160 enlisted men as they marched to the waiting transportation. They were going to be the first squadron to the front, the first to taste combat.

The reality of their journey to the town of Vertus, their final stop by rail, was less glorious than their send-off. They boarded a train that made its way slowly, haltingly, toward the front; they were repeatedly stopped and diverted for what someone determined was more important railway traffic. Excitement ebbed and gave way to boredom. "Hurry up and wait" was the name of the game once again. Reportedly, some of them proceeded to fortify their spirits, and the trip became punctuated by the crash of empty bottles well aimed at slowly passing telephone poles.

They stopped at Orléans, where the 103rd Aero Squadron left for Paris, then moved on to Montaigne for the first night and Chalons the second. There, Bill Taylor, Sumner Sewall, Chas Woolley, and others went into the center of town, found a small restaurant, sampled the local wine, enjoyed the fare of the day, and listened to the sounds of 75 and 100 mm antiaircraft batteries firing and the drone of German bombers overhead. Searchlights played over the skies, antiaircraft reports boomed, and German bombs flashed in the distance. The German night air raids seemed to be ineffectual. Ned Buford, the honorary Confederate Colonel from Tennessee, managed to consume more of the local wine than was good for him and kept poor Heinrichs awake in his rail *coupe* with his off-key renditions of popular songs. Among them was:

> Oh, I'm going to a better land; they binge there
> every night,
> The cocktails grow on bushes, so every one stays
> tight,
> They've torn up all the calendars; they've busted
> all the clocks,
> And the little drops of whisky come trickling
> down the rocks

Later, for reasons unknown, the train became sidetracked at Epernay, fifteen kilometers from the station at Vertus. Bill Taylor, with his imposing stature and excellent command of the French language, approached the stationmaster, and through demands and threats, found an engine that could deliver the squadron to Vertus. From Vertus it was six kilometers by truck to the airfield at Villeneuve les Vertus.

Two hours later, Major Atkinson, Captain Rankin, and Captain Roosevelt, the stalwarts who had worked so furiously to get everything in readiness, greeted them. Quentin's cousin, Phil Roosevelt, a gangly, Ichabod Crane sort, introduced himself and was later voted by the pilots to be the owner of the most disreputable overseas cap in the Air Service.

The camp, barring the usual mud, proved to be a promising place. The barren, barn-like barracks were divided into two-man rooms, each with two windows, and held twenty-five officers and three stoves. Hopes had been high that the fabled Major Raoul Lufbery would be their Commanding Officer, but that was not to be. Major Jim Miller, whom many at Issoudun had grown to know and admire, was the man. He, much to the relief of all, replaced the temporary commander, Lieutenant Roy Ripley, a non-flying officer who, because of his fervent opposition to alcoholic beverages, was dubbed "the Texas milkshake boy." The pilots scavenged Vertus for mirrors, lamps, and other homey effects to improve their new quarters. After the primitive conditions of Issoudun, it was nice to have a few creature comforts again. The only item they lacked was aircraft.

The 95th shared the field with the newly formed French flying unit *Escadre de Combat No. 1.* Under the much-decorated Commandant Menard, *Groupe Menard,* as it became known, earned a reputation as one of the finest organizations in the French Air Service. The Americans looked on enviously as the French pilots took to the air in their advanced Spad fighter aircraft. Despite their experience, the Frenchmen nevertheless had their share of accidents. One French plane bounced its wheels off the roof of the American barracks, fell, and was destroyed. The pilot, embarrassed, survived with nothing more serious than a broken nose.

The French airmen set out to make their Yankee cousins feel at home and succeeded only too well. Before the arrival of their aircraft, small detachments of the 95th, at any hour of the night, could be seen making their way quietly toward the French canteen, and a few hours later could be seen feeling their way home again—not nearly so quietly. When asked who was the greatest living Frenchman, Ned Buford unhesitatingly nominated Perronet, that peerless artist of the grape who managed Perronet's bar, the bar that became the "official" flying officers' headquarters. Our pilots without planes passed the time sharing bottles of champagne, called by the flyers "the local." They joined in singing hearty choruses of the British flyers' tune:

> *Take the cylinder out of my kidneys,*
> *The connecting rod out of my brain,*
> *From the small of my back take the camshaft,*
> *And assemble the engine again.*

The nearby town of Mesnil-sur-Ozer was given honorable mention, as it offered the charms of the fair and friendly Thérèse and her companion. The town became a favorite rendezvous for those who enjoyed the champagne, the well-known produce of the district. For those less nocturnally inclined, there were pickup football games played with a soccer ball, with participants like All-American Hobey Baker, fast and shifty Waldo Heinrichs, six-foot-five-inch Bill Taylor, and even a few Italian artillerymen who, without guns, had been sent from Italy to France as laborers. For those less athletically inclined, there were card games. Bridge tournaments abounded. Blackjack, red-dog, and an occasional game of craps could be found if one had some francs to spare.

The Villeneuve Gang, as the pilots called themselves, managed to keep up their appearance as well as their spirit of adventure. While waiting for planes they spent a great deal of time brushing their uniforms and polishing their boots and leather, cross-strapped Sam Browne belts, which were the dress symbol of the overseas commissioned officers. Occasional German air raids in the vicinity brought antiaircraft shrapnel raining down. But there were no direct attacks on the airfield, and damn little excitement.

The lack of airplanes frustrated Jim Miller, a man of action, as much as it frustrated the aviators under his command. Miller shared the feeling of many others that the French and the British had shouldered the burden of the war for too long. America's time had come. And yet the 95th had no aircraft! Announced the previous year, the much-heralded U.S. aircraft construction program, which was supposed to blacken the European skies with American flying machines, had as yet failed to deliver a single aircraft to the front.

Miller's 95th could have gotten into action much more quickly if Colonel Mitchell had followed the advice of the French commanders and allowed the American pilots to supplement the ranks of French squadrons. But General Pershing was adamant and told Mitchell that the Air Service, like all the other branches of the American military under his control, would fight separately, not under foreign commands. It may have made sense in principle, but in reality it left the 95th stranded in France with no equipment and no way to join the fighting.

With Major Atkinson's approval, Miller made numerous telephone calls to Paris and Chaumont demanding, "Where in hell are our airplanes? Do I have to call Pershing himself?" In utter frustration, Atkinson and Miller drove to American Headquarters in Paris on February 23 to plead their case and investigate firsthand the possibility of procuring suitable airplanes. Finally, they were told that they would get suitable aircraft. Limited numbers of Nieuport Type 28 planes were to be made available beginning February 27, 1918.

Two days prior to the promised date, the French authorities reported to Atkinson that five Nieuport 28s were immediately available and that four additional aircraft would arrive per day until the Americans received a total of thirty-six. Aircraft at last! They weren't the best—the Spad XIII was the most up-to-date fighter, flown exclusively by the first-rate French *escadrilles*, or squadrons. In fact, no one seemed to know much about the Nieuport 28s. The French had never flown any in combat. First Lieutenant Woolley did not care. It was an airplane, and he would be at its controls.

Captain Miller, my father, and eight other Lieutenants traveled to Paris to ferry the new aircraft to Villeneuve. On the day of their planned return, poor visibility forced the cancellation of all flying. That evening, the entire group bought tickets to La Femina Theatre, where they witnessed a show that the puritanical Heinrichs described as "the rottenest exhibition of naked women I have ever seen on stage." In all likelihood, Waldo had never before even seen such a show, but it's equally likely that his companions enjoyed the performance.

The following morning, barely recovered from their evening in Paris, the resolute nine traveled by truck to Villacoublay, the Nieuport factory testing field, to pick up the planes. Normally, aircraft were transported to Le Bourget, an enormous flying field six miles northeast of Paris, from which the planes were then flown to the front. But to save time, the Americans went directly to the testing field to collect their planes.

A high-ranking company official from the Nieuport factory met them, and presented a detailed lecture on the 160-horsepower Monosoupape, or single-valve Gnome rotary engine that powered the Type 28s. With instruction out of the way, each pilot took a short practice flight in a new plane. Grinning from ear to ear, they awaited the order to take off again in their new ships for Villeneuve-les-Vertus. The weather, with snow and rain, closed in again, making flying out of the question, but the pilots were treated to a sumptuous lunch at a fine hotel in Versailles, as guests of Nieuport. Following lunch a more detailed tour was given at the factory.

As a former engineering student, my father was fascinated by the design of and workmanship on the prototype planes still under development. From the factory floor, a visitor could see that airplanes supposedly designed for mass production were in reality anything but mass-produced. Each aircraft was literally handcrafted. Nieuport woodworkers—former cabinetmakers and skilled carpenters—pieced together the aircraft skeleton from stringers and struts of ash and silver spruce. The rigger relied on sight, feel, and experience as he brought the wooden skeleton into plumb alignment with more than a hundred wires. Only Swedish wire was strong enough to use. Excitement rippled through the wing room as the white-robed women workers noticed the rare visit of the American aviators, then returned to their work, stitching together the aircraft's skin. The production process reminded my father of the master canoe- and kayak-building practiced by the Native Americans in the interior of Maine.

Poor weather kept my father and his companions grounded for the next two days. It was pleasant to be in Paris, but expensive. Waldo's greatest luxury in Paris was a hot bath at night, a cold one in the morning, and reasonable meals. But "Women, wine and theatres are my companions' indulgence," Heinrichs wrote in his diary.

In Paris, pilots from the 94th Aero Squadron joined the now partied-out 95th to transport additional planes to Villeneuve-les-Vertus. The two groups of flyers knew one another from their final training days at Issoudun, and they were now to serve together as part of the embryonic First Pursuit Group.

Among the pilots of the 94th was Major John W. F. M. Huffer. Born of French and American parents, he had grown up in Paris, with all the attitudes and mannerisms of a Parisian. After a brief stint with the A.F.S., he joined the Foreign Legion; he then trained at the basic flying school at Pau, the gunnery school at Cazeaux, the "finishing school" at Avord, and was assigned to the front with N. 95. For his bravery in action, he earned the *Médaille Militaire* and the *Croix de Guerre* with three *Palmes* and two stars. With America's entry into the war, he, like Lufbery, was commissioned Major, U.S.A.A.S., and was appointed Commanding Officer of the 94th Aero Squadron.

Other members of the squadron included Captain Ken Marr, a San Franciscan, ex-ambulance, and ex-Lafayette Escadrille; Captain Dave Peterson, an ex-Lafayette Escadrille; and Captain Jim Hall, an ex–Royal Fusilier, British Army, and ex–Lafayette Escadrille. All were experienced, successful fighter pilots, bringing with them unprecedented talents to one new squadron. First Lieutenant Eddie Rickenbacker, the former race car driver, had been the Sergeant in charge of engineering at Issoudun. There he received his flight training, and was assigned to the ranks of the 94th Aero Squadron. With one of the best mechanical minds in the Air Service, he reportedly had started his military career as the chauffeur for General Pershing, but actually served in that position for Colonel Billy Mitchell.

The quiet, enigmatic Major Gervais Raoul Lufbery was also attached to the First Pursuit Group, but not specifically assigned to either the 94th or 95th, a phenomenon never explained. The thirty-two-year-old Lufbery had been born in France of French parents, but after the death of his mother, his father had remarried and left France for a new life in America. In his late teens, Lufbery traveled the world before joining his father in Wallingford, Connecticut. After a stint in the U.S. Army in the Philippines, Lufbery took to the road again, traveling to China, Japan, and India. There he met and worked as the mechanic for the famed French aviation pioneer Marc Pourpe. In 1914, while they were in France purchasing a new airplane, war broke out. Pourpe promptly enlisted in the French aviation service and Lufbery joined the French Foreign Legion. Within days, Lufbery was transferred to the *Armée de l'Air*, and served with Pourpe as his mechanic until the aviator's accidental death in December 1914. Deeply affected by the loss of his friend, he applied for flight training, and upon completion was assigned to a French bombardment squadron. In the spring of 1916, desiring more action, he enrolled in the fighter school at Pau, from which, after some difficulty, he graduated. Learning to control the nimble pursuit planes was vastly different from flying the more docile bombers. From Pau, he joined N. 124, the Lafayette Escadrille. With seventeen victories scored before America entered the war, Lufbery was the leading American ace, and in January 1918 he was commissioned Major, U.S.A.A.S.

On March 6, 1918, thirteen eager American pilots left Paris for Villeneuve-les-Vertus at the controls of their brand-new Nieuport Type 28 airplanes. It was to be an inauspicious beginning.

Six pilots, including Miller, Woolley, Rickenbacker, and Sumner Sewall, made it to their destination without mishap. The others were not so fortunate. A broken cylinder valve forced Dick Blodgett to make an emergency landing. Magneto trouble forced Hobey Baker down. Bill Taylor ran out of gas. One pilot got lost and three others were forced down by obscure mechanical faults. If they had such difficulty just getting their aircraft from the factory to the front, how could these delicate, temperamental machines hold up under the strains of combat?

They now had planes, but the planes were delivered without guns! The next step for each pilot was to sign Q.M.C. Form 242 and to receive:

> One fur-lined combination flying suit, new; one pair paper gloves, new; one fur-lined canvas helmet, new; one pair fur-lined boots, new; one map case, new; one watch, wrist, Elgin, new; one [watch] wristlet, leather, new, and one separate requisition form for one airplane Nieuport Type 28—new.

They were now equipped, thanks to Uncle Sam.

On the morning of March 9, Jim Miller traveled to Coligny to collect a repaired Nieuport, and while there was invited by Major Davenport Johnson to join him and Major Millard Harmon for a short patrol of the lines. Miller could not turn down the invitation. The Americans borrowed three Spad VIIs from a French squadron and took to the air. Very early into the patrol, Harmon was forced to drop out with motor trouble, but Johnson and Miller continued on past Soissons and Reims, over the lines. They spotted and attacked two German planes, with no German loss. Twenty minutes later, well into German territory, they encountered two more enemy fighters at 10,500 feet. Johnson reported that he fired twenty-five rounds at the higher of the two, but was forced to retire from the fight when his machine guns jammed. Miller continued the action, firing numerous rounds at the lower man, who went into a spin. He followed him down, spinning in pursuit. After two spins, the German looped, maneuvered above Miller and fired several long bursts. Miller made a series of spins and disappeared from Johnson's view at 3,300 feet above a forest north of Corbeny. Johnson's report ended, "I followed him down until he disappeared, but as my machine guns were broken, [I] could do nothing, so returned to Coincy, arriving at 5:05 P.M."

For days the squadron sought to confirm the fate of their commanding officer. It was their first experience with a combat casualty, and the first time they would search to piece together the scattered bits of the narratives of others. They were dependent upon the primitive condition of wartime telephonic communications; pursuit flyers had no radios in their planes, no means of communicating with either their companions in the air or their forces on the ground. The participants of an aerial combat were usually too absorbed in their tasks to observe what was happening to the others. The focus was on the enemy. Ground observers, if the action could be seen from the Allied lines, were the most reliable reporters. Surviving pilots all too often never learned how or where their close friends and comrades had died. Were they defenseless with jammed guns? Had the plane suffered fatal damage? Had the pilot received a wound? Had he been killed instantly in the air? Usually there was no answer.

Preliminary reports were that Miller had survived and was captured, the first American aviation war prisoner. Word was received in April from the International Red Cross that Miller was dead and had been buried in the military cemetery at Laon.

Research has since revealed that Leutnant Robert Hildebrandt of Jasta 13 (Squadron 13) was the German pilot responsible for Miller's death. It was Hildebrandt's fourth victory.

In one of my many conversations with Jim Knowles, he bristled at the memory of Miller's death. His complexion reddened with anger as he told of Miller's only combat:

> Harmon had engine trouble and turned back. Johnson and Miller ran into four Germans. Almost immediately, Johnson abandoned the fight and left Miller on his own. Miller went down with a German on his tail. After the war, the German pilot who brought Miller down told in a signed statement that he and his intelligence officer had rushed to the crash scene, where Jim, badly wounded in the crash and obviously dying, spoke his last words, 'Goddamned Johnson, he left me without warning. He's a yellow son of a bitch! You can tell him that and I hope he's stuck up against a brick wall and shot.'

"After that, the good Major was known as 'Jam' Johnson," Knowles muttered in disgust. "And to top it off, he replaced Miller as our commanding officer!" Miller's death was a blow to the squadron.

They now had everything, airplanes, pilots, mechanics, gasoline, oil . . . everything except guns! For some reason, the machine guns, the only weapon system on the fighter aircraft, had been left behind. The guns were simply unavailable.

By March 12, with enough planes on hand, the squadron was divided into three manageable subunits called "flights." Elected Flight Commanders were George Fisher, Bill Taylor, and Waldo Heinrichs. They chose men by turns and assigned each a machine. Fisher's First Flight included Charles Woolley, Sumner Sewall, Dick Blodgett, and Ted Curtis. Woolley was assigned aircraft #6149, the manufacturer's serial number. Sergeant Hammond and Privates Standt and Sullenger were assigned the job of maintaining his aircraft. These enlisted mechanics and crew chiefs were the unsung heroes of the air war. They were responsible for the fulfillment of the slogan featured on war-bond posters: "Keep 'em flying!"

The French and the Chief of Air Service agreed to have their pilots perform joint patrols over the lines, an agreement that caused some concern at Villeneuve-les-Vertus. Were the Spad Type VIIs and Nieuport 28s anywhere near compatible enough to fly the same patrols? Sumner Sewall and Dick Blodgett flew a trial patrol with a French aviator piloting one of Spa 81's Spads. The two Americans in their Nieuports found that they were able to climb faster than the Spad to 8,000 feet. The Nieuports could easily match the speed of the Spads and in further maneuvering, the Nieuports outflew them. The Nieuport landing speed proved to be slower, another plus. The Nieuports had passed their first test. The Americans and French could fly patrols together with confidence.

For the 95th the action could now begin. On May 15, 1918, the 95th was called on to provide three patrols of three machines each. Dick Blodgett took over as acting Commander of the First Flight, replacing Fisher, who had gone to Paris with a convoy of four trucks to get spare parts for the Gnome engines. "Being commander means nothing but a lot of hot air and written orders," Blodgett wrote. "It's more keeping track of machines and equipment than anything else."

At 11:30 A.M. Blodgett, Sewall and Woolley took off on the first patrol, accompanied by a French Spad. They flew their unarmed Nieuports at 16,000 feet between Epernay and Reims. Their mission: to observe the accuracy of Allied antiaircraft fire against enemy long-distance photographic airplanes. For the first time, my father headed out over the very lines that had been the focus of the world's attention for nearly three years. He looked down on two intricate trench systems stretching for miles. Separating the trenches was the pockmarked ground of No Man's Land, a lifeless ruin of wire, timber, and mud.

A haze hung over Reims in the distance. Here and there were smudges on the ground where villages had once stood, villages destroyed in the First Battle of the Marne in 1914, during which thousands of tons of shells ravaged the countryside and countless soldiers died in a vicious struggle for a few yards of real estate.

But this first patrol had no time for historical reflection regarding the seemingly quiet front. "You must constantly scan the skies for those black specks which could be the enemy," they had been warned more than once. First Lieutenant Charles H. Woolley was one of the first three American fighter pilots to fly a combat mission. How proud I am of my father, who was one of the first three Americans to cross the lines in the air, and with no guns to protect himself!

Equally proud of the accomplishment, Dick Blodgett wrote: "I am in the first American squadron to go to the front as a unit. I was also the leader of the first American patrol ever to patrol the lines. That's not so bad, is it?"

On that eventful day, not everyone in the 95th was physically up to the challenge. During the afternoon, Flight Commander Waldo Heinrichs was grounded by an inner-ear problem that destroyed his sense of balance. He assigned three of his men, Richards, Rhodes, and Quick, to fly on the second patrol over the lines. Heinrichs noted in his diary, "Ray Quick, who was forced on my flight as last choice and whom I always knew was yellow[,] turned and refused to fly. Said his motor wouldn't turn up more than 1250."

Waldo, disbelieving Quick, tried out the balky engine, which immediately turned 1280 rpm's on the ground. There is no record of what duties Quick performed in the squadron during the balance of the war, but it was certainly not combat flying. He was a "Kiwi," named after the flightless New Zealand bird, one without the nerve to fly. Dick Blodgett defined a Kiwi as:

> A bird that spends its time sitting on the ground, flapping its wings and making a lot of noise. These are barracks flyers, hot air heroes, the lowest regarded members of the Air Service.

On the same day that the first patrols were flown, Major Davenport Johnson reported in as the squadron's new Commanding Officer. The pilots were leery of "Jam" Johnson and his reputation after Miller's loss. And yet Johnson had his strengths. Harold Buckley noted Johnson's arrival:

The first night in the mess, Alex McLanahan had suggested deferentially as a lowly Lieutenant to a Major that a few light wines and beers (this was only a feeler) in the mess would add considerably to the health and happiness of the 'brave boys.' He intimated that it [the beverages] would help the pilots digest the bum food, and that they all might be dead in a few weeks anyway.

"I tell you, Major," said Lieutenant Ripley, the "Texas milkshake" boy, "I've had a lot of experience with the stuff and I'm agin it."

"Yes?" said the Major in his best West Point manner. "Well, I'm for it." Johnson's rating soared.

They had made the first patrols, but there was such a shortage of spare parts that the Flight Commanders decided to act in concert and refused to approve any further patrols until there were enough supplies to repair the aircraft properly. The supply officers complained to headquarters that "there are not enough shock absorbers, screws and wires to keep the Nieuports in the air." Heinrichs reported in his diary that, "Due to the fact that the Supply Office for the 95th was on a French-controlled field, the Supply Office at the First Pursuit Group Headquarters refused to fulfill the requisitions, because they were not ordered from an American-controlled airfield."

The next bit of red tape that entangled the Flight Commanders was in the form of orders from First Pursuit headquarters to report the number of every plane, the name of the pilot, the date, duration, location, and purpose of every flight taken. The reports were intended to locate the man or men who were reported to have been seen, acting without orders, in the air beyond the lines over enemy territory. This required interviewing every pilot and checking every "Pilot's Record" book, as well as interviewing the crews who had worked on the machines. No culprits were found.

If red tape were not enough to lower morale, a rumor began to circulate that the 95th was going to be pulled from the front and sent to the aerial gunnery school, *Ecole Tir Arien de Cazeaux,* just south of Bordeaux. "Every man in the Squadron would rather take a chance right now over the lines without any Aerial Gunnery than be sent back to Cazeaux," Waldo noted in his diary. "A very heavy gloom settled all over the 95th. Mechanics do not want to lose us nor we them."

On March 21, the men of the 95th learned that the rumors were true. To add insult to injury, all of their aircraft, the planes for which they had waited for so long, were going to be assigned to the pilots of the 94th Aero Squadron. In the same batch of communications came the message from Paris that only twelve machine guns would be available for the use of the two squadrons at Villeneuve-les-Vertus. On that note, Johnson and his adjutant departed for Paris to deal with this latest absurdity from headquarters. Before departing, Johnson promised his pilots that they would return shortly and would remain as a unit; the 95th was not to be compromised or broken up. They took final flights in their agile Nieuports and did a formation fly-by for Commandant Menard and their other after-hours companions, the French pilots of *Escadre de Combat No. 1*. Upon landing, the 95th reluctantly bid adieu to their planes and crews.

The 94th and the 95th spent their last night together at Villeneuve toasting to their luck, good and bad, while listening to the Germans bomb Chalons and Epernay!

# CHAPTER 7

# Guns, Champagne, and Spies

Unceremoniously yanked away from their precious Nieuports and action at the front, First Lieutenant C. H. Woolley and his fellow flyers of the 95th once again found themselves at the mercy of the French rail system. They stood in ancient railway cars packed with civilians carrying all their worldly belongings. Some of the cars belonging to the military were marked on their sides with *40 hommes—8 chevaux*, forty men or eight horses. In Paris, they found that mobs, panicked by the bombardment from the long-range German cannon called "the Paris Gun," had nearly filled all the trains headed out of the city, taking them away from the shelling. After waiting for hours and haggling with ticket agents and baggage handlers, the American flyers boarded an overnight train to Bordeaux.

At 7:30 the next morning, they transferred to a narrow gauge railroad for the final leg of the trip to the town of Cazeaux de Lac. At noon, after a grand lunch of eggs and oysters, they straggled into the gunnery school headquarters and reported to a Major Robertson. Casgrain concluded that the Major, "in spite of being a West Pointer, was a prince and sympathetic to our plight." With a minimum of red tape, Robertson signed the flyers in and released them for a quick tour of the facility. The equipment they saw was diverse: sorely used Nieuport 17s, their wings and fuselages showing the canvas patches of numerous repairs; French F.B.A. Type H seaplanes; and, to everyone's amazement, a small fleet of sleek, fast motorboats, tied up at the docks of broad, bright-blue Lake Cazeaux. Things did not seem so bad after all.

After the Gunnery School tour they were driven to the nearby town of Arcachon where they were provided billets in the modest Grand Hotel.

Classes started on the following day. My father assumed that hunting the Hun in the air must be similar to stalking live game. To make a kill, a fighter pilot needed natural instincts, quick reflexes, and total familiarity with his weapons. The bottom line: you had to be a damned good shot to down a Boche aircraft.

Gunnery training began with stripping and reassembling Vickers machine guns, the guns with which they would fight in the air. Survival would depend on thoroughly understanding the inner workings of the Vickers. The Vickers was prone to jams, the dreaded stoppages of the machine guns that were the curse of the fighter pilot in the midst of combat. Faulty ammunition and careless loading of the ammunition belts usually caused the jams. The aviator had to become so familiar with jams and their causes that he could clear them with one hand in mid-air. Clearing a jam required that the pilot reach around his windscreen with fingers numbed by cold, fighting 140-mile-per-hour winds, and fly the aircraft with the other hand. If the jam was particularly obstinate, he had to use both hands and fly the aircraft with the control stick between his knees.

The Vickers, however, was an improvement over the drum-fed Lewis gun that was attached on some aircraft to the top wing and fired above the arc of the propeller. To change an empty ammunition drum on a Lewis gun, the pilot had to retract the gun from its firing position on the wing, and bring it down the curved metal brace of the Foster Mount into the cockpit. In the lowered position, the pilot had to remove the empty drum, replace it with a full drum, and reposition the gun back up the curved metal mount to the top of the wing. A story has been told of a British pilot who undid his seat strap and stood up as he fought to free his empty but now immobile Lewis gun. His plane went into a dive, and the Britisher found himself dangling in mid-air, hanging on for dear life to the handle of his inoperative gun! Miraculously, the plane righted itself, throwing him back into the cockpit.

After the class in machine guns and ammunition, the students marched to the shore of Lake Cazeaux, where they were taught to fire little French 8 mm army carbines at one-foot targets set in the water 200 meters distant. This proved to be great fun, except that the carbines, despite their small size, had a ferocious kick. With sore shoulders, the pilots then fired fifty to seventy-five rounds from Vickers machine guns mounted in simulated airplane cockpits and aimed at the same one-foot floating targets.

After lunch came practice in the swift motorboats, each named after one of the Allied countries and armed with machine guns. Moving at high speeds across the water, they shot short bursts at red and white targets scattered about the surface of the lake. This was the first lesson in the art of "deflection." Deflection shooting is the aiming of one's fire in aerial gunnery beyond a moving airplane or target to compensate for its movement. It was a satisfying exercise, because the splash of each round could readily be seen and each fledgling marksman could assess his skill from the location of these miniature fountains of water in relation to the targets.

As the training progressed, a variety of weapons were fired at an assortment of targets: shotguns quickly brought to the shoulder and fired at soaring clay pigeons; snap-shots fired with revolvers and automatic pistols at fast moving pop-up targets. A fighter pilot had to be a good marksman as well as an aggressive flyer; and, most important, he had to know the elusive art of "deflection" to beat the Boche in the air.

The pilots were keenly attentive to the lectures of Sergeant Mantell, the French instructor with a splendid command of English, who was the management brains of this school. Mantell taught his students that airborne marksmanship required a unique combination of geometry, science, and calculus. The instability of the aircraft, the angle of fire, and the motion of the target all had to be taken into account when practicing deflection.

My father must have scratched his head as he studied the three mimeographed instruction booklets that dealt with various mysterious aspects of aerial gunnery. One booklet ended with: "Always keep cool-headed till the last moment. Do not be afraid or nervous if the enemy continues to shoot. Do not cease firing. Wait for the final fault in his manoeuvering." Easier said than done!

As I look through the thirty-four baffling pages of my father's training booklet entitled "Notes upon aerial shooting and deflectors," I am as confused today as my father must have been when he read the following:

> Given an aeroplane 'T' which travels with a speed 'Ts' in a straight course, a machine-gunner in an aeroplane 'S' going at a speed 'Ss'. At what point should one aim to hit the target plane? Also given the distance 'D' which separates the two aeroplanes, the initial velocity of the bullet 'VO', the time 't' taken by the bullet to travel the distance 'D'.

How anyone could have learned deflection from these notes is a mystery. I suspect few in combat would have had time to go through these calculations in the midst of shooting while flying upside down at over one hundred miles per hour.

On days when poor weather prohibited flying, it was wonderful to take a day trip to nearby Bordeaux. The complexion of the city had changed dramatically in the eleven months since my father had landed in France. Unloading their cargoes of war material, massive American cargo ships, camouflaged in "dazzle" patterns of vivid blue, lavender, white, and black, choked the piers as well as the waters of the harbor. In 1917, the British Navy had developed a disruptive paint scheme similar to that found in nature, which made it difficult for a submerged U-Boat to predict the exact course of the vessel it wished to attack. The camouflage (called "dazzle," from the American term "razzle-dazzle") was obviously effective—in 1918, 1,256 American ships were painted with this pattern, and only one percent were lost to U-Boats.

Disembarked from the troop ships at the piers, formations of young, khaki-clad American soldiers marched through the streets of the city on their way to war. The officers in charge had yet to purchase their Sam Browne belts and soft "overseas" caps, the symbols of an officer who had served at the front. Black U.S. Army troops worked as stevedores on the docks, unloading material needed by the hundreds of thousands of young American soldiers soon to arrive. Light Ford trucks, Hudson, Cadillac, and Packard touring cars, some in crates and some just under canvas, sat idly while lines of American five-ton White trucks moved supplies through the city toward the front.

Dad was not a particularly religious man, but he was fascinated with church architecture, and on one visit sought out the famous Bordeaux Cathedral. Above its buttressed nave soared the towering spire that dominated the skyline of the city. It seemed that even the cathedral had gone to war. Its lovely spire now supported a wireless-station antenna with guy wires fanning out from the tower for stability. Inside, the cathedral was unchanged, and he reflected on the stained-glass windows, the statuary, and the endless array of flickering candles lighted in prayer for so many of France's sons.

He traveled along the paved streets and large open squares, admiring the classic components found in most French cities: Le Grand Théâtre, Hôtel de Ville, the customhouse, and fine old houses with iron balconies recalling the wealth and aristocracy of times past.

The cuisine of Bordeaux was beyond compare. My father, with Alex McLanahan, found restaurants like the Le Champon Fin, Restaurant Dubern, and the Hôtel Biscouby, each with its own specialty, each exceptionally good. Connoisseurs ranked Bordeaux third behind Paris and Lyon for cuisine, enhanced in large part because of the incomparable wines of the Bordelais region. The region supplied sweet white table wines such as Château Raboud, Château d'Yuen, and Château Rieussec, and, yes, the reds from Médoc, Graves, and Saint-Emilion.

In Arcachon, in the continuing spirit of training, the gallant men of the 95th honed their palates by sampling as many varieties of these wines as they could find. As this education was proceeding, small groups who were friends and had compatible lifestyles began to secure more comfortable quarters. The French, always delighted to find a few extra francs, were renting their homes and small villas to the *"Bons Américains."* Alex McLanahan, Chas Woolley, and Bill Taylor formed one rental alliance, while Bill Casgrain, Ned Buford, and Russ Hall formed another. Others like conservative Waldo found living at the Grand Hotel pleasant enough, and less costly. Those with villas entertained lavishly whenever possible and were greatly appreciated by the area's vintners.

Alexander Hawley McLanahan was from a wealthy Philadelphia family, and before joining the Air Service, had been a member of the class of 1918 at Yale's Sheffield Scientific School. Upon enlisting, he was sent to the ground school at Cornell University, shipped overseas in July 1917, and for his flight training, joined the group at Tours and Issoudun. Alex was the epitome of a well-to-do young American. Tall and slender, with hair smoothly combed back from a middle part, he was full of fun and always ready for a party, either as a lavish host or an eager guest. Alex had superb taste; he was just the one to find the ideal quarters to share with Woolley and Taylor, to find an epicurean chef, and to fill a cellar with fine wines.

I never had the pleasure of meeting Alex, but after his death, I met his wife. After my initial contact with her regarding my interest in Alex's wartime experiences, I was invited to her Fifth Avenue apartment in New York for tea. Upon my arrival, a handsome woman of about seventy wearing a long, velvet hostess gown welcomed me. Obviously a former beauty, she graciously showed me into the living room.

There, over the fireplace, hung a portrait of the debonair Alex painted by the renowned French aviation artist Henri Farré. After the Great War, McLanahan commissioned other Farré paintings that depicted aerial combat. These graced the walls of a French château that Alex's family had purchased in 1919. The paintings showed planes with large German crosses on their wings falling in flames, while American planes with red-white-and-blue cocardes soared away in victory. During the Second World War, German officers occupied the McLanahan château. When the McLanahans returned to their château at the end of the war, the only things in the entire place that had been changed were the aircraft insignia in the paintings. The planes falling in flames were now American, and those victorious were German.

Scattered throughout the McLanahan apartment were smaller framed photographic portraits of Sewall, Curtis, and Woolley. As tea was being served, we talked about Alex and the others. With dramatic gestures and an occasional moist eye, she told me more about her glamorous and wonderful life with Alex. It was an interesting story, even if it wasn't germane to my research.

In *Squadron 95*, a light and irreverent history of the 95th Aero Squadron, Harold Buckley describes what some consider the most bizarre event of the entire Cazeaux period. It took place one evening at the McLanahan-Woolley-Taylor villa. Buckley recalls that McLanahan and his housemates had invited Russ Hall to a lavish feast where everyone "drank, and drank some more." Hall, for his safety, was pressed to stay the night, and all retired.

Back at Hall's villa, his roommates, Buford and Casgrain, as well as Buckley, were "brooding before their open fire over the need to go to bed and get up again so soon," when *"petit Georges"* the son of McLanahan's landlady burst into the room crying, *"Il est mort! Il est mort!"* "He is dead! He is dead!"

The boy was too upset to tell them exactly who "he" was. Rushing up the street toward the McLanahan villa, they met Bill Taylor, who indicated that the "he" in question was Russ Hall, and that he was "stretched out, cold and inert, lifeless and done for."

Buckley continued:

> Stricken with fear and wretched at the untimely end of the gallant Russ, we crept into the death-chamber to view the remains from which the gay spirit had so recently departed. We stared at the pale handsome face . . . and wondered who would get his Russian boots. But as we gazed, bowed down with the sadness of it all, the corpse suddenly sat up, all but causing

three or four more deaths from fright. We caught at him and held him up as if forcibly to keep him from the clutches of the other world. We gave him a drink, probably the last thing he needed, and gradually the truth was pieced together.

Hall explained that he had awakened in the middle of the night in need of a glass of water. Thinking that he was in his own room in his own villa, he walked toward what he thought was his door, but what turned out to be an open window on the second floor. Hall tripped over a suitcase, nose-dived out the window and landed "on his head on a cement walk fifteen feet below. By a miracle never since explained, he landed within a six-foot iron picket fence with points like javelins that was only three feet from the wall of the house."

"Strange as it may appear to be," Buckley wrote, "there were no ill effects from this crash. We watched Hall surreptitiously for a few days, apprehensive lest this fine mind be clouded at the outset of a brilliant career, but our fears were groundless. He remained quite rational, perfectly normal, boon comrade in the heydays, companionate grouser in adversity, *bon garçon toujours.*"

Waldo Heinrichs' diary entry on April 9 records: "Took Hall's place for practice shooting at balloons, since he was still too ill to fly. Drunk, fell out a window last night." Waldo disapproved of the drinking styles of both Hall and Buford. "I cannot trust men who drink as heavily as Hall and Buford. How will they ever be able to back me up in a fight?" Despite Heinrichs' concern, the noble grape did not seem to impair the flying ability of either man. Each pilot compiled an admirable record of time in the air, and each scored two confirmed victories.

The local French population, particularly those of the gentler sex, welcomed the brave American flyers and were often seen in many of the local drinking establishments, giving French lessons and possibly those of a more personal nature. Two particularly attractive young women who always seemed ready for fun and frolic resided near the McLanahan and Casgrain villas and became the particular favorites of Buckley and Woolley. The friendly girls favored the latest Parisian fashions, a marked contrast to the long skirts and cardigan sweaters of the girls at home, or the rather frumpy uniforms of the Red Cross nurses and YMCA girls. One day, much to the disappointment of the two Romeos, the girls simply disappeared. Perhaps that was part of the magic of wartime friendships and romances. These involvements tended to be transitory, as transitory as the life of a fighter pilot at the front.

As gunnery training at Cazeaux drew to a close, it was back into the air. No more nasty little carbines, no more lake-hopping speedboats; it was Nieuport 17s with real guns firing real bullets. Students had to concentrate on two areas: the varied targets that were offered, and their flying position in relation to the landing field at the aerodrome. This landing field was the only site in this beautiful landscape where they could safely alight. The only alternatives were water, salt or fresh, pine forests, or hillside vineyards.

Landing at the aerodrome had its own set of problems. The field was of smooth, clay-like soil, barren of grass. To keep this surface smooth and unmarred, the planes were fitted with broad, ski-like metal runners rather than the normal more pointed tail-skids. These runners, while protecting the field, made the landing run out much farther and made it more difficult to control the plane in a straight line. In an attempt to stay sharp and maintain his flying skills, anyone who had any type of landing mishap was fined a bottle of the best champagne. For several days in a row, constantly shifting wind conditions caused no fewer than seven magnums of the bubbly to be happily shared by all.

The aerial targets varied from tethered balloons to long fabric tubes or sleeves towed around at various angles and heights by an old Caudron twin-engine G4. The pilots also practiced on self-launched, slowly descending parachutes. At an altitude of 6,000 feet, Dad banked sharply and tossed out a parachute. Its paper cover was pulled off by the wind and a beautifully colored target about six feet in diameter slowly floated to earth. The object was to see how swiftly he could turn and dive, shooting repeatedly at the parachute, before it landed. Chasing it like an enemy Fokker, he maneuvered skillfully enough to make twenty passes. He was feeling better about his skills and knew that shortly he would need them. The 95th was not long from its return to action.

Training ended without warning when the 95th received orders on April 16 to report to the French airfield at Epiez. The squadron was given an hour and twenty minutes to pack its gear. Sergeant Mantell gave an hour-long oral examination. All received a passing grade and then proceeded to the rail station at Arcachon. After the usual delay and general confusion at the rail station, the 95th boarded a train bound for the front.

On the return trip, which took them back through Châteauroux, something totally out of character overtook Waldo Heinrichs. While he was waiting for the train from Châteauroux to Issoudun, he became aware of a striking French girl accompanied by her very dignified father. Waldo wrote in his diary: "Her eyes were very wonderful and never strayed from mine. I gave the woman ticket agent at the station a note with my address on it to give her after the train left. Of course I'll never see her again." She did write, but he never did see her again. Was Waldo's commitment to his engagement to Dotty weakening? He continued to complain about the attitudes of the others toward women, as partially evidenced by the racy papers and magazines stacked in the barracks. "It is little wonder that our fellows, lonely and without distractions, fall into sin which entices everywhere," he piously lamented. On the other hand, while in Paris, he purchased a book entitled *L'Education Sexuelle* which, he explained in his diary, was for him and Dotty because it contained so much information that they needed to learn. Ribbed unmercifully by the others when he was caught studying it, his only riposte was "Libertines!"

The 95th Aero Squadron was reformed in its entirety at the aerodrome near Epiez, as Johnson had promised. This amazed everyone. The Air Service had finally kept their word. Bill Casgrain arrived at Epiez a few days later than the rest and informed my father and Buckley that the two oh-so-friendly girls from Arcachon who had wilted under their charms had been arrested. The French authorities had declared them spies and had set a date for their trial. Casgrain reported that the girls undoubtedly would be shot. No one in the squadron felt that Buckley and Woolley had any information that could possibly have rendered aid to the enemy. They felt that the whole affair seemed to be a senseless loss of two lovely girls. *C'est la guerre.*

# CHAPTER 8

# Losses, Victories, and a Mule

As the 95th settled into the comfortable barracks near Epiez, the pilots of the 94th had been flying patrols since April 9 from their base at the Gengoult Aerodrome near Toul. The quarters at Gengoult were sturdily constructed of cement, and included finished two-man rooms, enclosed sanitary facilities, and showers with hot running water. The landing field was long, flat, and grassy, the roads were good, mud was nonexistent, and the surrounding countryside was beautiful. The pilots joked, "This has to be the promised land!"

Major Lufbery had the first recorded combat of the 94th Squadron, when at 12:25 on April 12 he took on three Albatros fighters at 10,500 feet near the town of Xivray. The leading American ace with seventeen victories to his credit, "Luf," as he was known to most of the pilots, was a great one for answering alerts and flying alone. During his highly successful service with the Lafayette Escadrille, flying alone was his preferred style, and this day was no different. The operations report of the combat was as terse as Lufbery himself:

> Major Lufbery attacked a group of three Albatros. About forty cartridges were fired on one of these planes, which appeared to be seriously damaged and which fell, nosediving into a vrille. Major Lufbery was

prevented from following this plane down on account
of the other two planes.

The final result of this fight was never confirmed, but a study
of German records after the war revealed that he was fighting
men of Jasta 64, a unit new to the front, and that they had reported no losses for the day. But more important, the 94th was in
action. They had leaders like "Luf," Jim Hall, Dave Peterson,
John Huffer, and Ken Marr—proven fighters with proven victories who had transferred from the Lafayette Escadrille and
French *Spa 62 Escadrille de Chasse*, fighters who were to lead
the 94th to the top position of all air-service squadrons.

Major Huffer, in command, advised French Aviation that, as of
April 14, the 94th was ready to fly regular patrols and respond to
alerts. That first morning Doug Campbell and Alan Winslow were
scheduled for alert duty from 6:00 to 10:00 A.M. Their planes
were wheeled out of the hangar, motors were tested, and guns
were loaded; in the Alert Tent they, too, were primed and ready.
At 8:45 the telephone rang. Doug received the message that two
Boche had been sighted fifteen miles away and were heading directly for Gengoult, their mission unknown.

During one of my visits to Doug in Cos Cob, Connecticut, he
told me about the fight that ensued:

> At 8:50 I took off and had to make one round of the
> field at 1,500 feet before Winslow got into the air. He
> was to lead, and when he reached 600 feet, I was just
> getting into position behind him. It was quite misty.
> All at once he turned and I saw him chase a plane
> which was not over 900 feet high. I was astonished
> that it had black crosses on it! I heard him shoot and
> they both went out of sight under my wings. I banked
> up 90 degrees and turned to get a view below so as
> to help Winslow, if necessary, and it was lucky I did,
> for just as I turned I heard the pop-pop-pop of a ma-
> chine gun behind me! There was another Boche and
> he was shooting at me! For some unknown reason I
> thought his tail was turned toward me as he shot and
> the thought, 'Bi-place, a two-seater, keep under him,'

flashed into my brain. He turned out afterwards to be
a single-seater Albatros.

When Doug first told the story, hoots of derision rose from the
other pilots, who razzed him about his inability to tell a two-
seater observation plane from a single-seat fighter. He admitted
he had guessed wrong, and continued his story:

"Instead of getting above him, which would have been easier,
I kept below him, maneuvering so as to try to get under his
tail without letting the gunner point at me or get a shot at me
broadside."

He had been taught that the enemy gunner, facing backward
in a two-seater, could shoot a 180-degree arc behind the wings
and above the tail and through large arcs down each side of the
plane, but not below or behind the tail. The pilot could also operate a machine gun, but as it was fixed, it could only be fired
straight ahead in the same manner as the Nieuports that he and
Winslow were flying:

It took me over a minute to maneuver into a position
behind and under his tail, without exposing myself to
his fire I thought, but I finally found myself right under him. Then I pulled my nose straight up into the
air and let him have the bullets and I think he got
some in his motor, for I saw some tracers hitting his
nose. The next thing I knew, he was diving at about
45-degrees and I was behind and above him, but behind his tail. Then I got a good aim, pulled the trigger
and held on to it. Two or three tracer rounds hit him,
and after about fifty rounds had been fired, a streak of
flame came shooting out of his fuselage near the motor. I ceased firing and watched him land and crash in
a ploughed field, his plane a mass of flame and wreckage. The pilot had sense enough to unfasten his seat
belt and was thrown clear of the machine, escaping
with some bad burns and broken bones. Winslow had
shot down his Boche; it landed and turned over in a
ploughed field on the other side of the Airdrome. I was
so excited that I was afraid to land until I made a slow

tour around the field. When I rolled up to the hangar, everybody who had not run to the fallen Boches was on hand to help us out of our planes and give us a congratulatory slap on the back.

Corporal Prince, one of Doug's mechanics, forgetting military protocol, pounded him on the back and shouted, "Damn it! That's the stuff, Lieutenant, old kid." The whole camp was pouring out to see the Boche and their victors. They were whizzing by Winslow and Campbell, some on foot, some on bicycles, others on motorcycles with sidecars, and automobiles—Colonels, Majors, soldiers, both French and American, all a sea of horizon blue and khaki. As he approached the downed Albatros, Alan noticed a crowd surrounding one slightly built man in a gray uniform. Someone in the crowd said triumphantly in French to the prisoner, "There he is. Now you will believe he is an American."

The German pilot looked Winslow over and asked in perfect French, "Are you an American?" *"Oui."* When he heard the answer, the stunned prisoner fell silent. The rumors he had heard were true. The Yanks had arrived. The captured pilot declared that his name was Vizefeldwebel Antoni Wroniekci, a German Pole flying with the Royal Württemberg Jasta 64. Later, he explained that he had actually been trying to defect to the Allies when Winslow shot him down. He explained the reason for his defection was that he had been badly treated by the Württembergers because of his Polish heritage and had been passed over many times for promotion. He subsequently assumed the alias of "Wroblewski," joined the Aviation Française, and flew with a French *escadrille* of other Polish expatriates called the Escadrille Polonaise.

Pathé newsmen took motion-picture footage of a parade held shortly after these first two victories. The film showed a French officer decorating the two flyers with the Croix de Guerre. Campbell and Winslow were relieved when the French officer did not try to kiss them on their cheeks. Later they joked, "They give out so many of those medals, I guess they save their kisses for more important occasions."

The pilots of the 95th, now finished with their gunnery training, were anxious for victories of their own, but by the end of April they were still temporarily operating from the airfield at Epiez, previously occupied by a French bombardment *escadrille*. There, they eagerly awaited orders to proceed to the Gengoult Aerodrome at Toul to join in the action with the 94th Aero Squadron.

The problem, once again, was equipment. By April 27 there were only three brand-new Nieuport 28s at Epiez ready for action, but enough for "Jam" Johnson to lead George Fisher and Bill Taylor on a patrol over this quiet sector of the front. There was one antiaircraft burst, but no enemy aircraft to be seen; here was the perfect place to gain confidence and experience. Other Nieuports finally began to arrive daily, and the Flight Commanders assigned them to pilots of each flight. This assignment provided the pilot with a chance to become familiar with his plane, to watch his mechanics tuning its engine and flying wires and performing those adjustments necessary to make each plane a fighting extension of the man at its controls.

Flight Commander George Fisher assigned Nieuport Type 28, Serial Number 6194 to First Lieutenant Charles H. Woolley, who was thrilled! His own plane! One he would personalize with improved gunsights, customized seat belts, and a rearview mirror. His improvements would make fighting easier and more deadly. He spent hours with his new crew, Sergeant Les Hartnett and Privates Joseph Lewis and Guy Talmadge. They installed a meticulously calibrated compass, an altimeter, a clock, that rearview mirror, and that special improved ring-sight for the single machine gun mounted on the top of the fuselage just to the left of the cockpit. They spent the hours necessary to tune the Le Rhône rotary engine to perfection—perfection that would bring the plane and its pilot back safely after long patrols and violent combat.

During this time of working together, a team spirit and partnership evolved between the officers and the men. They developed a truly warm feeling for one another as individuals, each doing his very best to make the partnership move toward achieving its goal of besting the enemy. Still, they had to maintain an artificial distance that befitted the difference in rank. Officers and men, no matter how close, did not and could not socialize.

Bonds of friendship formed among the flyers gathered strength with each passing day. Waldo Heinrichs and Bill Taylor, temperamental opposites, had a surprising alliance. Taylor was a big, fun-loving sort, who loved to tease and wrestle playfully with the straitlaced Heinrichs. One evening returning from dinner in Neufchâteau, Taylor, at the wheel of a borrowed staff car, swerved madly down narrow French roads, doing his best to unhinge the unflappable Waldo. "Came home at tremendous speed but I took things as they came," Heinrichs noted in his diary, "and enjoyed it thoroughly."

Ned Buford and Harold Buckley became inseparable, prowling the finer nightspots of the Toul–Nancy area. John Mitchell, who joined the squadron late in April, teamed up with Curtis, Sewall, Woolley, and McLanahan to form a "band of brothers," friendships that would last for more than forty years.

The 95th finally went into action on May 2 and mounted two separate patrols. The first of four planes flown by Buckley, Blodgett, Taylor, and Johnson ran into two German two-seaters over the lines. Buckley aggressively dove first, fired a short burst, and had to retire with a jammed gun. Taylor followed with a ten-shot burst, but then his guns jammed at the very same moment as Johnson's. Three pilots now had retired, leaving "Dauntless" Dick Blodgett alone on the attack.

Realizing that he could easily outmaneuver the German two-seater but had to avoid the fire of the gunner in the rear seat, Blodgett positioned his aircraft under the tail of the German, pointed his nose up and managed to fire more than a hundred rounds into the Boche. He saw the observer throw up his hands from his guns and topple backward into the rear seat. Smoke was pouring from the engine as the German pilot went into a steep dive. Blodgett followed him down, continuing to fire until *his* gun also jammed! Deep into enemy territory now, he broke off the attack and headed for home.

Exhausted and nearly out of gas, Dick made it back to the field. He managed to land, but somehow tipped up on his nose, breaking the propeller and seriously crumpling the engine cowling. Somewhat chagrined by his poor landing, he nevertheless congratulated himself. He was the first pilot of the 95th to score a victory in the air!

A little late for dinner, Blodgett walked into the officers' mess, and was greeted with a standing ovation from the other pilots, who clapped and shouted and congratulated him on his first kill. Embarrassed by it all, he simply said, "I really didn't do anything except what any of you would have done if you had been in my place." He joked about his good luck to the excited group around him, but later during the meal he soberly reflected upon what it was like to kill another pilot and his observer: "I kind of feel sorry for the Germans now . . . but during the fight I didn't have time to think about anything but bringing the Hun plane down."

Two days after this event, the squadron departed from Epiez and joined the 94th as part of the First Pursuit Group, U.S. Army Air Service, under the control of the French Sixth Army headquartered at Gengoult Aerodrome. Gengoult actually lay at the base of Mont St. Michel near the town of Toul, not too far from the city of Nancy. They had flown nine Nieuports to the new field with only one mishap, when Heinrichs' motor died as he was preparing to land. He landed too slowly and stalled, wiping out the undercarriage and cracking one of the ribs of the fuselage. Waldo blamed the whole affair on a "bad fuel mixture"; others claimed, good-naturedly, that he had cut his engine too soon and should by rights owe them a bottle of champagne.

The sights, sounds, and smells of Gengoult were a tonic to the pilots of the 95th. The fast-paced activities of the 94th and a French photographic squadron at the other end of the field inspired them. Here was the pace they were to thrive on—planes overhead, planes taking off and landing, patrols departing for the lines, pilots visiting from up and down the front with news of friends and whopping tall tales, the roar of rotary engines as they burst into life, the sharper bark of Harley-Davidson motorcycles, and the rattling of machine guns being tested out in the gun pits. The very smell of the castor oil in the exhaust of the engines had become intoxicating. It was enough to quicken their pulses and lure them into the air. Enlisted men who were electricians, riggers, mechanics, stitchers, and welders worked from early morning until late at night.

When the 95th ran short of aircraft spare parts, Waldo and two enlisted men drove to the First Air Supply Depot at Colombey-les-Belles in a three-ton Dennis truck. There he found the depot woefully short of spares, with less than a quarter of what was needed. The French had supplies of everything at an aerodrome near Nancy, but unfortunately, U.S. Army regulations did not allow the Americans to order what they needed from the French. As they had discovered before, only U.S. depots could supply U.S. forces.

After they had personalized their airplanes, aligned their machine guns, and zeroed in their Reille Soult sights, it was time for the final step—adorning the aircraft with national, squadron, flight, and personal insignia and markings. The Germans and the French allowed their squadrons and individual pilots great latitude in decorating their aircraft. French squadrons had specific squadron markings that appeared on all planes of that unit, while the pilots were allowed smaller individual markings of their own. The Germans were even more colorful than the French, painting their aircraft in vivid reds, blues, yellows, and greens to indicate the specific Jasta to which they belonged. The outlandish markings were not just for vanity. They helped German pilots more easily identify one another in the air. The Boche pilots chose their own individual symbols—dragons, shooting stars, geometric figures, names of lady friends, anything that had meaning for them personally.

The Allies identified the nationality of their planes with roundels, or cockades, in varying combinations of red, white, and blue. The American combination was white in the center, then blue, then red for the outer ring; the British, red in the center, next white, and blue on the outer ring; the French, blue in the center, next white, and a red outer ring. The German aircraft began the war painted with a black Maltese cross insignia outlined in white, and by early 1918 changed to a straight-sided black cross, also outlined in white. The U.S. Air Service handed down a directive that after a pursuit squadron had scored its first victory, it could choose a unique insignia to be painted on both sides of the fuselage, as well as numerals for the aircraft to be applied on the fuselage and the upper wing. The 94th, after the victories of Campbell and Winslow, opted for a design created by First Lieutenant Johnny Wentworth, an architect by training and a descendant of "Long John" Wentworth, the six-foot-six-inch first Republican mayor of Chicago. The design was the *Hat-in-the-Ring* insignia, signifying America throwing Uncle Sam's red-white-and-blue hat into the ring of the Great War. The pilots of the 94th were so pleased with their insignia that several months later they ordered sterling silver "Hat-in-the-Ring" squadron pins from Cartier's in Paris.

After Dick Blodgett's first victory, the 95th immediately began to consider their choice of insignia. Major Johnson suggested an Army mule, the symbol used by his alma mater, West Point. He further suggested that it be a kicking mule, stubborn and defiant. The squadron approved the selection, and squadron painters went to work applying to the sides of their Nieuports the kicking mule surrounded by a blue oval background. It was a good insignia—tough, humorous, not as artistic as the hat-in-the-ring, but just as striking.

The squadron approved of the mule idea so much that they decided to find a live example as a mascot. Buford and Buckley spied a handsome mule pulling the wagon of the French garbage collector who serviced the American airfield. Inspiration struck the intrepid twosome! They offered the owner a large bundle of francs, and the sturdy mule was theirs! The 95th insignia in the flesh! They named the mule "Jake" for reasons unknown, and included the cantankerous beast in most squadron social celebrations. On one particularly festive occasion, Jake found himself standing in the officers' bar.

With great pride they began regular flights in the newly decorated Nieuports. Each flight had its own colored cowlings; red and white checkerboard for the First; maroon and gold spirals for the Second; and white and blue alternating rings for the Third. Their first duties were "alerts," standing by with pilots and aircraft ready to take off at a moment's notice upon report of hostile aircraft over the lines. Near the hangars stood a small alert tent in which the pilots read, napped, or played cards, awaiting a call to action. Dressed in flying clothes, they were prepared to climb into the cockpits of their readied and warmed-up planes standing by. As soon as the Germans crossed into Allied territory, notification of pending action would be forwarded by telephone from frontline observers, giving the type, number, and direction of the enemy intruders. Those on alert would immediately depart the field in search of the enemy.

The first group to stand on alert for the 95th was called at 4:30 A.M. on May 11; every single pilot was eager to be selected for that duty. During one of our visits, Ted Curtis told me with a grin, "For the first few days we were on alert from daybreak until sundown, hopping off several times a day to give chase to enemy planes reported up and down the lines. The truth was, we were never 'alert' enough to find one of the bastards."

When the 95th had close to its full complement of eighteen Nieuports, they began protection patrols as well as alerts. Protection patrols meant shepherding slower-flying observation, photographic, and bombing planes through their assigned missions along the front. They also flew protection patrols intended to meet Allied bombers just exiting the German lines and returning to their bases from missions deep into enemy territory. The bombers, often attacked by Boche fighters during their difficult return flights, were normally fighting heavy headwinds, and the patrols were in the air to drive off the attackers. The bomber types were the French Breguet 14 B2 with a forty-seven-foot wingspan, a 300-horsepower Renault engine with a speed of 110 miles per hour, and a 520-pound bomb load; and the British-designed de-Havilland DH 4 with a forty-two-and-a-half-foot wingspan, a 400-horsepower Liberty engine with a top speed of 120 miles per hour, and a 460-pound bomb load. Depending on the specific mission, four to eighteen planes flew these patrols. Both the 94th and 95th pilots initially detested the protection duty for outbound missions. It was nearly impossible to locate and link up with the other aircraft. Finally an arrangement was made to have the two-seaters land at Gengoult and then the entire mission would depart as one. A fine idea, but with the fragility of the aircraft, one out of three would blow a tire, spring a landing gear, or

develop motor trouble, and the patrol would be called off. Officials at Air Service Headquarters would not have been happy to
see the spectacle of their brave boys cheering lustily as some unfortunate pilot of a photographic plane slated to be protected ran
his wheels into an unseen hole in the field and ended up on his
back. The patrol would then be cancelled.

*Chasse* patrols were flown at both high and low altitudes to
intercept any enemy aircraft intruding over Allied lines. These
were usually routed over a triangular course between three
identifiable towns close to the lines where ground fighting was
heaviest.

High-speed *chasse* patrols uncovered a flaw of the Nieuports
that soon became a major concern. Jimmy Meissner of the 94th
went on patrol on May 2 and later described what happened to
his Nieuport after a violent clash with an Albatros:

> The enemy was going into a spiral when two of my
> tracer bullets went straight into its fuselage right back
> of the motor. Flames broke out from the cockpit in-
> stantly, as I had struck his tank, but to be certain the
> pilot was not alive and suffering, I kept up shooting.
> Diving with full motor in the excitement of the mo-
> ment, I got so close that a sudden lurch by the blazing
> enemy made me plunge almost vertically to avoid a
> crash. The strain was too great; with a crack, my top
> wing seemed to break loose and whip back overhead at
> the instant I shot under the Boche, so near I thought
> we had met. I wondered how soon the bottom wing
> would fold up and leave me in a wingless fuselage,
> pointed at the ground 15,000 feet below. What beastly
> luck to die just as my first victory had been won!
>
> But suddenly I realized the top wing wasn't all
> gone, and the bottom wing had not folded up yet, the
> plane was still diving with the motor cut off, still an-
> swering to the controls as I gently rocked the stick
> and pushed on the rudder. Surprised at still being
> alive, I looked up to see what really had happened to
> the top wing. All the entering edge (leading edge) back
> to the main spar, had torn off, to take the linen com-

pletely off the upper surface from wing-tip to wing-tip so that only about two-thirds of the covering on the lower surface was held against the ribs by wind pressure alone.

Four weeks later, Meissner was flying the same aircraft—Nieuport 6144—when, in a violent fight, he lost the leading edge and the entire upper fabric of his top wing. Once again, he managed to survive.

Rickenbacker had a similar experience. He dove at prolonged high speed on a Boche aircraft, and when he pulled his stick back to his lap to begin a sharp climb, Rick recalled, "a frightening crash that sounded like the crack of doom told me that the sudden strain had collapsed my right wing. The entire spread of canvas over the top wing was torn off by the wind and disappeared behind me." Rickenbacker's Nieuport turned on its side and spun down over 10,000 feet. At the bottom of the spin he put the Nieuport motor onto full power, leveled off, and managed to reach Gengoult.

Then it was Heinrichs' turn. He was diving on a Boche, when . . . crack—a rending smash seemed to hit his top left wing. He fell 9,000 feet in a violent *vrille*, but managed to gain control, level out, and safely land his Nieuport. Once on the ground, he discovered, as did the others, that the leading edge of his top wing and the fabric were gone. What had happened? Had he hit a German? No. He was another victim of the design weakness of the Nieuport 28.

Several days later, Captain Jim Hall lost his upper-wing fabric while diving after a Pfalz of Jasta 64W. Hall had double trouble; as he was trying to nurse his crippled plane home, an antiaircraft shell hit his engine. Miraculously, the shell failed to explode, but without power, he was forced to land behind enemy lines. Hall remained a prisoner of the Kaiser until the war ended. In prison, Hall sharpened his writing skills, skills that he would later use to craft, with fellow aviator Charles Nordhoff, the definitive history of the Lafayette Flying Corps, as well as the historical novel *Mutiny on the Bounty* and other literary treasures about the South Seas.

There was indeed a flaw in the upper-wing design of America's gift from France, the Nieuport Type 28. No French squadron had ever been equipped with 28s, nor had any been delivered to other Allied countries. Was the French government aware that there was something wrong with these latest models from the Nieuport factory? Were the Nieuport engineers and aircraft testers aware of the problem? We will never know the answers. Strangely, the U.S. Air Service was quiet about the entire matter. By June, all 28s had beefed-up wings and, at last, two machine guns. These modifications finally made them competitive with fighters flown by the Germans. On May 30, 1918, before all the modifications could be made, however, another pilot suffered from the Nieuport's faulty wing construction. It was Bill Casgrain.

Almost fifty years from that nearly fatal day in May 1918, Bill and I were enjoying gin-and-tonics on the patio of his summer home in New Hampshire. Bill had his wartime diary on his lap and laughed to himself as he recounted the events of that Thursday morning:

> It happened on the first patrol of the day at about 8:15. Johnny Hambleton was leading a patrol of five consisting of Harold Buckley, John Mitchell, Stu McKeown, and me. We were coming up to the lines from Pont-à-Mousson when we sighted two bi-place Boche over to the left about 900 feet above us, traveling east. We turned around and started to climb above them into the sun. Before we could reach them, they had separated, the highest one going straight into Germany and the other turning back toward St. Mihiel on his side of the lines, heading hell bent for election due north.
>
> This is the bird that Hambleton and I picked on. I could see Johnny diving down to come up underneath him, and I was trying to get over and attack from his left, but in a minute he was directly underneath me, so I had to dive on him straight from above with full motor. I let about fifty rounds go at him, but I don't think I led him enough. [Deflection!] My shots seemed to fall behind. At this point I became alone,

alone in the big blue sky. Suddenly I felt a hell of a thud and the next thing I knew, I was in a *vrille*, the French word for a corkscrew spin. The Rhone rotary engine spinning from right to left set up a tremendous torque, compounding the problem caused by my broken left wing. It was then that I first noticed that all the canvas was gone from my upper left wing! I had to throw my control stick way over to the right in order to come out of the spin. I was about 3,000 feet high then and I gave her the gun and started due south. But the hell of it was that although I had all the controls as far to the right as I could get them, my machine was still turning to the left. That was turning me back into Germany, so there was but one thing left to do and that was to cut my motor and make a glide for it back to our lines.

The ground beneath me was a mass of trenches. By this time I was at 1,800 feet. Straight ahead of me the ground looked clear and I made for a field between two woods. I was as far south as I could get. I was certain I had crossed all the trenches and that I was going to land safely in France. In landing I ripped off the landing gear and my wings collapsed, but I was okay. I unstrapped myself and got out of the wreck. Shortly I heard a voice calling, 'Hello.' Turning toward the sound, I saw a head and shoulders sticking out of a trench and an arm waving me to come on. When I got to the trench, I found myself staring into a row of Mausers, all nicely aimed at me. One of the men behind the rifles said with a smile, 'Kamerade,' and allowing they were the damndest bunch of comrades I ever had seen before, I reluctantly climbed over some barbed wire and joined them. 'Amerikaner?' Amerikaner, I replied. A prisoner! Good God! I thought this can't be true.

When he had finished his story, I admired the glasses that contained our drinks. They were beautifully etched with the design of the 95th's kicking mule. A month later, unannounced, a box clearly marked *Tiffany and Co., New York,* arrived at our home near Boston. The box contained eight lovely highball glasses etched with the design of Jake, the squadron's kicking mule. Bill Casgrain was that kind of guy.

My father and his Nieuport were fast becoming as one. The plane was quick, maneuverable, and yet, because of the torque caused by the rotary engine, tricky to handle. He stood ready for alerts, and flew his share of protection patrols and *chasse* patrols. When in the air, he would fly an irregular course to throw off the aim of the enemy antiaircraft gunners. He was vigilant, sharply attuned to his surroundings, constantly checking his rearview mirror, searching for "the Hun in the sun," and dodging "Archie"—fire from below. (Antiaircraft fire was called "Archie" after "Archibald, Certainly Not!" a popular London music hall refrain sung by a woman fending off an overly amorous suitor.) He loved being in the air and he reveled in the experience despite the constant possibility of an enemy attack.

Flying a patrol seemed much different from his work with the Ambulance Service. There he had been part of a team, and there they were saving lives, not focused on taking them. In the air, a pilot was alone, unable to communicate with anyone except by crude wing movements or flares. German planes could appear from anywhere—above, below, or behind. In the air, a flyer was an individual combatant, whirling about, unprotected, in a spherical field of potential fire.

On May 17, the cheerful, generous, and companionable Dick Blodgett completed one of those detested protection patrols and then set off to hunt alone. Two hours later, about a mile from the field, his charred and broken body was found in the wreckage of his plane. No one could know for certain how he had died. The best guess was that Dick had been wounded either by Archie fire or an enemy aircraft, and that during his return to Gengoult, had fainted and crashed. He was buried the next day in a small cemetery near the field. The members of the First Flight, Dick's own, served as pallbearers. Flying officers of the 95th and many from the 94th were present at the service which was conducted by a Catholic Army chaplain. As an honor guard fired volleys and "Taps" was played in the distance, the service closed. Many of the men wept openly. Grimly, they turned from the grave and left the once vital Blodgett in his final resting place. Dick had left a note for the squadron that, in part, read:

> In case of my death, will some public-spirited bum please do the following. First send a cable to Blodg-ham, Boston, [telling] of my death . . . Send home what stuff I have at the Front, especially all pictures and films. Keep what flying clothes and odds and ends anyone wants. Fill out the enclosed check for enough to cover all expenses and set the gang up to a bottle of champagne apiece. Good luck to you all. I'll see you later one day. Show them we can fight like hell—a hard, clean fight. Give 'em hell. So long. Dick.

Ted Curtis, who had known Blodgett well at Williams College, packed up his friend's clothes, pictures, uniform, and violin and sent them to his parents in Newton. "I counted him among my best friends, so I can share a good deal of your grief," Curtis wrote to the parents of the twenty-one-year-old. Dick Blodgett, the first pilot of the 95th to score a victory, had become the first pilot of the 95th to give his life.

At 8:55 on the clear morning of May 19, Woolley and other members of the First Pursuit Group heard the sounds of Nieuports roaring from the field on an alert and rushed out of their barracks to see what they could of the action. They spotted the white puffs of smoke from Allied antiaircraft guns at about 5,000 feet over St. Mihiel. There! There it was! The black silhouette of a German observation plane could be seen headed for Gengoult.

Three pilots of the 94th, First Lieutenant Gude, Major Huffer, and Major Lufbery took to the air in pursuit of the Boche. Gude and Huffer departed ahead of Lufbery. Gude closed on the German two-seater Rumpler, but not close enough. At a distance much too great to be effective, Gude fired off his entire supply of ammunition and fled back to the field. The Rumpler turned and retreated toward Germany. Lufbery, now in the air flying a Nieuport that was not his own, sped after the departing Rumpler and when in range, fired a short burst. Then he swerved away.

Jammed gun! Lufbery cleared the jam quickly and rushed at the German again.

There—flames! But not from the Rumpler. Fire engulfed Luf's fragile fighter, and the flaming aircraft plunged down to 2,100 feet, headed in the direction of the village of Maron. Those observing from the ground watched in horror as the Nieuport turned on its side over a small stream, and a tiny figure leapt or fell from the flaming plane. Major Lufbery's body landed on a picket fence surrounding the garden at the rear of a widow's home in the village. The leading American ace was dead. Shortly thereafter, Lufbery's victors, Vizefeldwebel Kirschbaum and Leutnant Scheibe of Reihenbildzug Nr. 3, were shot down by French fighters at Mars-la-Tour and taken prisoner.

Lufbery's death struck a severe, gut-wrenching blow to the entire Air Service. He had been their hero, the most experienced and successful of all American flyers. As unsettling as his death were the questions that surrounded and continue to surround the incident. Did Lufbery jump or did he fall from his plane? Where was Major Huffer who had been in the air during the fight? Why did Gude ineffectively fire all his ammunition and flee? The only question that could be positively answered pertained to Gude's actions. He was a coward.

Lufbery's funeral was the equivalent of a state burial. Floral arrangements were banked in abundance around the grave. During the service, American and French aviators stood at attention. General Edwards of the 26th Yankee Division and General Passage of the Eighth French Army delivered powerful eulogies. At the conclusion of the service, five Nieuports flew low over the cemetery and dropped further bouquets of flowers, and the sound of "Taps" echoed solemnly from the surrounding woods.

Several weeks after the funeral, Marr replaced Huffer as Commanding Officer of the 94th. Huffer was assigned to liaison duty between the Americans and the French and appointed Operations Officer for the First Pursuit Group. Huffer's bravery was never in dispute. He was highly decorated while serving with the French and later was given a new command with the 93rd Aero Squadron. During his duty as Operations Officer, Huffer had a disagreement with Davenport Johnson, Commander of the 95th, whom Huffer had felt compelled to put on report. The tension between the two men was to take an interesting twist at the war's end.

The 95th continued their patrols over Commercy, St. Mihiel, and Flier, where, looking north toward Verdun they could see the evidence of some of the war's most ferocious fighting—ruins surrounded by a vast sea of lifeless gray mud. These frigid high patrols were physically challenging and it seemed as if it took an eternity to restore feeling to the face and hands after no more than an hour flying at 18,000 feet.

One morning, as Woolley was taking off for one of these patrols, his engine, without warning, quit. His Nieuport with the red and white checkered cowling plunged to the ground and rolled end over end, tearing off the wings, shattering the propeller and crushing the metal checkerboard into a twisted ruin.

After somehow walking away from the incident unharmed, Woolley explained to anyone who would listen, "It was bad gas."

"Sure, sure," they razzed him. "We all fly with bad gas, but not with the same results."

Two days later, in a new Nieuport, it was business as usual. Dad had become separated from his morning patrol team, and took on a Rumpler two-seater alone. Realizing that he had enough altitude to attack before the German got out of range, he dove on the two-seater and opened fire at an altitude of 17,000 feet. The German gunner in the rear seat replied with a stream of lead from his Maxim machine guns that flew wide of the mark. Woolley made several more passes at the German, but was unable to inflict any serious damage. The Rumpler sailed serenely back across the German lines while Charles Woolley returned to lunch at Gengoult empty-handed, outraged by his lack of results.

Later that same day, Sewall, McLanahan, and Woolley flew a protection patrol for an observation plane. As they were returning to Gengoult, they chanced upon a Rumpler that they attacked unsuccessfully. Dad, flying at 15,600 feet, the preferred altitude for enemy observation planes, glimpsed another Rumpler over the lines calmly taking photos. Quickly maneuvering his Nieuport into a position behind and slightly above the Boche, he dove sharply and came up under the tail of the two-seater, firing fifty rounds into its fuselage and wings. After his first pass, banking and looping, he got back on the German's tail for one more attack and forty more rounds from his Vickers gun. His adversary fell into a sharp dive.

First Lieutenant Charles H. Woolley had scored his first kill! Upon landing, Sumner Sewall jumped out of his plane and ran up to him, laughing, to slap him on the back. "You got him! You got him! I followed him down to below 3,000 feet and he was still in a *vrille*."

Woolley's reconnaissance report was the essence of brevity. "Combat with German bi-place 2 kilom. West of Thiaucourt— German plane fell in spin—Time 10.55—Approximate altitude 15,600 feet—90 rounds of ammunition fired. Confirmation Requested."

That evening the pilots stood at the 95th bar as Sergeant Diamond, the wizard bartender, mixed his famous Bronx cocktails: equal parts of sweet and dry vermouth, orange juice, and many parts of gin, to taste. All toasted Woolley's entry into the ranks of victorious fighter pilots! Dad was more than a little delighted with his success.

The kill was never confirmed. His victory did not appear in the *Compte-Rendu* of the Sixth French Army. But that did not matter. My father knew he had brought down that plane. He had brought down a Hun behind German lines.

# CHAPTER 9

# Tempered in Battle

**D**ad was in his mid-thirties when I was born, older than many new fathers in those days. As I was growing up we did have occasional times together as father and son, but they were too infrequent for a slightly timid only child. I adored my father, but he seemed a distant figure with little time available for playing catch or tossing a football. I don't know if any son really knows and understands his father, but in my search for the history of the 95th Aero Squadron and in talking to his old friends and wartime comrades, he has emerged for me as a powerful person, an individual whom, from another perspective, I have learned to know and admire. There was great humor in the man. He was also a little daring, but he was not reckless. He was a storyteller par excellence—often using dialects to enhance a tale. He was honest almost to a fault. He appreciated fine things, but he was not driven by the accumulation of wealth. Through his squadron mates, I began to see him as a man who was loved and admired by all who knew him well, a loyal friend, a strong leader.

My father also had a keen appreciation of the opposite sex. In the spring of 1918, the dashing young men of the 95th occasionally turned their thoughts to the fairer sex. They discovered an American hospital near the airfield that housed a swarm of beautiful nurses. This discovery elicited considerable excitement among many of the group. At the end of the day, some shined their boots, donned their best-pressed uniforms, plastered down their hair, tilted their caps at a jaunty angle, and disappeared in the direction of the hospital. Ed Thomas, the Supply Officer, was the first to discover this treasure trove of maidens and surreptitiously shared the wealth with Bill Taylor and Russ Hall. The secret was not kept for long. Soon the nurses caught glimpses of Curtis, Fisher, and Woolley, and the first prospectors of passion were quickly deprived of their exclusive rights and with the second wave, a friendly intimacy was established by the nurses.

Next came the discovery of a nearby maternity hospital that provided a ward to care for war babies, some of whom the nurses facetiously named after Allied commanders. On more than one occasion, after what they described as a "hair-raising" patrol over the lines, McLanahan and Mitchell could be seen wheeling Pershing, Joffre, Pétain, Foch, and other high-ranking infants around the sunny hospital grounds. The aviators were also enthusiastic attendees at the dances sponsored by the hospital.

To repay the many kind favors bestowed on them by the nurses, my father and "Jam" Johnson decided to put on an afternoon tea party outside the squadron alert tent for six or so of their lady friends. While Dad was busy making tea and dainty sandwiches, his flight, which was on alert, was called to action. Absorbed in his teacups and *pâté de foie gras*, he was convinced that this call to arms was a hoax, a trick concocted by envious souls who had not been invited to the tea party. Fisher, Curtis, McLanahan, and Buford of the First Flight dashed to their Nieuports and took off, with zooms and climbing turns. Returning to the tea after a half an hour in the air, they explained to the breathless, admiring female guests that they had most "opportunely" engaged two enemy two-seater aircraft and shot them down in a thrilling combat. Curtis described the fight and its results in a letter to his parents.

> We got around into the sun and I dove first on the leading Boche. I saw a couple of his tracer bullets fly past my wing, and the observer stood up as I went down past his tail. I pulled up underneath him, fired a burst and pulled away as he tried to get a shot at me,

but all of a sudden he burst into flames and fell like a
rock—about the most thrilling sight the world affords.
We all came home together, and the girls decided we
were pretty good entertainers.

Woolley did not find them the least entertaining. He was convinced that the whole thing was a fabrication. And, indeed, no
confirmation of the "downed Boche" was ever forthcoming.

When bad weather kept them from the air, the pilots took advantage of the opportunity on the ground to tour the front. Officially these field trips were for "ground orientation," but many
went more out of curiosity to observe up close the results of the
ground war and to collect souvenirs.

Riding in the squadron's Hudson touring car, they toured artillery positions sixteen kilometers from the field. Equipped with
gas masks and trench helmets, the curious airmen visited the
gun emplacements for two enormous 240 mm guns nicknamed
"Ignatz" and "Krazy Kat." They next inspected "Hun Hunter,"
"Wild Liz," and "Gyp the Blood," 155 mm guns manned by former Coast Artillery gunners. They traveled to a French forward
artillery observation post and a French antiaircraft battery and
talked with the French crewmen about how they confirmed claims
for aerial victories and under what circumstances they fired
bursts of Archie to reveal the location of approaching enemy
planes. Thunk! Thunk! As they talked with the Frenchmen, German shells hit, not more than twenty yards away. Several picked
up empty shell casings from the famous *soixante-quinze*, the
French seventy-five millimeter cannon that was the backbone of
the Allied field artillery. Later, they hired a French *poilu* who was
an artisan to engrave the shell cases with the Kicking Mule insignia and to flare their tops to form them into flower vases—
great souvenirs for the family back home!

They drove along part of the twenty-kilometer section of the
front controlled by the U.S. 26th Division, 37,000 men strong.
They entered the trenches, stepped along the wooden duck-
boards that kept the feet of the Army out of the mud and entered
a thirty-foot-deep dugout manned by American infantry. Some
infantrymen were said to resent what they perceived as the soft

billets and easy work of the "flyboys." But most of the ground troops understood the dangers involved in fighting in the air. One doughboy, who had witnessed the crash of an American airplane, summed up the feeling of many infantrymen when he admitted to the pilot of the twisted aircraft, "Jee-zuss Kee-riste. I'll take mine on the ground."

Perhaps no pilot who flew with the First Pursuit Group was more concerned about the dangers of flying than Lieutenant Joseph H. Eastman. A Californian who had attended Stanford University, Eastman drove an ambulance for the American Field Service, SSU 14, prior to joining the Air Service in Paris. He had trained with the others at Tours and Issoudun, and was delighted when he was assigned to the 94th Aero Squadron.

I came across Joe's diary in the holdings of the Hoover Institution on War, Revolution and Peace at Stanford University. As I read the pages that were covered with a strong clear hand, I realized that Eastman had been tortured by a lack of confidence, a tendency toward indecision, and an obsessive distrust of his aircraft. Yet he stuck it out.

One entry in his diary describes a combat while on patrol with Doug Campbell and Bill Loomis:

> Very much war today. In conjunction with an American trench raid at 3:00 AM—Doug, Bill and I went out on a 7:15 AM patrol for the purpose of snaring Boche that might be up surveying the aftermath. After about an hour Doug wig-wagged [his wings] and pointed at a heavy barrage of black shrapnel mixed with a few whites. (Note: the black bursts were German, the white French.) He chose [to dive on] one of the two gray spots [enemy planes] which appeared suddenly below and I lost track of him for the rest of the shift. He was merely bringing down a Boche bi-place which makes the sixth he has handled in that manner and therefore somewhat a commonplace affair for Doug.
>
> On the other hand, I had the extremely important task of learning another lesson—a not altogether rare thing with me at that. Yet the tale is not without its merits. One machine left and curved over our terri-

tory back to Germany—at an altitude about 900 feet less than mine. I *piqued* (a banking turn) around and [got] under his tail—merrily fidgeting with selector, gas throttle, and gun lever the while. My two mistakes were in *piquing* too far under and too far behind—to the end that by that time I had used up my surplus speed and I was still at too great a distance to maneuver effectively. This was really poorer judgment than it was my conservative nature . . .

For my part—and this has been on my mind ever since—I actually passed up the one instant of a good target offered me. There *was* an instant when he exposed a three-quarter broadside so that—had I pulled up my nose, I could have gotten off a burst or two. But as I say, that *might* have happened. As an actual fact, he ran square into the sun where I could see him in a *renversement* [a 180-degree change of direction] starting to dive on me. Other than that, I had nothing to do with combat. It was a bi-place, higher than I, *piquing* down on me. Also, it was my first combat—so I chose to have no more dealings with him and turned homeward with a fair show of energy. We haven't met since, but I sincerely hope soon again to have the pleasure.

Eastman exhibited his fine sense of humor when he described a protection patrol he and two others flew as an escort for an American two-seater photographic plane seven or eight kilometers behind the German lines:

In a way the two-seater needed it—the protection—as six of the 95th planes mistakenly tried to embarrass [attack] us from the rear. Then someone made a false move that sent all nine of us swooping at one another like a swarm of bees. We must have thought that there was a German in our party as we spent fifteen minutes in the silly game of *'Cherchez le Boche!'* I inadvertently, like others present, lost track of which was the plane we were to protect, and the next event was a grand diversion of five of the pack dropping on two slow moving and unoffending French A.R. observation planes. Bill Loomis and I untangled ourselves from this affair and set off on another fictitious Boche. We dove on him only to discover him to be a friendly Spad! It's high time this foolishness is stopped . . .

Several days later, Eastman, Doug Campbell, Bill Loomis, and Phil Davis got into a battle with six Pfalz single-seat fighters of Jagdstaffel 64:

Three of us were all taking an afternoon nap in our room—when Doug called us out to meet the British bombers returning over the lines—eleven of them, and a promise of any number of Huns tagging after them. My mechanics weren't there when I started off, so for some reason everything sounded wrong after leaving the ground. I imagined a knock, a trace of smoke in the *nacelle* [motor covering]—so I left the three others to return to the field. Over the camp I decided I was apprehensive without reason—and again, turning, soon rejoined the others. Five minutes later Doug waggled his wings, and all four of us dove.

I was three quarters of the way down when I discovered our objective. There were six enemy planes at about 7,500 feet, and in another instant I was close to one, shooting away with my gun. It jammed and I *viraged* [banked and turned] away, and quickly fixed it. In the *virage* I could see what a wild melee we had dropped into. Our planes, Boche planes, swooping and firing, smoke ribbons of tracers up, down, at you and away from you far and near. I had always known that the first big fight I ever got into would be my last, and there, quite a way from me, was a biplace peppering me from his side, and here another swinging around on my tail. Another thing I had always known was that in a real fracas I'd be helpless because of my poor execution of acrobatics. This man on my tail was at the point of straightening his turn to fire on me when without figuring how to do it or where it led, I did a *renversement* that brought me out in a slow dive directly in a head-on flight toward the enemy. He was a trifle lower and diving beneath me. He gave me a vivid impression of red. Red on his tail, red upholstering in his seat, and then he passed under me directly through my line of fire. I swung on down after him to get in a short burst and then another gun jam; his plane limply fell in a long wing slip. At the moment he appeared about to crash—still wing-slipping at about 150 feet altitude—a brilliant explosion somewhere to my starboard brought me to my own precarious predicament. My altimeter read 2,400 feet, and as I gave it full motor, I looked around to see not a plane of all the combat in sight, but there was a terrifying barrage of 'archies' all around me. If I wasn't frightened in combat, certainly I was now, jackrabbiting at 2,400 feet over all those guns which had to have me in their range.

Racked with self-doubt and constantly tortured by thoughts of real and imagined equipment failure, Eastman displayed a dogged courage that permitted him to fly patrols whenever they were required. Every time he flew, he questioned his ability as a pilot; he questioned his judgment, and yes, even the cause of his timidity. Yet he stayed with the responsibilities presented to him. Joe may have held the all-time record for wrecking Nieuports, but he was always ready to climb into the cockpit and try again. His attitude endeared him to his fellow pilots, who warmly accepted him and his frailties, and in all probability protected him in a brotherly way. If he had been a real coward, they would have instantly known and for their own protection they would have rejected him from their midst.

On the other hand, Sumner Sewall had few doubts about his ability as a flyer. In contrast to Eastman's tentative diary entries, Sewall's letters back home eloquently evoke his self-confidence and sense of adventure:

You and Father can cheer me just as much as you want to now for today I brought down a German plane and what is more he fell inside our own lines. Believe me it was one fine little fight . . . We started at 15,000 feet and it ended when he burst into flames just before he struck the ground. And what a run for my money he gave me. He really out maneuvered me, and I am convinced he had the better plane but he did not put a single bullet in my plane and his, as I afterwards found, had three of my bullets in his engine, three in his gas tank, one right through his radiator and propeller and a goodly fat number through his wings and fuselage.

It was a photographic plane, a 'Rumpler,' a bi-plane having pilot and observer with both having splendid machine guns as I learned by seeing a few tracer bullets go by. But you see the fight lasted nearly a half hour which is awfully long and after a little while I noticed the observer had stopped shooting for I could see the poor fellow huddle down in his cockpit every time I attacked. So then I knew he was either wounded or out of ammunition. Even after that however, the pilot gave me an awful fight, but at last I got a good burst of tracers right into his engine and he started going down in a *vrille* or spinning nosedive. I knew I had him then, for if he did not come out, that would be the end, and if he did, I knew I could get a burst into him while he would still be dizzy. He did come out, and I did get my burst in, which got his gas tank. He then blossomed into flames, landed and tipped over. Both pilot and observer were thrown out over the top wing and to my surprise, got up and started walking. I don't know what made me do it, but when I saw them get up, I swooped down on them and waved my hand, and one of them waved back. I am glad I did not kill them, but I guess I [had] tried hard enough. Anyway, two live German prisoners are worth a darn sight more than two dead ones. Prisoners mean information. I wish you could have seen the poor old French woman who was minding her own business when she suddenly looked up and saw this huge plane all covered in black crosses come piling down, crash and burn in the middle of her potato patch!

Sewall went on to describe cutting off "three beautiful big black [canvas] crosses" from the wings of the fallen plane. He explained their rarity: "Mr. Boche prefers to play over [on] his own side of the lines so that if he does fall, he falls home. . . ." He kept one of the crosses for display by the squadron and sent the other two home by American Express to his parents. They both exist today, one in the Owl's Head Transportation Museum in Maine and the other on loan to me.

The following day Sewall received a large bouquet from a ten-year-old French girl, addressed to: "The Great American Bird who struck down the Boche over my head." The other pilots were much more impressed with the case of rare champagne sent by the city of Toul to the "brave American aviators."

Sewall wrote of his accomplishment in a letter to his parents, "Before, I always warned you not to let any of this, 'Bath boy under booming bombardment' stuff get into the papers, but now I have actually accomplished something, and I must admit I am kind of proud of it and hope all my friends hear about it."

Decades later, on one of our visits to the Sewall family in Bath, Maine, Sumner's son Nicholas entertained my wife and me for lunch at the family-owned Montsweag Restaurant. On the second floor of the restaurant building, the Sewalls maintained an informal family museum. Nick gave us a tour and pointed to the ceiling. There in a large frame was stretched a mammoth black German cross, and next to it, also framed, was a large piece of fabric bearing the "Kicking Mule" insignia on a blue oval background. Here before me was a memento from Sumner's first victory, and the original insignia later cut from the Nieuport he flew when attaining that victory.

It is noteworthy that Sewall did not take pleasure in killing his opponents. This was true as well of other American flyers. In a combat against a German two-seater, Doug Campbell noticed that the gunner had exhausted his ammunition and in his rear cockpit was standing arms folded, next to his empty guns. Rather than shoot down a defenseless adversary in cold blood, Doug broke off his attack and allowed the German to retreat to his lines. Was this an act of foolish sentimentality inappropriate for a warrior whose primary mission was to kill the enemy? Or was this a demonstration of gallantry and protective kindness toward the weak and generosity to defenseless foes? To this day, the fighter pilots of the First World War are still considered "knights of the air."

The arrival at Gengoult of two new American fighter squadrons, the 27th and the 147th, brought the First Pursuit Group up to full strength. The seasoned aviators of the 94th and 95th derisively called them the "Canadian Circus" because the newcomers had received part of their training in Canada under the British system. With its emphasis on rapid production of new pilots, the British flight schools graduated pilots with notoriously little flying time and experience. At one point in 1916, the life expectancy of these inadequately trained British pilots flying outdated aircraft at the front was less than six days. The pilots of the two new Squadrons were extremely cocky and were convinced they would soon out-fight and out-score the old pros at Gengoult. Their attitude, as well as their very presence, which caused the doubling up of living quarters, did not endear them to the old guard.

Each squadron of the First Pursuit Group developed its own personality, and that personality did not necessarily reflect the personality of that squadron's commanding officer. Major John W. F. M. Huffer, first Commander of the 94th, spent his entire life in France and was a living example of relaxed French attitudes, morals, and way of life. The 95th's first commander, Major Davenport Johnson, was a West Point–trained martinet who tried to lead his squadron strictly by the book. Yet the men of the 95th under the straitlaced Johnson behaved in a much more loose and cavalier manner than did the men of the 94th under Huffer. The men of both squadrons came from similar socioeconomic backgrounds, but for some unknown reason, parties at the 95th became the focal point of the social life of the entire First Pursuit Group.

With the arrival of the new Canadian Circus squadrons, Heinrichs, Buford, Sewall, and Hall were assigned to lead the less experienced aviators in training flights, familiarizing them with the countryside around Commercy, Menil-la-Tour, and Doullard. The new men needed to learn the terrain of the front by heart; there would be no time for studying maps in the air. In combat, a pilot must watch for the Boche on his tail, keep an eye out for the patrol leader, check instrument readings for altitude, pressure, and fuel, and avoid antiaircraft fire. During this introductory training, the newcomers practiced dives, turns, *renversements,* barrel rolls, and mock attacks on one another. After a week of this enlightenment, even Heinrichs, the perfectionist, grudgingly admitted that the Circus was catching on.

While the Circus was being put through its paces, regular patrols continued to be conducted by the First Pursuit. Woolley flew many of the squadron's dawn patrols, awakening at 3:30 A.M., downing a breakfast of toast and coffee, and then taking off at the first dim morning's light. As he reached the lines he could see hundreds of brilliant little flashes, winking and twinkling out of the ground mists. These tiny lights were the explosions of artillery shells pulverizing the earth below, literally burying men where they stood in their trenches. His orders were to patrol the lines and attack any Hun aircraft that might attempt to observe Allied ground movement and direct German artillery fire. He flew back and forth over the lines looking for that small black speck that might be the enemy he sought. Flying at an altitude that made him vulnerable to the heavy Archie fire from below, he twisted and turned his tiny Nieuport, making every effort to avoid the constant black bursts and the small clouds of deadly shrapnel. His plane bounced and rolled in a macabre dance induced by the concussion of the bursting artillery rounds. As the sun rose in the east, he could see the outlines of the trenches more clearly. Exploding shells threw tall fountains of dirt, dust, and unspeakable debris into the air. Sometimes he saw clouds of poison gas drifting over the battlefields, reminding him of the day when he, the ambulance driver, had hauled those suffering *poilus* away from similar attacks.

At that time my father had been fighting a losing battle with a condition rather unpleasantly called scabies, a skin irritation caused by tainted water, which resulted in extremely painful blistering and eventual scabbing of the infected areas, and that became serious enough to require his hospitalization. He cursed his bad luck.

Doug Campbell had preceded him to the American Evacuation Hospital No. 1 near Menil-la-Tour. "Good maneuvering on the part of my two-seater adversary, and rotten shooting on my part" was the explanation Campbell gave for his wound. Doug had been in combat with a German two-seater. When the Boche gunner's Maxim gun jammed, Doug swooped in for the kill, dangerously exposing his own aircraft. The gunner somehow cleared the jam and poured a stream of explosive bullets into Campbell's attacking Nieuport.

Campbell heard a loud crash and felt a sharp pain in his back as an explosive bullet hit him. The bullet had struck a wire just behind him, exploding and lodging fragments in the flesh of his lumbar region. He managed to return to the field and, unassisted, climb from the cockpit. Inside a half-hour, the bullet fragments had been located by X ray, and refusing ether, Doug was put on the operating table and given cocaine as a local anesthesia. The fragments were removed, and because the wound was perfectly clean, he was sewn up and sent to recover.

Campbell was discharged from Hospital No. 1 not long after Dad was admitted; he went on sick leave to the Riviera, and then, much to his disgust, was sent back to the States to teach the art of combat flying. The Army felt that Campbell, one of the first American aces with six confirmed victories, could do much to support the war effort back home.

# CHAPTER 10

# Newcomers in Their Midst

**W**hile Woolley was being treated in the hospital for his persistent infection, replacements joined the ranks of the First Pursuit Group. Among the most celebrated arrivals were Quentin Roosevelt, assigned to the 95th, and Hamilton Coolidge, to the 94th. The good friends were disappointed at not flying with the same squadron, but were pleased to be billeted close to each other on the same airfield where they could frequently be together.

Both men, in their respective squadrons, promptly began closely monitored patrols over the lines. Although Coolidge and Roosevelt were experienced pilots, they quickly learned that flying under combat conditions was uniquely challenging.

Ham described these new experiences to his brother, still at Groton School:

> How staggering all this is to the newcomer, and really I still place myself in that class. I have not as yet had any combats, but I have had some interesting times over the lines looking for Huns and dodging 'archie.' No longer are there any of these trips alone over the lines; a lone man is practically certain to be nailed. On all our voluntary patrols, we must go at least six strong in formation. As *chasse*, or fighting planes, our function is to patrol certain areas between certain

times in search of the Boche, and to offer protection
to Allied reconnaissance, *réglage* [spotting], and photographic planes.

For the novice, the toughest part of the job was locating the
enemy. Ham learned just how tough it was when he flew a mission in which he was to act as a decoy to lure German aircraft
away from the protection of one of their observation balloons,
while other pilots in the 94th patrol attacked the *drachen*, or
German kite balloon:

> I performed my [decoy] duty exceptionally well, as I
> afterwards found out, though I must make the admis-
> sion that it was entirely unknowingly that I did so. I
> had never been over this part of the lines before, so
> I did not realize it when we reached them. Moreover, I
> didn't see any of the black 'archie' puffs that generally
> inform one that he is over hostile territory. A few
> 'onion,' or incendiary, rockets and incendiary bullets
> came up, but it still didn't dawn on me where I was.
> My flight leader seemed to be acting queerly, too, and
> I, a few minutes later, lost sight of him. I circled, hop-
> ing he would pick me up again, and in the meantime I
> saw a distant plane that might have been anything.
> But no, it was one of five Boche machines who had
> their eyes on us and were looking to bite if we crossed
> their lines. They must have known I was lost more
> or less, because later my flight leader, who saw them
> all the time, said they all started to get together and
> come my way.
>   About five minutes after sighting the enemy, my
> flight commander found me wandering around and
> motioned me 'home.' Upon landing he told me how
> they were planning to trap us! It shows how little the
> green fighter sees! At least I did distract them for a
> while.

Roosevelt wrote to his mother:

I've had my first real fight. I thought I might get cold feet, or something, but you don't. You get so excited that you forget everything except getting the other fellow, and trying to dodge the tracers, when they start streaking past you. The real thing is that I'm on the Front—and I'm very happy.

Woolley's condition improved enough so that he could return to the squadron, where he found the Kicking Mules trying to make the best of life near the front. Things on the ground were really quite pleasant. They had discovered and dined in many small restaurants, and in the evenings after flying was over, congregated in the cozy bars in the town of Nancy.

One such evening, after dinner at the Stanislas Café, a group repaired to the Hotel Angleterre for drinks. In one of his moral tirades, Waldo Heinrichs complained that the hotel proved to be "a regular whore house" and that this particular evening, five different women were "dragged in" to a suite taken by a pilot from another squadron and there was some "fooling around." He, although present, "drank but little." On another evening, a well-lubricated Russ Hall threatened to take on the entire force of the combined Allied Military Police while protecting the honor of the Royal Flying Corps. With some difficulty his squadron mates restrained and evacuated him to safer ground.

Heinrichs was continually troubled by the recreational pursuits of his squadron mates, but he was even more infuriated by many of his superior officers. Complaining bitterly of his commanding officer, he wrote in his diary, " 'Jam' Johnson is a joke! He has only had 22 minutes of air time and that was on a trial flight. He's a Major because he's a West Pointer and the only reason he's commanding a squadron of flyers is because of his rank."

When Johnson was named to head up the new Second Pursuit Group, the 95th gave a farewell dinner for their departing Commanding Officer at the Stanislas Café. Others shared Heinrichs' disapproval of Johnson, but they were more than willing to celebrate his departure, a departure that would include a fine meal arranged by that gourmand Quentin Roosevelt, complemented by the wines, liquors, and champagne selected by the oenophile Ed Thomas, the squadron Supply Officer.

The festivities began auspiciously enough with a boldly political toast to President Wilson, the great politician who was making "the world safe for democrats," a play on his comment about, "making the world safe for democracy." Following this closely were toasts to the Air Service, to General Mitchell, to the First Pursuit Group, to the 95th Aero Squadron, and to the Allies, first collectively, and then individually. By the time the toasts got down to the Prince of Wales, things were out of hand. Captain Harry Lyster of Group Headquarters deemed it time for speeches, not toasts, and rose majestically, only to find he was unable to choose a good topic, and so proposed a cheer for Madame Hélène, whose feminine charms were familiar to more than one in the room. Speech followed speech, each surpassing the last in good will and exuberance, many of which were given, out of turn, by Quentin's cousin, Phil Roosevelt. Captain Walter Rankin, First Pursuit Group staff, whose feelings toward Davenport Johnson were those of a mad dog, had a complete reversal of attitude. Rising to his feet, he declared, "Johnson, you little son of a bitch. I like you." He then collapsed into his chair.

Waldo Heinrichs had this to say about the party: "I refused to give honor to a man whom we despise and never can respect . . . The 'party' at Nancy for the Major was a wild drunken carousal and I'm glad I didn't go."

The following evening there were more festivities. The officers of the First Pursuit Group gave a dance for the officers and ladies of the surrounding stations, hospitals, and Red Cross units. Johnson noticed Major Huffer, with whom he had frequent differences, arrive in the company of a rather brightly dressed Frenchwoman. Huffer commanded the 94th in a relaxed manner that the West Pointer Johnson detested. On the other hand, Huffer, in the role of Group Operations Officer, had actually reported Johnson's lapses in leadership to the head of the Air Service, Billy Mitchell. Johnson privately noted that the woman accompanying Huffer, "was heavily made up, not the sort of woman that proper officers should invite to U.S. Army functions." Even in the midst of the festivities, Johnson laid future plans to make Huffer pay for his apparent disregard of protocol, as well as his uncomplimentary report to Mitchell.

The next morning, much to the relief of all the revelers, a thick, sodden layer of clouds rolled over the area, negating any possibility of a dawn patrol. Later in the day, the pilots of the First Pursuit Group turned out for a band of Army Signal Corps photographers who were shooting still photos and moving-picture footage for home-front consumption. The Signal Corps cameramen captured, in jerky black-and-white film, images of the young officers with confirmed victories, smoking and smiling, standing self-consciously beside their aircraft. Then the entire First Pursuit Group posed for still photos with their various mascots and pets gathered next to one of the enormous canvas hangars at Gengoult. For the movie camera, the Second Flight of the 95th responded to an alert, ran to their planes from the alert tent, taxied out onto the field, and took to the air. It was propaganda, ridiculous nonsense, but still, no one could resist the fun of being in the movies.

A few days later, rumors had it that the group was going to be on the move again. Upon receipt of the confirming official orders, the Group Adjutant departed Gengoult to inspect the new field and prepare the way for an orderly transfer. The enlisted men packed up the squadron records, ordnance equipment, tools, and luggage, and loaded it all onto large trucks and trailers in preparation for the move. The personnel of the U.S. 26th Division presented a talented farewell musical performance for the departing flyers, complete with an old-fashioned vaudeville show.

On June 27, 1918, the group left the Gengoult airfield and moved en masse to the old French field at Touquin, some twenty-five miles south of Château Thierry and nearer the front. Flying between the two fields, most found the route simple enough to follow on the aerial strip maps carried in their planes. Ned Buford was assigned to lead a flight of the still-untested 27th Aero Squadron, but during the trip, he lost his motor and was forced to make an emergency landing. By a prearranged plan, a pilot of the 27th then took the lead. To signal the other pilots about the change, as instructed, the new leader promptly fired off a Very flare pistol, which kicked back in his face and knocked out one of his front teeth. So the First Pursuit Group arrived at the new airfield minus one tooth, but no further harm done.

A French bombardment *Escadrille* flying large French Breguet aircraft had previously been stationed at the field and had erected numerous large canvas hangars; the Americans could wedge three of their small Nieuports into one such hangar. One hangar was used for the Officer's Mess and four were used by the squadrons for basic living quarters. A vicious three-day flu attack on most of the personnel, along with a total lack of gasoline, prevented all flying for several days. The missing Buford spent some time relaxing in Fontainebleau, and was then returned to the squadron in the Hudson touring car, which was more reliable than his Nieuport.

Morale brightened considerably when the 95th moved their quarters to a large estate at the north edge of Touquin. Called Le Château Mal Voisin—or, as dubbed by the pilots, the "house of the bad neighbor"—the château was the property of a wealthy olive oil merchant who had closed it in 1914 and moved to Paris during the early, seemingly unstoppable German advance.

As was usually the case, Group Headquarters officers immediately installed themselves in the best quarters. In this case they chose a large apartment of fine rooms on the ground floor. The flying officers then scrambled for the next best rooms and the best furnishings before someone decided that Ed Thomas, the Supply Officer, would assign rooms to officers according to the date of their commissioning. Sumner Sewall thought that was a lousy idea. He thought that the original Villeneuve gang should get first choice on general principles.

The grousing began to subside when the pilots took time to inspect their new quarters. Marble statuary and Göbelin tapestries graced two huge salons, complete with mahogany and gilt chairs and a grand piano. The château was surrounded by gardens, untended since the beginning of the war, but still fragrant with roses and other blossoms and abundant with fresh vegetables, including squash and tomatoes. Stone steps led down through an oak glade with a panoramic view to the banks of a small stream, swirling with fish. A pond offered its refreshing waters for swimming and outdoor bathing. "Ah, the hardships of war," the fly-ers joked as they changed for a swim near a lilac bush bursting with early summer blooms, and then gleefully dove into the cool water.

The officers took their meals at a massive table in the enor-mous dining room, the walls of which were paneled in dark wood adorned with tapestries and paintings. A great chandelier of fifty lights glowed overhead. Unfortunately, a blue-and-white-checked oilcloth cover intended to protect the priceless dining table marred the illusion of grandeur. Much of the food prepared by Mess Sergeant Diamond, a better bartender than cook, was sent up from the basement kitchen by hand-operated dumbwaiters, and left a great deal to be desired. Several of the pilots even sug-gested that charges be brought against poor Diamond for "the horrible stuff" he served them. When they needed a change from Army fare, the pilots tumbled into the squadron's car and drove at breakneck speeds to the town of Melun for a decent meal, or possibly to locate a keg of beer for the mess. Or on to Versailles for a visit with the 27th Aero in their quarters, or even a quick visit to Paris, only thirty miles away, for just about everything.

On July 4, a great many members of the First Pursuit Group headed to Paris to celebrate Independence Day. Commandeer-ing the Hudson touring car, Mitchell, Hall, Buford, Sewall, and McLanahan hurried to join the 94th, lest they sweep up all the Parisian ladies and leave nothing in their gallant wake for them. Woolley, usually part of this gay group and their festivities, was forced to his bed with further complications of his pesky skin in-fection. His roommate, Heinrichs, who had no interest in joining the Paris contingent, did all he could to make Dad comfortable, which was a kindness typical of Waldo. The others later reported they had "an interesting trip." Buford insisted on driving; his questionable ability at the wheel added greatly to the zest of the occasion. On their return, the trusty Hudson developed a me-chanical problem, delaying them until dawn. They arrived just in time for the First Flight to go on patrol.

First Lieutenant James Knowles, replete with trunks and a large collection of duffle bags and musettes, joined the 95th at the château. Knowles, an Andover school graduate, had enlisted in the Air Service from the United States and trained in France; he was fresh and eager for action after serving as a ferry pilot at Orly. Delighted to finally be at the front, he flew patrols with the other pilots as they took the war to the Boche, penetrating the German lines by six to ten miles. At first they believed this sector of the front would be much the same as that at Toul, at least with respect to the activity level and the caliber of the enemy pilots. They were sadly mistaken on both counts.

On the morning of July 5, Heinrichs, Mitchell, Rhodes, and Thompson took off on patrol. They were flying above another formation of four Nieuports, which were probably from the 94th, when they ran into a group of five or six German Albatros D. Va scouts. Heinrichs quickly noted the enemy's markings: red noses, white tails, scarlet diagonal stripes on the wings, large black crosses with white backgrounds on the wings and rudders. Waldo wondered if the aircraft belonged to Rittmeister Manfred Freiherr von Richthofen's famed "Scarlet Scouts," some of the most experienced air fighters in the German Air Service.

The four Americans attacked the superior number of Germans, and a whirling dogfight began at once. Waldo took four machine-gun bursts into his plane from one Boche, and then, for just an instant, the twisting German flashed across his sights. It was long enough. Heinrichs fired. The enemy fell in a spin. Frightened, but with adrenaline flowing, Waldo then climbed to attack another Albatros, which proceeded to out-climb and out-distance him. It was time to head for home. Upon landing, Waldo learned that two from the patrol, Thompson and Rhodes, had gone down in enemy territory. He and Mitchell each received credit for one Boche. During the fight, Waldo's Nieuport was holed three times and Johnny's wings were so badly shot up that they had to be replaced. Mitchell and Heinrichs agreed that these German pilots were the best they had encountered.

At this time, the Germans had unleashed a great new offensive. Realizing that the German army could not win a war of attrition with America entering the fray, General Erich Ludendorff, the commander of German forces on the Western Front, was preparing to unleash an attack on Reims, hoping to capitalize on the gains made in the earlier offensive and to divert attention from his planned attack on British forces to the north. To support Ludendorff, the Imperial Air Service had moved several of their more experienced Jastas, or squadrons, into the fight to support the new German push.

The French may have been the ones to introduce fighting in the air, but the Germans were the ones who had perfected it. In 1915, German fighter pilot Max Immelmann introduced the famed "Immelmann turn" and other air-fighting techniques that became standard operating procedures for pilots on both sides of the lines. After Immelmann's death, Oswald Boelcke, perhaps one of the greatest fighter tacticians in aviation history, refined and codified Immelmann's teaching: "Climb before the attack and dive from the rear"; "Use natural cover—clouds and the glare of the sun"; "Foolish acts of bravery are fatal." These and other of the "Dicta Boelcke," Oswald Boelcke's air fighting rules, are still followed today.

After Boelcke's death in a collision with his good friend Erwin Böhme, his talented student Manfred Freiherr von Richthofen, a former cavalry officer who became perhaps the most renowned fighter pilot of all time, took the lead of Jasta 11. Von Richthofen, "The Red Baron," was given command of JG 1, comprised of four squadron groups in June 1917. Richthofen, who flew in an all-red Albatros D.V and later in a Fokker Dr 1 triplane with a red upper wing, cowling, tail and wheel covers, encouraged his pilots to decorate their aircraft with wild colors, stripes, and checks for easy identification in the air. His "flying circus" could pack up their tents and quickly move up and down the line, wherever the German command needed control of the air. On April 21, 1918, after eighty combat victories, Richthofen's plane was shot down and he was killed, in all likelihood by ground fire from an Australian machine-gun unit. The Australians buried the war's highest scoring air ace with full military honors.

By July 1918, the First Pursuit Group faced Richthofen's successors in the air. One of these successors was Oberleutnant Ernst Udet, a handsome, slender youth from a well-to-do landowning Frankfurt family. Like Quentin Roosevelt, Udet's first love was motorcycles, and he served first as a motorcycle messenger

in the German Army before requesting a transfer to pilot training. He was so eager that while waiting for acceptance, he paid
for his own flying lessons. He then gained admission to the training program at Darmstadt. Udet was credited by some as the flyer
who forced down the aircraft of France's first ace, Roland Garros.
When German technicians, including Anthony Fokker, perfected
the "interrupter gear," invented by Schneider, a Swiss, Garros's
metal-wedge deflection system became obsolete. This new technology allowed a machine gun to shoot through the arc of the
propeller; the air-war playing field was leveling out.

By the summer of 1918, the twenty-two-year-old Udet was one
of Germany's most accomplished pilots and most charismatic
leaders. He was the Commander of Jasta 4, and flew a Fokker D VII with a red fuselage and red-and-white candy stripes on
the upper wings. The fuselage of his aircraft carried the nick-
name of his fiancée, Lo. On the upper side of his tail surface, visi-
ble to any attacker, were painted the words *Du noch Nicht!* Not
you yet!

Thirty-five-year-old Carl Menckhoff, another seasoned ace,
the Commander of Jasta 72, led his unit into combat against the
First Pursuit Group. From a Westphalian family, Menckhoff,
strong-willed and independent, volunteered and joined Infantry
Regiment Number 106 in August 1914. Within three months, he
had been seriously wounded and decorated. Refused for further
duty at the front in the infantry, Menckhoff volunteered for pilot
training, was accepted and served in a two-seater on the Eastern
Front. He quickly earned a reputation as a skillful and fearless
fighter, but a man who was disdainful of military etiquette and
protocol. Like Waldo Heinrichs, Menckhoff had nothing but con-
tempt for the arrogance of many of his Prussian-style noncom-
batant commanding officers. "Besides fighting a war against the
Russians," Menckhoff recalled of his service at the Eastern Front,
"we fought a second one against the Army Post Commander."

While stationed in Russia, Menckhoff noted that his egotistical
commander renamed the squares and streets in a town after
himself and his fellow staff officers. When that commander was
replaced, the new commander promptly renamed the squares
and streets once again, after his own staff officers and himself.

After a night on the town, Menckhoff and his friends removed the newly posted signs and returned them to the new commander, noting that a "traitor" as a "wicked act of sabotage to lead our troops astray must have posted the false signs."

Like many of their American opponents, Udet and Menckhoff were well educated, courageous, and came from respected and successful families. Unlike the men of the First Pursuit Group, Udet and Menckhoff had considerable combat experience behind them, both on the ground and in the air. They were both recipients of the coveted *Pour le Mérite*—the "Blue Max," Germany's highest military award, created by Frederick the Great in 1740, an ardent admirer of all things French.

July 7, 1918 dawned brilliant and clear. A cloudless sky permitted the early sun to burn off the morning mist. The 95th was called upon to mount a ten-plane patrol over the lines; in fact, every available Allied asset was going to be put into use to help blunt the hammer blows being struck by the German offensive. General Ludendorff's all-out attack had pushed several deep salients—bulges caused by the offensives—into the Allied lines, and the German forward observers, on this lovely late-spring day, could almost see the spires of Paris.

That morning, Sumner Sewall was flying his Nieuport, identified by his personal number "0," when he and the others sighted six brightly colored Albatros fighters patrolling three miles inside their lines. Without hesitation, the Americans attacked, and a battle royale ensued. Sixteen planes zoomed, dove, and climbed; some were upside down, some were in a steep bank, and all were attempting to get a clear shot at the others. It was the "darndest stew" that Sumner had ever seen. The "Brave Bath boy" took potshots at planes darting past, then decided to stick with a single target and fastened himself to the tail of one German aircraft. It was quickly apparent that he had picked out an inexperienced pilot, as the German attempted no evasive moves and just headed farther behind his lines. Both planes plummeted down and down, deeper and deeper into Germany, with Sumner determined to get the "birdy," even if it meant shooting the German down over his own airfield.

Sewall gained on his prey, but he shot poorly. He simply could not hit the German. Flying into Germany at an altitude of about 150 feet and at 120 miles per hour, Sewall in desperation sailed right up to the German's tail, close enough to look the German pilot in the eye as he twisted around to glance at his pursuer. Sewall opened fire. He watched tracer bullets slam right into his adversary. Pieces flew from the Albatros. Its nose dropped suddenly. The pilot must have fallen forward lifeless onto his control stick. The aircraft dove straight down totally out of control and smashed into a small town.

Sumner took one last look at the crash site of his enemy. He then realized he was totally lost, and fought to find his bearings. Dodging housetops, he took a concentrated look at his compass. Locating his course, he headed for the lines, praying that his engine, now at full speed, would get him back. It roared faithfully as he hedgehopped along—too low for Archie, but well within range of Maxim machine guns on the ground. The weather had changed. He now had cloud cover protecting him from the high patrols. He swerved his plane from side to side to avoid ground fire, wondering if he would ever reach his own territory. Minutes seemed like hours, but finally shell holes began to appear on the ground, and he tore over No Man's Land at 1,500 feet to safety at last.

A large protection patrol of eleven Nieuports of the 94th took off that same morning to protect a single Salmson two-seater of the First Aero Squadron. The First Aero was an observation squadron, the oldest in the Air Service, dating back to Pershing's Mexican expedition against Pancho Villa. The observation aircraft was trying to determine the location of German troops and artillery that were reportedly massing for a large attack in the area around Reims. The Allied commanders needed this information desperately, so desperately that they assigned eleven *chasse* aircraft to protect the single Salmson.

While on this patrol, Ham Coolidge, Jimmy Meissner, and two others attacked a two-seater Rumpler; all fired away without any success. The Rumpler, whose pilot flew like an old pro, gave the foursome more than a run for their money. Two of the Americans broke off the fight with jammed guns. Ham decided it was time to get under the enemy's tail where he would be out of range of the rear gunner, and at the same time, be able to shoot at close range. Just as he got into position, the Rumpler dove and Meissner appeared on his left. They both opened up with their Vickers guns. "I shall never forget the sensation of seeing a stream of flaming tracer bullets from my guns sink into the German plane's body and almost instantly great hot, red flames bursting out from beneath his fuselage as we dove at great speed through the air," Coolidge later recalled. The German aircraft plunged like a fiery comet, exploding on impact with the earth, 9,000 feet below.

Rushing back to protect the Salmson, Coolidge did not have time to contemplate the killing. He discovered his guns had jammed; he was defenseless, and was now being pursued by a group of Fokker D VIIs, among the fastest and best-designed fighter aircraft of the Great War. A particularly persistent Fokker fastened itself onto his tail. Meissner, seeing Ham's predicament, peppered the German with a few well-directed bursts. The Americans raced toward the lines, outdistancing the swarm of angry Fokkers in pursuit. The undamaged First Aero Salmson returned to its field with its precious intelligence.

Smoking a Fatima, his favorite brand of cigarette, as he reclined in a gilt eighteenth-century chair in the salon of the grand French château that served as his temporary home, Coolidge felt pleased with himself. After months of training, with the frustrations and delays of duties at Issoudun, he was finally in combat. Coolidge's ambition, to be a fighter pilot, had been fulfilled.

When the American pilots left the serenity of their comfortable quarters, they would, within twenty minutes, be flying over the front looking down on the most wretched war the world had ever known. From 12,000 feet in the air, they patrolled over Château Thierry and Belleau Wood. The American forces there were on the attack. Towns burned all along the lines. Others were blown into splinters as giant shells landed on tiny houses, which would just roll up into the air. The bombardment was so heavy and the dust and smoke so thick that it became difficult to see the ground. Americans flying protective patrols of three planes were set upon by droves of Boche aircraft—twelve, eighteen, twenty aircraft at a time. At eight o'clock one morning, Waldo Heinrichs counted fifty Germans in three formations crossing the lines. But they kept patrolling, driving back the German observation aircraft, prohibiting them from spotting the Allied guns and ground forces. Flying back to their airfield, then dining at the château, the flyers enjoyed their good fortune to be airborne rather than earthbound, and toasted the spirit and grit of the "poor bloody infantry."

In the second week of July, the First Pursuit Group received orders to move again, this time to the airfield at Saints, two and a half miles to the north of Touquin. A British wing was moving in and taking over Touquin, which did not please the Americans in the least. The once comfortable pilots now were rudely ejected from their feather beds and dismissed from the grand château. They found the prospect of billets in the rather shabby town of Mauperthuis, located near Saints, a decidedly unpleasant prospect. The short hop with their Nieuports to Saints had only one minor casualty. Soon after Buckley departed Touquin, motor failure forced him to land in a wheat field. This he did without incident. Elated, and believing himself a true pioneer in successful wheat field landings, he was hauled out of the wheat by the farmer, and he took off again. Two minutes later he was given another opportunity to prove his new expertise. This time the results were not as good: One brand-new Nieuport was demolished, and Buckley had a long tear in his new whipcord breeches.

Each pilot was eager to secure the best new billet—until Supply Officer Ed Thomas informed them that there was no rush. He was, again, going to allocate billets in local homes according to seniority. After what seemed a long delay, Thomas passed out the assignments to the waiting pilots.

Jim Knowles was well pleased with his room in the home of the village blacksmith. The house itself was nothing special, but it did afford the company of a *jolie fille*, the blacksmith's lovely daughter. Hall, Buford, and Buckley were comfortably installed in a large bedroom overlooking a garden, with a motherly old landlady who had been forced to billet Germans during the Franco-Prussian War of 1870. Just across the way from them was a small yellow house on wheels, where the gallants of the 95th focused a great deal of interest. It sheltered a beautiful French girl of gypsy origin, who was usually clad in highly colorful attire complete with gaily hued bandanas. This situation afforded a splendid opportunity for further investigation and intrigue. Headquarters had—by their divine right, of course—settled in most comfortably at a respectable château whose gardens faced the town's main square.

If anything, their situation in the French village was even more incongruous than their life in the château had been. They were amazed at the warm reception they received from the villagers, who were forced by military law to take them into their homes. Far from resenting the intrusion of the uninvited guests, the villagers greeted them with wine and cakes. Sitting in their billets, looking out at tidy flower gardens, they found it difficult to believe that the war was raging only a few minutes away by air. But it was. After spending two hours a mile or two above the earth behind two machine guns hoping to down an enemy, the Americans returned to their peaceful surroundings and whiled away their off-duty hours, perhaps playing a game of billiards at the town restaurant or hunting rabbits with their .45 automatics.

No one took to the village of Mauperthuis quite as readily as Quentin Roosevelt. He enjoyed entertaining his landlady, an aged woman bent almost double, who nevertheless managed to make her gossip rounds every morning, hunched over her walking stick. The villagers were thrilled when Quentin accompanied the elderly woman. *"Roussefel,"* they whispered. It was the one American name familiar to the French villagers. And to think that "Meestair Roussefel," the handsome young flyer with the famous last name, was so fluent in French! *C'est la Guerre!*

# CHAPTER 11

# A Death in the Family

**A**t the same time that Quentin Roosevelt was charming the aged ladies of Mauperthuis, my father was back in the hospital. Being inactive and separated from his squadron was a great deal more painful to him than the stubborn abscess on his leg. But while he lay in hospital, Sewall, Heinrichs, Curtis, and others visited him regularly and brought him up to date with the latest news from the First Pursuit Group.

On July 10, Roosevelt flew as a member of a morning patrol with others of the squadron. As an unpracticed fighter and patrol participant, he experienced difficulty keeping a tight position in the formation. That morning they were flying at very high altitudes, and the small wing surface of his Nieuport Type 28 lost some of its lift capability in the thinner air. Due to this problem, Quentin momentarily lost control of his aircraft and dropped deeply before the formation in a *vrille*. Regaining control and pulling out of the spin, he realized that he had lost sight of his patrol. Estimating that he still had about an hour's worth of fuel, he decided "to fool around a little before going home."

He circled the area for about five minutes until he spotted three planes flying in formation. Initially he thought they were Germans, but as they ignored him, he concluded they were part of his crowd and started after them at full throttle. He thought it strange that they should be going almost straight into Germany with the wind at their backs, but he kept on.

Quentin was nearly into the formation when their flight commander led them into a turn. Horrors! He discovered that the planes had white tails emblazoned with large black crosses. They were Germans. Roosevelt did not panic. He still had altitude on the other aircraft. Either they had not seen him, or they thought he was a friend. He pulled closer, put his sights on the end man and fired a long burst. He saw his tracers going into and around the Boche, but the German never even turned until suddenly, his tail went up and he spun to earth in a *vrille*. Quentin wanted to follow him down, but by then, the remaining two enemy fighters had started after him. He reversed his course, fully opened his throttle, and outdistanced the slower Germans, landing safely back at Saints.

When they heard about his adventure, the other pilots joked, "Next time you won't catch your mistake, and you'll land back at a German aerodrome." Nevertheless, Coolidge and the other members of the patrol slapped Roosevelt on the back and congratulated his splendid *coup de main*.

Roosevelt's victory was confirmed and the press quickly got wind of it. The next day a reporter approached the twenty-year-old pilot, wanting an interview and an opportunity to take his picture. Roosevelt simply stated that his Boche was no better than the others shot down by his squadron, and he flatly refused to pose for a photograph. The reporter persisted. "Look, whether or not you shot down a Boche doesn't really make any difference. The real reason I want a picture is because you're a Roosevelt."

Quentin turned angrily on the newsman. "Why do you single me out? Is it because I happen to show good taste in the selection of my male progenitor?" End of discussion.

Three days after his first victory, Roosevelt was hard at work arranging an entertainment program for the following day—July 14, Bastille Day, the French Independence Day. Aware that the French loved ragtime and banjo tunes, he drafted a few talented musicians from the squadron and rehearsed them for an American-style variety program. In this role, Quentin was at his best—lively, funny, charismatic, and entertaining.

The pilots suggested, half in jest, that such an important French holiday was a good reason to cancel flying for the day and that a proper celebration was in order. The United States Army Intelligence, on the other hand, believed that the Boche were going to start another drive. Orders from the French Sixth Army requested flights of the 94th and 95th go on high patrol between Dormans and Belleau Wood at 11:00 A.M. on July 14. The American pilots were disappointed to be missing the holiday, but not terribly so. They would be flying comfortably at a high altitude. They would be traveling east to west with the sun at their backs. That alone would give them the advantage if they were to run into any Germans. And what better way to celebrate "Le Quatorze Juillet" than by shooting down some Germans.

The day dawned clear and warm with a light southerly wind. The French tricolor flew from every cottage in Mauperthuis. Some villagers raised delicate glasses of light-golden, locally distilled *eau de vie de cidre* in a toast to the holiday. Many of them gathered at the American airfield to watch the action, the most exciting local attraction.

More than fifty years later, Jim Knowles remembered the morning well. As we talked about the events of that day, he referred to his well-worn photo album, its pictures detailing his entire period with the Air Service in France. He also produced his *Carnet d'Emploi du Temps*, the original logbook in which he had recorded every flight he had made, from his first at Tours as a passenger in a Caudron G3, to his last, flying a Spad XIII ten days after the Armistice.

As he consulted the July 14 entry, it almost seemed as though he had stepped back in time, back into the cockpit of his Nieuport 28, to grip the control stick in his leather-gloved hand. He then began to tell me the story, slowly and deliberately:

> By the time we were ready to leave the Aerodrome, the clouds had gathered and thickened until the blue of the sky could only be seen in spots. The wind freshened considerably, which we did not enjoy because it meant that it would blow us deep across the Boche lines. Coming back we'd have to head straight into a strong wind.

By ten of eleven we were dressed and in a tent on the field, listening to our Flight Commander's orders. Everyone agreed to meet over Coulommiers at 1,800 feet, then climb steadily to 13,500 feet over Château Thierry. Ten of us met without mishap, then started to climb through the clouds at a very steep angle. One pilot got lost in the clouds. Two others had to drop out because of engine troubles. The rest of us reached Château Thierry. We turned and followed the Marne River, which was No Man's Land, toward Dormans. We arrived over Dormans at 14,000 feet. We were just ready to turn to go down the river to Belleau Wood, when Ted Curtis signaled that he saw an enemy formation, and fired his guns in their direction. At the same time, the French antiaircraft batteries pointed out the Boche by firing an arrow-shaped barrage of white smoke shells. We all turned toward our own lines, climbing steadily to gain the advantage of altitude and maneuvering into the sun so that the Huns could not see us.

After reaching 15,000 feet, we turned back to attack. The Boche were 1,500 feet below us, and two and a half miles behind Dormans, which was just between the lines. We dove on them, with every advantage except the wind, which was blowing us straight into Germany.

Knowles paused for a moment in his description, obviously full of emotion at his recollections of the brutal fight that followed:

Quentin and I picked a machine apiece and immediately attacked. Our opponents dove, and we followed them, not realizing that they were luring us down into a position from which we could be attacked by the remaining Huns above us. The other more experienced pilots had pulled up after a short burst, maintaining their superior position. When they saw our predicament, they dove again, and fourteen machines mixed in a general melee, rolling and circling and diving, some on their backs and others cocked up at an angle of 90 degrees, but all trying to get in a burst and still remain out of range [of the enemy]. The sky looked as if it were covered with a huge tangled cobweb, which in reality was caused by the white trails left by incendiary bullets. Suddenly a plane flashed in front of me, with two fiery ribbons streaming from its machine guns, and a goggled pilot hanging his head over the side of the fuselage to get a look at his victim. Bullets were flying everywhere and added to the roar of the motors and the wind winging through the wires was a continuous tat, tat, tat, tat of the machine guns.

After fifteen minutes of this sort of fighting, we were widely separated and all bucking a headwind as we started back for home. When I got back to the aerodrome I taxied up, got out and asked who had not yet returned.

It took some time to determine exactly who was missing. Coolidge and Richards had run out of gas, but had landed safely near small towns. Buford unsteadily returned to the field at about 7:00 P.M. He had also run out of gas, landed at Villers St. George, and spent the afternoon celebrating Bastille Day by drinking with the famous French ace George Nungesser of Spa 56. "Nungesser flies with a 37 mm cannon, three machine guns and a movie camera," Buford explained blearily to Coolidge, deeply concerned about his missing friend.

"Yes, but did you see what happened to Quentin?" Coolidge snapped.

Sobering a bit he replied, "No. I did see one machine go down in flames. But it was so far behind the lines, it couldn't have been Quentin."

If it was not Quentin, then who was it? Headquarters had called all the American and French landing fields nearby. No. They had not seen Roosevelt. Still, hopes remained high.

Jim Knowles momentarily gazed out the window and then continued with the story:

Everyone still believed that he was alive. No one thought for an instant that he had been shot down. Pilots are peculiar in that way. They will never believe that a man who is very dear to them, as Quent was, has been shot down until they receive absolute proof of his death.

The next morning, doubts arose. Captain Peterson, the commanding officer of the 95th, telephoned Quentin's cousin Captain Philip Roosevelt, who at that time was attached to Air Service Headquarters of the Sixth French Army. Peterson gave Roosevelt details of the fight and asked if any observation posts had seen a plane fall at about 12:15 P.M., July 14. Two balloon observers had noticed a plane fall at about that time. They had followed it down until it went behind a clump of trees, where it probably crashed. But the observers could not tell whether the plane was Allied or Boche.

It was not until two days later that we knew the truth through the German communiqué for July 14, which was intercepted by wireless. It read as follows: 'On July 14 seven of our chasing planes were attacked by a superior number of American planes north of Dormans. After a stubborn fight one of the pilots (Lieutenant Roosevelt), who had shown conspicuous bravery during the fight by attacking again and again without regard to danger, was shot in the head by his more experienced opponent and fell at Chamery.' Heaven knows how such a communiqué ever slipped by the Boche censor. As a rule, they did not praise their enemies.

But Roosevelt was no ordinary enemy. The Germans identified Quentin by his silver identification bracelet. It was later reported that German soldiers stood at attention as the young American aviator was laid to rest in a simple grave next to his fallen aircraft. At the head of the grave, the Germans placed a rough cross marked in English, "Lieutenant Roosevelt, buried by the Germans, July 14, 1918."

A few days later, the German press, looking for anything to bolster the sagging morale of their troops, as well as the morale of the war-weary civilian population, printed an article in the *Kölnische Zeitung*, the Köln daily newspaper, about Quentin's death. The headline blared "The Son of Former President of the United States of America, Roosevelt, Found Death in an Aerial Fight on the Marne." The article reported:

> . . . seven German planes were attacked by a group of twelve Americans. After a short struggle Vizefeldwebel Gräper of Jasta 50 succeeded in bringing the brave American before his sights. After a few shots, the plane went out of control, the American began to fall and then struck the ground near the village of Chamery about six miles north of the Marne . . . He was buried with full military honors.

The propaganda backfired, particularly among the frontline soldiers. A German prisoner of war later confessed to an American lieutenant:

> No sooner had Quentin fallen but that it was whispered from ear to ear, from trench to trench . . . In it one could see how in free America everybody was fighting . . . The son of an American President, engaged in one of the most dangerous lines of service, was lying back of enemy lines, while their country had been at war three years and . . . neither the Kaiser, nor any of his sons were ever so much as scratched . . . It gave the soldiers a vision of the democracy of America, and helped to deepen the feeling that they, the common soldiers, were only cannon fodder for the Kaiser.

Upon hearing of Roosevelt's death, his elderly French landlady went into deep mourning, lamenting the loss of her honorable "Roussefel." The village of Mauperthuis quickly honored him by immediately renaming the town square "Place Roosevelt."

At home, newspapers across the country lamented the loss of a well-known son. On July 21, 1918, a headline on the front page of *The New York Times* declared: "Oldest Roosevelt Son Is

Wounded: News of Theodore's Injury Comes on Heels of Confirmation of Quentin's Death."

The nation remembered Quentin as the young lad whose White House pranks brought the first family into the hearts of every American family. He was the boy who had once managed to get a hive of bees into a Washington streetcar to take them home to the White House. He was the impish youth who led a pony up the stairs of the presidential Pennsylvania Avenue home to his brother Kermit's room to keep him company when he was confined to his bed. Across the country, folks reacted to Quentin's death as if they had lost one of their own, "Hell! They got the president's son."

After the death of his youngest son, Theodore Roosevelt felt even more deeply the words he had written to all his sons on September 1, 1917:

> My disappointment at not going [to war] myself was down at bottom, chiefly [due to my] reluctance to see you four, in whom my heart was wrapped, exposed to danger while I stayed at home in do-nothing ease and safety. But the feeling has now been completely swallowed in my immense pride in all four of you. I feel that *Mother*, and all of *you* children, have by your deeds justified *my* words!

Nine months later, he was engulfed in grief.

An irate Jim Knowles gave me his final words on Quentin's loss:

> There was a story started by a yellow YMCA bastard who stated the Boche attacked *us* in superior numbers and that all the rest of the patrol except Quentin turned and ran, leaving him alone. If the rest of us had stayed, Quentin would never have been killed. All of that was a rotten lie! We attacked them in the first place, and secondly, because of the clouds, no damn YMCA man could have seen the fight.
>
> In answer to the charge that we all ran away, let me tell you who took part in the fight. Besides me and

Quent, there was Ted Curtis, later to be made a Major and an Ace, decorated with the Distinguished Service Cross and the Croix de Guerre three times; Sumner Sewall, later a Captain and an Ace, awarded the Distinguished Service Cross twice, the Légion d'Honneur, the Belgian Order of the Crown, and the Croix de Guerre twice; Johnny Mitchell, later our C.O. and Captain, awarded the Distinguished Service Cross and Croix de Guerre twice; Alex McLanahan, later Captain, awarded two Croix de Guerres and two American citations; Ned Buford, later a Captain, awarded the Distinguished Service Cross and the Croix de Guerre twice. These guys shot down twenty-six planes among them by the time the war ended. Sure as hell these people were not the kind to run.

No, they hadn't run, and they continued to fight. "It would be useless for me to attempt to eulogize Quentin in any way," Jim Knowles wrote in July 1918. "Anything I could write would sound mean and small in comparison with what he did and how he died. I can only say that he died fighting, and when he was gone, no one was ever more missed than he."

Perhaps no one missed Quentin more than Hamilton Coolidge, his best friend, who had gone to school with Roosevelt, trained with Roosevelt, struggled with the problems at Issoudun with Roosevelt, and finally, fought with Roosevelt. Shaken by his friend's death and by the painful necessity of being the one who had to collect Quentin's belongings for shipment home, Coolidge nonetheless took to the air in his new aircraft, one of the long-coveted Spad XIIIs, which had begun to arrive about July 17.

With the loss of his closest friend, the war to Ham had suddenly become terribly personal. On a seven-man low patrol, the 94th encountered six Fokkers. Coolidge, with newfound combat savvy, coolly sized up the situation: the Germans were in their own territory, and the wind was blowing hard, pushing the Americans farther into Germany. All the Boche had to do at that point was to engage them in acrobatics for a short while and, without even shooting them down, the Germans would be victorious; the Spad's gasoline supply would be insufficient to bring the 94th home against the heavy head winds. They would have to land in enemy territory. Through these tactics, the Germans might have acquired a new Spad or two, plus their pilots, with little investment. Ham thought, "This is probably how poor Quent was lost; he fought splendidly, but he was too far into Bocheland, the wind was too strong and with insufficient fuel, he was cruelly hounded until they brought him down."

Coolidge's patrol headed for home. They had learned when *not* to fight, even when they wanted so desperately to avenge a fallen comrade.

A few days later, Coolidge took a short leave in Paris, where he visited with Quentin's sister-in-law and his brothers, Ted and Arch, both of whom were recovering from slight wounds received at the front with the A.E.F. As he talked with Quentin's family, his anger and grief remained, but he had his emotions under control and was able to offer comfort to the others:

> Death is certainly not a black unmentionable thing. And I feel that dead people should be talked of just as though they were alive. Back at the Squadron, we speak all the time of the boys who have been killed when any little thing reminds someone of them. To me Quentin is just away somewhere. I know we shall see each other again and have a grand old 'hoosh' talking over everything together. His personality and spirit are just as real as they ever were.

In mid-July the Germans launched their Fifth Offensive, a push across the Marne River near Château Thierry, their last desperate push of the war. This three-day offensive is known to history as the Second Battle of the Marne, or Champagne-Marne. Nine American, two Italian and twenty-three French divisions fought to halt the advance of German General von Hutier's Eighteenth Army offensive. The First Pursuit Group, as well as all other Allied air and ground assets, were thrown into the fray. The Germans were successful at first and managed to cross the Marne, but after several days of fierce fighting, they were pushed

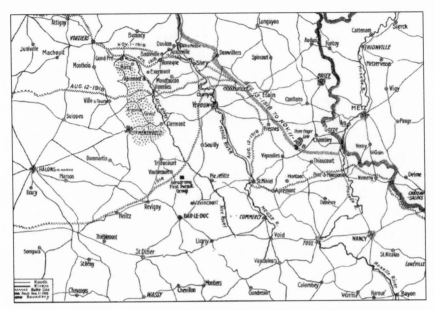

Area of operations—First and Second Pursuit Groups

back beyond their departure point. During low-level protection missions by artillery-spotting planes, the pilots were exposed to clear, close-up views of the action below. The war, no longer static, had broken out of the trenches; soldiers fought now from woods, shell holes, and the protective ruins of French barns.

From the air the American flyers could see entire houses disintegrate, fires break out in others, and, on occasion, entire villages smoldering in ruins. John Mitchell counted, at one time, more than fifty Allied planes in the air covering an area of only a few miles. Major formations of German fighters tangled with the Allied forces in massive dogfights. At one point in such a fight, Mitchell found himself battling three German Albatros scouts over the Marne River. One of the Germans was able to maneuver behind and below John and put a long burst into his wings and motor, crippling the aircraft.

Frantically looking to see if there was anyone to help him, Mitchell spotted a friendly aircraft, but it was too far away. He realized that he would have to continue to face the Germans alone in a damaged aircraft. As the three Boche took several more passes at him, John waited for the end. To his surprise,

Charles Hildreth Woolley,
age twelve, with his
brother, James, and
his mother.

The Woolley home
on White Street,
in east Boston,
built by
Donald McKay.

Charles Woolley and an SSU 9 friend after a boxing match.

The Ford Model T
ambulance was
versatile but not
indestructible.
Number 301 has
thrown a rear
wheel.

An SSU 9 crew loads wounded French soldiers into the ambulances.

The front gate of the basic flying school at Tours, France.

Blériot clipped-wing "Penguin" at Tours.

A Caudron GIII trainer coming in for a landing.
(*Musée de l'Air*)

Dick Blodgett, while in training at Tours, October 1917.

Captain James Miller, the first C.O. of the 95th Aero Squadron, was killed in action.

Major Davenport "Jam" Johnson took over from Miller after his death. (*Signal Corps photo*)

The first Nieuport 28s were delivered to the 95th at Villeneuve les Vertus unarmed.

Speedboats at the aerial gunnery school, Lake Cazeaux.

The 95th Aero Squadron—the Original Villeneuve Gang, March 1918. (*Left to right*) Russ Hall, Larry Richards, Harold Buckley, Jam Johnson, Reed Chambers, Stuart McKeown, Gene Jones, Harry Lyster, Charles Woolley, Raoul Lufbery, Sumner Sewall, Louis Schultz, Ed Thomas, Alex McLanahan, Bill Casgrain, Waldo Heinrichs, Dick Blodgett, Seth Low, Ted Curtis, Carlisle "Dusty" Rhodes. All were First Lieutenants except for Johnson and Lufbery, who were Majors.

Ned Buford buzzes a Signal Corps movie cameraman, Gengoult Aerodrome, May 1918. (*Signal Corps photo*)

Lieutenants Buford, Richards, McKeown, McLanahan, Curtis, and Heinrichs waiting for a mission at the 95th's operations tent, Gengoult Aerodrome, May 1918.

Jake the mule, the 95th's mascot, performs for the pilots of the First Pursuit Group, Gengoult Aerodrome, Spring 1918. (*Signal Corps photo*)

Woolley's and Johnson's tea party for the Army nurses, Gengoult Aerodrome, spring 1918.

Jim Knowles guards the 95th Bar, complete with captured German sign over the entrance.

Waldo Heinrichs's Nieuport minus the upper left wing fabric—a not uncommon occurrence with the 28s.

First Lieutenant Waldo Heinrichs, Saints, July 1918.

Charles Woolley, Ted Curtis, John Mitchell, and Alex McLanahan, Gengoult Aerodrome, June 1918.

The remains of Woolley's Nieuport 28. Bad gas, perhaps?

(*Left*) Quentin Roosevelt at Issoudun. (*Right*) Roosevelt in his Nieuport 27 trainer at Issoudun.

Quentin Roosevelt lies beside the remains of his wrecked Nieuport 28, July 14, 1918. Although the Germans buried him with military honors, they made postcards out of this photograph.

Quentin Roosevelt's first (*left*), and second (*right*) grave markers.

(*Left*) Ham Coolidge. (*Right*) Coolidge in the cockpit.

Major Raoul
Lufbery

First Lieutenant
George Fisher
(*Signal Corps photo*)

First Lieutenant
Ned Buford
(*Signal Corps photo*)

First Lieutenant
Bill Vail

First Lieutenant
John Mitchell

First Lieutenant
Peter Puryear
(*Signal Corps photo*)

First Lieutenant
Walt Avery

Captain James
Norman Hall

Captain Hobey Baker

Eddie Rickenbacker and the famous Hat-in-the-Ring logo of the 94th Aero Squadron.

Twin Vickers guns on a Spad XIII

The 94th visits the front. *From left to right:* First Lieutenants Cunningham, Chambers, unknown, Rickenbacker, Meissner, unknown.

Major John Huffer,
Commanding Officer, 94th
Aero Squadron.

Lieutenant Oscar Gude

Major Huffer's
Spad after
Lieutenant Gude
landed at the
German airfield
at Mars le Tour.

The personally
marked Fokker D
VII of Ober-
leutenant Carl
Menckhoff,
brought down by
Walt Avery of the
95th.

Brevet 9634 belonging to First Lieutenant Dave Backus.

Charles Woolley stands next to his plane as a Flight Commander of the 49th Aero Squadron.

Fritz, the German shepherd mascot of the 49th, and his handler.

Ground crews show the troublesome twenty-five-pound bombs forced on the pursuit pilots.

First Lieutenant Sumner
Sewall, 95th Aero Squadron.

Sumner
Sewall
cuts out
a black
cross
from his
first kill.

Maine Governor Sumner Sewall, with his wife Eleena, son David,
daughter Alexandra, and son Nicholas.

Charles Woolley's identity-card photograph, March 1918.

Major Charles Woolley with Amelia Earhart and her mother on her triumphant return to Boston.
(*AP/Wide World*)

Colonel Charles Woolley, 1950.

none of their fire inflicted any further serious damage. Then, for
no apparent reason, they broke off the chase and headed back
into German territory. With a smoking engine and bullet-riddled
wings, he limped back to his aerodrome.

A few days after this event, Mitchell enjoyed some well-earned
leave in nearby Paris. While walking just off the Champs Elysées,
a long-range German gun dropped a shell into a side street, just
two blocks away from where John was walking. It tore an enormous hole in the street, killed a horse and a taxi driver, and shattered windows in shops and houses. Mitchell was stunned that no
one seemed to pay any particular attention to the event. Life in
Paris seemed to be proceeding in a normal way. He tried to imagine people at home in Boston calmly eating dinner or sitting in a
theater, with large shells exploding every fifteen minutes a few
blocks away. John somehow felt he was much safer in the air,
where he could at least *see* the enemy and *fight* him.

On the second day of the Second Battle of the Marne, Ted
Curtis and Sumner Sewall were on a low patrol with orders to
strafe or shoot at any "targets of opportunity" on the ground.
While searching for earthbound targets, they caught sight of three
German Albatros single-seat scouts. Curtis, the patrol leader, singled out one of the gaudily painted enemy fighters and led the
others in an attack. Sumner later commented:

> I dived to see if I could not stick a finger in some-
> where when all of a sudden another strange-looking
> ship appeared directly in front of me. He was in such
> a position I could not see his insignia, but he looked
> 'Bochey.' I did not worry long, however, for he flashed
> past in a second, a two-seater with a big black cross
> on his tail. Well, I had the darndest time getting under
> that fellow's tail, which I guess accounts for the fact
> that when I at last did get my sights on him and saw a
> beautiful stream of bullets going straight home, I sim-
> ply could not change for a better position, although I
> knew I was a perfect shot for the observer . . . It was
> the darndest predicament I have ever been in. Here
> we were getting nearer and nearer and I could see this

damn Dutchman shooting at me, but yet I could see
my stream of tracers flying through his fuselage . . .

Sewall knew something had to give; either he was going to
be shot down by that gunner or he was going to hit some criti-
cal point of the Rumpler and it would go down. He kept waiting for the gunner to fall over the side or crumple into his
cockpit, or for the pilot to collapse on the controls sending the
plane into a dive from which the two-seater would never recover.
But to his astonishment, the plane suddenly burst into flames,
flames that engulfed the enemy almost instantly. To Sumner's
horror, the gunner was still at his guns, doomed by the fierce fire
around him.

Banking away and heading for home, Sewall took one last look
at his victim and saw the German jump from the rear seat, falling
away from the burning plane. He was then no longer human; he
was just a small ball of flame windmilling through the sky. Sumner recorded:

> When I turned, however, I noticed I had troubles of
> my own . . . My motor was missing and getting worse
> and worse, and as I was not sure just whether I was on
> the side of the lines or not, this was my first worry . . .
> Then I suddenly looked out on my wing to find my
> second worry; namely, that a bullet had gone through
> my front strut, cut a stagger wire, (wing support
> wire) and had completely cut as [by] a knife, my rear
> strut . . . The only thing that was holding the thing to-
> gether was pressure of both ends and a little friction
> where it was cut . . . I saw the darn thing slowly slip-
> ping and I saw that if it slipped much more, my style
> would certainly be cramped, so without the slightest
> hesitation, down I started, and oh! so gently.
>     It was then that I noticed my third worry, for I ob-
> served that there was much loose gasoline running
> around dripping on me and especially into my mag-
> neto (electrical switch) where there was an excellent
> spark.

The spark did not ignite the gasoline, and Sewall managed to land his crippled Spad yards from the enemy lines.

When Sewall, on foot, eventually returned to the field, he was met by his greatly relieved pal Ted Curtis, who thought he had been shot down in enemy territory. Curtis told him that he had driven his own opponent back and had come to Sewall's assistance, and without caution had attacked the two-seater from above and from the front. In this instance, teamwork had paid off, and both pilots were credited with the victory.

"This is getting to be the most natural life in the world," Curtis wrote. "Climbing into a 220-horsepower fighting plane and hunting Boche around the skies. It's like shooting at a target which gives satisfactory and obvious results. Combat aviation is by all odds the best way to go to war."

As the Allies advanced north and northeast of Château Thierry and took the ground over which Quentin Roosevelt had fought and died, Ham Coolidge set out to find the grave of his friend. He flew to a small field near Chamery, where the grave was reported to be. There he borrowed a motorcycle and set off to search the area. As he passed through a small ruined village, he was amazed to see an American nurse calmly walking down the devastated main street. Even more amazing, the nurse was a girl he knew, Rose Peabody, from Boston, who was serving in a mobile hospital in the town. After a brief conversation with her and promises to meet again, Coolidge set off once more on his quest.

He found his friend's grave overlooking rolling grassy hills and scattered woods, a grave marked with a plain wooden cross. The twisted axle and wire wheels of Roosevelt's aircraft rested at the foot of the cross. A few other remains of his Nieuport lay nearby next to the savage gouge in the earth dug by the plane in its fall. American troops had built a stick fence around the grave and decorated it with wildflowers. Well-worn footpaths marked the routes that other mourners had taken to pay their respects.

As Coolidge stood near the rough grave of his dearest friend, he could hear the pounding of the big German guns and the sudden shallower whang of Archie. Looking up, he watched black Boche antiaircraft shells bursting around a group of American planes as they flew over the sausage-shaped observation balloons that marked the front lines.

Coolidge later wrote, "Bursting shrapnel, onion rockets, machine gun bullets and Boche planes give you a start at first, but you get used to all that. What you can never get used to, though, is to have your very best friends 'go West.' "

Later when Theodore Roosevelt was asked by the American Graves Commission if he wished to have his youngest son's remains returned to the United States, he simply said, "No, let the oak lie where it fell."

# CHAPTER 12

# From Joy to Despair

Quentin Roosevelt was not the only 95th pilot with limited front-line experience to fall in the summer of heavy fighting along the Marne River. Irby "Rabbit" Curry was killed after less than a month in action; Bill Russell met the same fate; Clarence Gill was badly wounded after three weeks; Norman Archibald, Walt Avery, Granville Woodard, and Peter Puryear went down behind enemy lines and became prisoners of war. Four out of eleven assigned to the 95th was not a good survival rate for replacement pilots, but it proved what most pilots knew, that experience in the air was the key to survival in the air.

After the loss of so many new friends, the First Pursuit Group flyers sorely needed something, anything, to lift their sagging spirits. And nothing could lift their spirits more than the arrival of their new, long-awaited, up-to-date flying machines. For weeks, rumors had circulated that the 94th and the 95th were about to be equipped with the most modern fighting aircraft available: the Spad XIII, which promised to be stronger, faster, and more deadly than the fragile Nieuport 28. The Spad, with a top speed of 130 miles per hour, featured a 220-horsepower Hispano-Suiza V-8 water-cooled engine, mounted in a fixed inverted position. "Spad" was an acronym for "Société Anonyme pour l'Aviation et ses Dérives," the French company that first designed and built the aircraft. The 94th and 95th pilots, the old hands, were particularly pleased to present the upstart pilots of the 27th and 147th Squadrons with their old Nieuports.

By the end of the war, the Allies had taken delivery of 8,472 Spad XIIIs, making it one of the most widely used aircraft of the war. Woolley and the other pilots felt confident that with the new Spads, they would be able to fly rings around the German Fokker D VIIs, and that they would be equipped with a fighter plane superior to any other.

On July 13, fourteen new Spads were delivered to the field at Saints. The thrill of receiving the new aircraft quickly gave way to consternation, and the hard work began as the pilots, mechanics, and armorers toiled to make the machines reliable and combat-ready. The Operations Report from the 94th Squadron for July 13 stated the situation simply. "Spads available, 1; Spads unavailable, 13; Total, 14." The next day's report showed the same statistic. The Spads had proven to be a mechanic's nightmare.

The Engineering Department had to deal with multiple mechanical difficulties. In the 94th alone, the ground crews were faced with 124 major mechanical problems between July 18 and the end of the month on these brand-new airplanes. The Spads had problems with overheating, leaking oil pipes, faulty oil pumps, faulty carburetors, faulty magnetos, faulty gas tanks, nonfunctioning gauges, poorly designed reduction gearing, and on more than one occasion, completely worthless engines that had to be totally replaced. Major Harold E. Hartney, who became the Commander of the First Pursuit Group in August, described the new Spad aircraft as "a catastrophe."

Shoddy workmanship was the major cause of the difficulties. Spads were built, under contract, by nine companies, and Spad itself built only 1,141 of the more than 8,000 in existence. The quality control everywhere was atrocious but somewhat understandable, because the French aviation industry production capacity was stretched to the limit.

The confidence of the American pilots did not improve with the mounting number of inexplicable problems with their planes. A patrol would leave the field with a group of ten to twelve functioning Spads, only to have six fall out with mechanical problems before reaching the lines. Without question, the heroes of these terrible weeks in American aviation were the engineering divisions of the pursuit squadrons and the individual mechanics assigned to each plane, who worked tirelessly to solve countless problems not of their making.

Heroic efforts by the enlisted men did not make the situation of the faulty aircraft any less frustrating for the pilots of the 94th and 95th Squadrons, however. Ham Coolidge's experience was typical. His first Spad was a total lemon. The second ran fine for a short time, then a valve disintegrated and tore the engine to pieces. His mechanics installed a new one and tuned it to what they thought was perfection. A cheerful Coolidge flew off for the lines. A furious and frustrated Coolidge returned and described what happened:

> A few minutes [after taking off] I felt a drizzle of water in my face and suspected it was raining. But no, the water was hot. Then a pipe burst and the cockpit was flooded with boiling water from the cooling system. Luckily I was able to land at a French field where they fixed the pipe, and I gaily started out a second time. Again a drizzle of water, this time from a different place. A plug had come out of the water jacket and let it all out again. My temperature began to rise and before I finally made a good landing field, the poor old motor was almost *grillé* (fried). A wooden plug in the hole held the water sufficiently for me to limp back home. I'm the most disgusted man you ever saw. I've been cheated out of a lot of action.

One of the causes of Coolidge's continuing mechanical problems was the Spad's Hispano-Suiza engine and its propeller reduction gearing. Aeronautical engineers had discovered that propellers, when turned too rapidly, actually lose effectiveness. To overcome this, engine designers placed a gearing system between the engine and the propeller that reduced the propeller's revolutions and maximized its power. The reduction gearing, unfortunately, caused many water-cooled engines to vibrate excessively. The engine's radiator was bolted directly to the front of the fuselage, and the vibration quickly caused leaks at attachment points on the pipes that circulated the cooling fluids. Stronger radiators mounted to the fuselage with flexible rubber mounts quickly solved this particular problem.

No one was more tortured by the Spads' failures than Joe Eastman, whose diary revealed his total lack of confidence in his machine as well as in himself. "The run of luck that I have been experiencing as a pilot is soon due to alter for the better, or it will finish me in some manner," he confided to his diary. "The madhouse looms up as an imminent possibility."

Eastman's mechanics changed the oil pump on his Spad five times! Finally, after all these changes, he took off on a patrol, but had just cleared the field when whack—something broke, smoke surrounded him, and the entire plane vibrated violently. Eastman was barely able to regain the field. First Lieutenant Charles Rankin, the Engineering Officer, was aware that Eastman tended to be an accident-prone pilot who seemed to have black clouds of trouble hanging over his head. Nerves coupled with bad luck were an unfortunate combination. "Take Number 10," he told Eastman. "It's in top condition. It will serve you well."

Eastman went out to his newly assigned aircraft and found that it was inexplicably under repair. "The damn motor is a make we've never heard of," the mechanics complained. "The throttles are offset and difficult to control. You need a pair of pliers to move its gas thumb-lever and neither the guns nor sights have ever been tested. Coolidge and another pilot had this plane before you. Never could get the machine to work right."

"Just my luck," Eastman thought as he finally sat in the cockpit of Number 10 preparing for takeoff. "Although my habitual appearance is one of cow-like docility and temperamental imperviousness, I left the ground in a state of mind that jumps out of its chair when a door is closed above a whisper."

After two minutes in the air, he checked his gauges. The oil and air pressure were less than half of what they should be. The engine was running hot. A few minutes spent hopefully in pursuit of his patrol failed to influence the gauges for the better:

I *piqued* for the field, and instead of the temperature cooling, it continued to augment in its own cheery fashion. The motor stopped firing over Coulommiers; I jiggled it to life; it coughed, missed and revolved feebly by turns letting me down nearer and nearer to an unpromising landscape—which by the grace of God, I was enabled to clear.

At the hangar I climbed out of the boiling creature of misfortune and was able only by a considerable effort to keep myself from breaking down completely. It bothers me no little to find that my nervous force is bordering the point where it can't be held in leash by willpower . . . everything I touch or fly seems to suffer as from the plague of ill fortune with my contact.

Eastman reportedly told himself that in the same planes the same thing would have happened to anyone else. But did he really believe it?

A few days later, on takeoff, Eastman blew out a tire. After repairing the tire, he finally caught up to his patrol, where he quickly became engaged with five Boche machines in a dogfight. He found himself entirely surrounded by the smoke of Hun tracers, which he described as "like being in a Boche pretzel shop." His motor began to knock. He had no idea where he was. He had to leave the fight, and managed to make his way to a French airfield and land without further incident. From July to August, Eastman's Spad 15004 was unavailable on twenty-six out of forty-five days. In stark contrast, Rickenbacker's Spad 4523 was down only one day during the same period, and that was not due to mechanical failure. Was the problem entirely one of Eastman's equipment? Or his nerves? Did Eastman ask his mechanics for solutions to problems that were only imaginary?

While the Air Service was attempting to get and to keep their Spads in the air, the American infantry was advancing, retaking the territory given up in the German attack earlier in the summer. Despite their mechanical difficulties, patrols of the 94th and the 95th managed to take to the air to cover the American advance. Both squadrons formed a combined patrol of nineteen planes that fought a furious dogfight with Jasta 74 over the woods north of Château Thierry. During the height of this action, Jim Knowles was attacking an enemy Fokker, when out of the corner of his eye he saw a fireball flash less than ten feet from the tail of his plane. It was the Spad of Grover Vann, who had been with the squadron only three weeks. "Just those few seconds, as I watched that plane come down, added about thirty years to my life," Knowles told me, adding:

> With a rare presence of mind, which consisted of keeping my guns wide open all the time in the dogfight that followed Vann's death, I got my first official [victory]. One unlucky Jerry just happened to wander in front of me and got the full benefit.

The 95th's fresh pilots were now becoming comfortable with the new Spads. Walt Avery was one. The thirty-year-old Avery joined the squadron from French Escadrille N 471, a squadron manned by American pilots charged with the air defense of Paris. Avery's combat report of the same fight in which Vann had been lost was terse: "Brought down one Fokker bi-plane in the woods north of Château Thierry: Pilot Capt. Menckhoff." On his first flight over the lines, Walt Avery had shot down Carl Menckhoff, one of the most experienced and successful German fighter pilots of the Great War.

Climbing down from his shattered aircraft, which had landed in a tree, Menckhoff was quickly surrounded by French troops. During the fight he had noticed that there were French wing markings on the machine that had brought him down, markings that Walt Avery's mechanics had not had time to change to the American combination of colors.

"Who was the French pilot who maneuvered and shot so well?" the German ace later asked his interrogators in perfect French.

"An American, Lieutenant Avery," he was told. "It was his first time flying over the lines in a Spad. And his first time in combat."

"Impossible!" the proud Menckhoff fumed. "Now I know it was ground fire that brought me down."

Peter Puryear had been the last man off on the massive patrol, but he had to turn back with an overheating problem. First Lieutenant George "Peter" Puryear, before joining the Air Service just out of law school, had been practicing law in Memphis. He was a dark, attractive, athletic young man, aggressive almost to a fault. In order to solve the temperature problem of his motor, he landed at the field of the 12th Aero Observation Squadron, poured seven gallons of water into his overheated radiator, and quickly took off again in an attempt to rejoin the patrol. He was unable to locate the others, and not finding any Boche in the area, finally headed for home.

Puryear was serenely flying along, when he noticed a British single-seater Sopwith Camel approaching. He was unconcerned about the Allied aircraft, until it positioned itself three hundred feet above and behind his tail and opened fire! Three bullets from that burst hit his Spad. Puryear immediately maneuvered his plane onto his attacker's tail and fired a short warning burst. Alarmed as well as fuming at the situation, he zoomed and circled, and with adroit diving passes, finally drove the "Brit" to land on the ground near Lucy-le-Bocage.

After the Camel was on terra firma, Puryear dove on it a few times from a low altitude "to scare him a bit" and to gather further identifying data. The number on the plane was "945"; the cocardes were unquestionably British, and there were two diagonal white stripes on the upper wing. After landing, a phone call was made to the British Wing at Touquin; Puryear was furious to learn there was no such numbered and marked machine on the British field. Adding insult to injury, Knowles and Curtis razzed him without mercy. "You damn fool," said Knowles, "that was without doubt a German pilot in a captured English machine. He didn't know how to handle a Camel or else you never could have done what you did. You, in a Spad, outmaneuvering a Camel! Imagine your doing that to an experienced Camel pilot?" It was well known that several prominent German aces flew captured Camels and Spads in combat.

Curtis heaped more abuse. "What you should have done was to have landed, taken his name, rank, and outfit, and reported him with all the details. I would have taken him bodily back to his group if I had been you."

"If it happens again, I'll certainly land right beside him," Puryear vowed.

Knowles recounted the events of the following day. Suffering from a victory celebration that had lasted well into the early morning, Knowles led a patrol that departed the field at what he felt was the ungodly hour of 6 A.M. In his company were Peter Puryear, Waldo Heinrichs, Sumner Sewall, Ted Curtis, and the married squadron elder, Charlie Gravatt. Knowles paused for a moment, remembering the men, then continued the story:

> Near Château Thierry and coming out straight from behind the German lines, I spotted what appeared to be a Fokker. We, at least this other machine and I, were at almost the same altitude, so I couldn't see its markings, but it had the short lower wing typical of the Fokker D VII and I couldn't figure that any Allied machine would be coming out of Germany that early in the morning. Therefore, without further ado, I started firing . . . The rest of the crowd, being higher than I, could see the machine's markings, but because they thought it a huge joke and knowing that there wasn't much chance of my doing any damage, let me go ahead and continue shooting at a French Breguet bombing plane. After a couple of hundred rounds, the two Frenchmen finally realized that someone was shooting at them and cocked up to show the [French] cocards on their machine's wings. When I saw these, I quit, but good old Charlie Gravatt, imbued with that spirit that makes men follow their leaders blindly, and possibly thinking my guns had jammed, started firing at this machine when I stopped, although he was the last man in the formation and at least as far away as I was. The poor Frenchmen twisted and twirled, showed their colors, and did everything to prove they were friends of ours, but Charles was not satisfied until he had chased them all the way back to their field.

Things went along peacefully for a bit, when suddenly I found myself deserted by my young charges. Nowhere could they be seen. 'Where the hell have they gone?' I worried. 'Perhaps they haven't any confidence in me after the way I just performed.' I hadn't thought of looking below, but finally decided to, and what a sight! One poor Boche Rumpler with Curtis, Sewall, Heinrichs, and Puryear all breaking their necks to get a crack at it and only succeeding in getting in each other's way. Being leader that morning, I considered I ought to have first crack and so dropped down to add to the confusion. Somehow or other a little order was restored and we took turns in dropping down on this bird's tail, firing a few rounds, then pulling away so that the next could try his hand.

Fortunately the Rumpler pilot was a rotten one, and even more fortunate for us, the Rumpler observer was a rotten shot, otherwise the Jerry plane would have flown home in good shape and the observer would have gotten at least three of us. It took us five brave boys about ten minutes to force him down when one man alone could have knocked him off in fifteen seconds.

I believe it was a burst from Heinrichs' guns that finally stretched the observer over his gun turret, and when this happened, the pilot decided to find a good smooth spot and land. He took his time finding one, too, which hurt our pride considerably. He headed for a field behind a small farmhouse which had a fairly high wall around the barnyard. As soon as he landed, the pilot hopped out, threw the observer over his shoulder, and started running for the farmhouse. Heinrichs, having popped the observer, thought he had a first mortgage on the pilot, and dropped down to give him a few rounds. It appeared the pilot didn't last as long on the ground as he had in the air, but we discovered later on that he was playing possum and had not been hit. In the meantime, I had flown over the house to see if there was anything to shoot at in that vicinity, or get some clue as to just where we were because the American attack was in full swing and

American troops were advancing rapidly in spite of tremendous losses, and no one knew exactly where the lines were . . . I got over the house, flying at about 75–100 feet altitude and found the walled courtyard filled with German infantry. 'O, ho,' I said to myself, 'I have you boys where the hair is short. As soon as I can roll this bus over and come down on top of you, you're going to have both guns opened up on you.' Just as I was about to do this, I happened to see Puryear's plane nosing down with the prop idling as if he were going to land. 'What's the matter with him,' I thought, 'he can't be foolish enough to land without knowing where he is. His motor must have cut out.'

Peter kept on going, leveled out, made a beautiful three-point landing, rolled slowly across the field, hit a hidden ditch, and then slowly, oh, so slowly, went up on his nose and then dropped back; but his prop had been broken, which cut out any chance of his taking off again . . . [His landing] cut out the most beautiful opportunity I had had up to that time of running the Dutch lads a little ragged on the ground. For the minute I thought more of my disappointment, rather than of Peter's predicament, and was pretty sore.

His plight was very forcibly brought back to my mind by a German reception committee issuing from the house to receive him. Any one of us could have dispensed them in a few minutes, but it would have meant Puryear's instant death if we had so much as fired one shot into the crowd. We were forced to fly around overhead, absolutely helpless, and watch him be taken away.

The Germans captured Puryear, and the Boche pilot, who was highly indignant that Waldo Heinrichs had fired on his wounded gunner, vented his anger on the American. Adding to Peter's problems, the Germans checked the ammunition in his machine guns and mistakenly identified the incendiary rounds, which had flat noses, similar to the dreaded dum-dum bullets that were intentionally blunted so that when they struck they mushroomed, causing dreadful wounds. The dum-dum bullets were outlawed by the Geneva Convention, but occasionally found their way into use fashioned by bitter soldiers on both sides. Fortunately Puryear was whisked away from the angry infantrymen and taken to the rear. There he underwent intensive interrogation by two intelligence officers before being sent to a prisoner of war camp at Rastatt in Baden, Germany.

With the heavy movement of men and materiel necessary for the Allied advance, the air above had to be kept clear of prying enemy eyes so that some degree of secrecy could be maintained. But the front had been advancing so rapidly that the American pilots could hardly locate it, much less protect it. Flying a simple protection patrol from their base at Saints to the advanced lines now required the pilots of the First Pursuit Group to make a re-fueling stop at Coincy. This stretched the total flying time per patrol to over four hours. The additional takeoffs and landings added to the maintenance woes, because the Coincy field was pockmarked with repaired shell holes that caused both tire blow-outs and undercarriage troubles.

Pilot losses from accidents were the most tragic casualties. Coolidge was in a formation flying toward the lines when he spotted a group of "Huns in the sun" above. The Americans started to dive down away from them. Coolidge related the outcome in a letter home:

> As our boys dove they were naturally looking back over their shoulders watching the enemy when suddenly two of our best pilots collided. The wings were stripped cleanly from one machine. It fell like a stone. The other had the wings on one side badly damaged. I watched him go down in a slow spiral more or less under control. Everybody hoped that he might have landed safely, but later investigation proved that they were both smashed to pulp. It's such a hideous way to lose men. . . .

Allied fighter pilots did not carry parachutes because of limited cockpit space and their perceived unreliability. Parachutes were used regularly by balloon observers on both sides, and as the war neared its end, the German pilots began to use newly designed parachutes with some degree of success.

Because the Spads "were continually breaking down and causing endless problems," regular flying operations had been suspended. The men spent their duty time practicing mock battles in the air, which were to prove helpful, but Coolidge and the others grumbled about the "dreary, monotonous place" in which they lived.

One of the bright spots of the summer was a lavish banquet hosted at Fontainebleau by the recently well-heeled Johnny Mitchell. All the pilots and ground officers of the 95th—Major Harold Hartney commanding the First Pursuit Group, Captain Ken Marr commanding the 94th, and Jim Meissner of the 94th— gathered to celebrate the awarding of the "Tilton Prizes." Established by Mr. Curtis Tilton of Philadelphia and Biarritz, France, in May 1918, the prize was money—a king's ransom at the time, donated by several individuals—totaling more than 10,000 francs. It was to be divided among the first five pilots of the American Expeditionary Forces to bring down three German airplanes. Mr. Tilton mandated that, "An aviator claiming the prize should send one copy of his official record to *The New York Herald*, Paris Office, and one copy to Mr. Curtis Tilton, Lloyds Bank, Biarritz."

Four pilots qualified: Doug Campbell and Jimmy Meissner of the 94th, Sumner Sewall and Johnny Mitchell of the 95th. Mitchell spent his prize money, and probably more, on the bountiful banquet.

Lieutenant Eddie Butts, the 95th Squadron Operations Officer, summed up the event in his brief diary entry: "August 24, 1918, John Mitchell gave a banquet at Fontainebleau. Everybody got gloriously drunk. We had a wonderful time."

Buckley rendered a more stylish description of the evening's festivities at the Hôtel de France et Angleterre in his book *Squadron 95*:

> In the pleasant summer evening, we passed the time before dinner in the garden, drinking whiskeys and soda, waving grandly at the waiter, 'Lieutenant Mitchell, my

wealthy American friend, will pay for all. Let's have another drink.' Dinner was at eight, a superior meal, which would have won a tribute from a hardened gourmand. To us, teeth sharpened on bully beef and horsemeat, palates crying out loud at the mere sight of a carrot it was—well, here's the way it went, as far as we can recall:

> *Porto Flips*
> *Hors d'Oeuvres*
> *Sole Meuniere—Graves Supérieur*
> *Caneton—Sauce au Rhum*
> *Filet Mignon*
> *Pommes Souffles—Pommard*
> *Asperges Hollandaise*
> *Crêpes Suzette—Château Yquem*
> *Fromage*
> *Café*
> *Cointreau—Grand Marnier—Bénédictine*
> *Chartreuse—Anisette*
> *Vodka*
> *Brandy*
> *Brandy*
> *Whisky and Soda*
> *Wiskey Soda*
> *Whishkey—Shoada*
> *Wishshisk Shohd sh sh odddd*

Eddie Butts's description about the level of alcoholic consumption had to have been correct.

Sewall was frequently uncomfortable with the coverage he received in the stateside press. "People are making a little too much of the Boche party of mine," Sumner complained when he learned that one of his previous letters home had been printed in the local Bath, Maine, paper:

> They put that letter of mine in the *Independent* . . .
> I must admit I think the world is better off minus a
> couple of good fat dutchmen and I am not in the least

sad because I have perhaps hurried a few of them down, but as for being in any way connected with bravery, it is all wrong. I know personally whenever I see one of those horrible black crosses, I get so darned excited I forget everything, even to be afraid. And when the old tracers start to sail through the air and the machine guns start hammering, then everyone just goes crazy and the fun begins. It is simply a good game, the point of the game being to knock down the black cross which is done by throwing so many bullets into the right spot . . . It was nothing but pure luck that my bullets happened to be the ones to bring out the flames . . . It is the sort of thing that happens every day and they shouldn't have stuck in my picture and written all that junk. It's a pity.

In another letter home, Sewall wrote:

Oh, Mother, won't you please doubt these rumors and absolutely disbelieve the newspapers? I write you everything without modesty because I know you want to know everything as it is, and yet, here comes a cable from you congratulating me on something I have never mentioned and never received . . . It is not right, Mother, that you or my friends should think I am doing these things when I am not, so please, for my sake, deny everything and don't get hopeful on a little clipping.

The other pilots agreed with Sumner's negative stand on the "hero and the other rah-rah stuff" regarding their exploits that appeared in the popular American press like *Collier's* and *The Saturday Evening Post*. Aviators made great press, but the details in many of the articles were incorrect, exaggerated, and terribly embarrassing to those who were the actual participants.

While the pilots of the First Pursuit Group waged the battle with faulty equipment, my father was to face new and different challenges. Finally free of his pesky infection, he had been released from the hospital at the end of July. He found himself promoted to the new role of Flight Commander assigned to the 49th Aero Squadron, the latest addition to the Second Pursuit Group.

The Commander of the Second Pursuit Group was Major Davenport Johnson, the same "Jam" Johnson who had formerly commanded my father in the 95th. Although a questionable air fighter, Johnson was an excellent administrator. He asked First Lieutenant George Fisher, Dad's Flight Commander from the 95th, to take command of the 49th Aero Squadron. Fisher readily agreed to take command of the squadron and requested that Woolley and Buford from the 95th and John Wentworth from the 94th serve as his three Flight Commanders.

It was difficult for my father to leave his close friends—the "Villeneuve gang," the "Kicking Mules," the men with whom he had first served and with whom he had learned the art of combat flying. On the other hand, he was honored by the appointment to the duty of a Flight Commander and felt well prepared to take on the responsibility of that position. Friends at the 95th joked, "The real reason you took the job was because of Fisher's new Cadillac touring car." A few days later, he and Buford left in the Cadillac to join the 49th and the Second Pursuit Group, the newest squadron of the rapidly expanding American aviation presence on the Western Front.

# CHAPTER 13

# *Flight Commander*

Lieutenant Woolley's new assignment to a new squadron was one small part in the overall blossoming growth of the U.S. Air Service. New squadrons were being created almost daily. On the ground, segments of the American Expeditionary Force had previously operated under various French and British commands. The American Supreme Commander, General John "Black Jack" Pershing, strongly believed that American forces should operate under American commanders in an all-American army. Pershing's drive to change the command structure caused considerable friction with French Field Marshal Ferdinand Foch, but eventually Pershing won the tug of war. The Joint Allied Command agreed that United States troops would fight as a unified force under Pershing's command. On August 10, 1918, the American Expeditionary Force became the "First American Army," responsible for a twenty-mile section of the Western Front.

While the Americans were reducing the salients on their front in the Champagne region, the British and French were hammering away at their objectives in Belgium to the north. In Flanders, the British launched a surprise attack supported by 456 tanks, the largest tank corps ever assembled. Advancing behind noisy, smoke-spewing, clanking armored vehicles that lumbered forward at three or four miles an hour, the British broke through the German lines on August 8, 1918, quickly capturing 12,000 men and

400 artillery pieces. For the first time, whole German divisions gave up their positions. Mutiny was in the wind. German foot soldiers greeted their replacements with cries of "You are prolonging the war." Erich Ludendorff called August 8 "The Black Day of the German Army." The German Field Marshal realized that the era of stalemate and trench warfare was over. No longer would bullet-spewing, concealed machine-gun nests and long-distance artillery duels be able to hold back armies indefinitely. A new era, the era of the tank and the airplane, the armored and air cavalry, had arrived.

Prior to the September attack on the St. Mihiel salient, Pershing had named the visionary airman Colonel Billy Mitchell Chief of Air Service, First Army. Brigadier General Benjamin D. Foulois, who had taught himself to fly the U.S. Army's first aircraft in 1909, was Chief of Air Service, American Expeditionary Forces, but Mitchell had the top combat position and reported directly to Pershing. Mitchell, who had arrived in France as a Major and an "observer" in March 1917, had been promoted to Lieutenant Colonel by May 1918, and two months later became a full Colonel. His star was in ascension.

Pershing did not have the mind of an airman. He had seen aircraft operate ineffectively during his hunt for Pancho Villa. He was aware that pilots in aircraft had found it impossible to communicate from the air with the artillery and infantry commanders on the ground. Pershing, nevertheless, believed that control of the air was necessary for victory, even if he could then visualize only limited use for the squadrons of flying machines under his command.

Mitchell, on the other hand, was convinced that aircraft would play a vital role in winning the war, but he was hampered in building his case by the lack of frontline operational aircraft. American industry had promised to "blacken the skies with aircraft" but was unable to deliver a single serviceable fighter aircraft to the front during World War I. The United States did manage to build and deliver the British-designed deHaviland DH 4 powered by the American-designed, 400-horsepower Liberty engine. The aircraft saw only limited service during the war, due to its tendency to catch fire in flight. Pilots abhorred what they called the "Flying Coffin." Upon investigation, the Air Service found that the fires were caused by gas-line leaks ignited by the long, red-hot exhaust pipes. They then experimented with pipes cut off short, only to discover that flames pulsing from the ends of the short pipes blinded pilots during night operations. Despite the fact that his airmen had to fly primarily French aircraft, Mitchell was determined to prove to the world the importance of airpower provided by Americans in the skies over France.

Woolley took his place as a Flight Commander of the 49th, one of the four squadrons that made up the Second Pursuit Group. The early days of the 49th, as it was forming up in Texas, were fraught with organizational delays, as were those of other squadrons in these first efforts at mobilization. The 49th officially began to form on August 6, 1917, when an all-volunteer group of enlisted men from Fort Leavenworth, Kansas; Columbus Barracks, Ohio; and Fort Slocum, New York, arrived at Kelly Field in San Antonio, Texas.

These enlisted men traveled from Kelly Field by train to Garden City, Long Island, New York, where they boarded the ancient U.S.S. *Carmania* for Liverpool, England. They traveled from Liverpool by train to Castle Bromwich, England, then across the English Channel to France. After some delays at Issoudun, the men of the 49th were issued their Spads and spare parts at Voucouleurs, and then traveled overland to Gengoult Aerodrome outside the town of Toul, where their pilots joined them.

Fisher, the commanding officer, Woolley, Buford, and Wentworth, the flight commanders, were the professionals, having been part of the First Pursuit Group at Gengoult from April to June. They knew firsthand the superb facilities available at the Aerodrome; there were excellent maintenance shops and comfortable housing for both pilots and enlisted men. The nearby Army hospital and its staff of fair maidens certainly enhanced the overall appeal of Gengoult. Woolley and the other old hands immediately became reacquainted with their charming neighbors, even as they went about their business of forging a new fighter squadron.

The 49th organization was like the 94th, 95th, and the other squadrons of the First Pursuit Wing. An officer headed up each of the seven support sections, or departments: headquarters, operations, engineering, armament, supply, transportation, and mess. These seven departments supported three "flights" of aircraft: A, B, and C. Each flight was made up of eight sections. Each section consisted of one Spad XIII and pilot, a crew chief, and two crewmen. In total, it took more than 200 men to maintain and operate the squadron's full quota of twenty-four aircraft.

As each new Spad XIII arrived at the field, the pilots and their crews prepared them for action. They aligned and sighted the Vickers machine guns, tuned the engines, and finely adjusted the flying wires for proper flying characteristics. During many of the necessary test flights, the pilots often just managed to nurse their temperamental machines back to the field.

The crews painted squadron identification numbers on the upper-right and lower-left wings and on both sides of the fuselages, large black numerals edged in bright yellow. Ned Buford's number was 1. Wentworth's was 9. My father accepted the last number available, 24.

One of the Flight Commander's most important jobs was to evaluate the new pilots in his Flight as quickly and as thoroughly as possible. A careful study of their logbooks disclosed where they had trained, what kind of aircraft they had flown, how many hours they had in the air, and how they had fared at gunnery school. The new pilots of the 49th had trained at flying schools in the United States, Canada, Great Britain, Italy, and France, and each school, of course, employed its own training styles and techniques. The pilots with the least airtime arrived fresh from advanced training, while others had spent hours airborne, temporarily assigned to French squadrons or ferrying planes to the front. The Flight Commander's task was to take these flyers with such disparate backgrounds and forge them into a coordinated team of fighter pilots.

Hugh Bridgman, from a long line of Salem, Massachusetts, sailing ship owners and captains, was one of the first new pilots assigned to the 49th. Hugh had left Harvard in February 1917 to volunteer for the American Field Service and was assigned to SSU 19 (Section Sanitaire 19) serving the French Army during the

desperate campaigns in the Argonne. Leaving the A.F.S., Bridgman was accepted into the Air Service and trained at Tours, Issoudun, and Cazeaux. He was several classes behind those who
went out to the 94th and 95th, so no openings were available at
the front at the time he graduated. After waiting for six weeks, he
became a "ferry," flying aircraft from the American equipment
depot at Orly and Colombey-les-Belles to the front. Later, in a
stroke of good luck, he and nine others were assigned to French
units, Hugh to Escadrille Spa 98 stationed near Château Thierry.
Bridgman thoroughly enjoyed his service with the French; there
was excellent food, an orderly who cared for his personal needs,
a private room, the latest Spad XIII, and experienced French mechanics. He was particularly delighted with the unlimited access
to Paris in the squadron touring car. In a letter home he described his fine surroundings, ending with: "I tell you, the French
really know how to fight a war."

While on leave in Paris to be treated for an ailment he referred
to as "the itch" (the same ailment, though milder, that had plagued
Woolley), Bridgman received orders to join the 49th. He was reluctant to give up the many amenities of his French *escadrille*,
but felt much more at home flying under the American flag.

Another of the new pilots to be evaluated was Percy W. "Red"
Graham, a redheaded Chicago native and one of that city's most
celebrated collegiate athletes. He was a pole-vault champion, a
sprinter, a hurdler, and a star football quarterback at the University of Chicago before he volunteered for the Air Service. When I
interviewed Red in Chicago, he told me about some of his misad-
ventures in the Air Service prior to his assignment with the 49th:

> I went to ground school at the University of Illinois
> and was then scheduled for flight training in England.
> I was delighted because I was a little unsure of my
> French. But somehow I got misrouted and wound up
> in Paris billeted at the Hotel de Paris. This was nifty,
> but we had not received any pay for weeks. Luckily, a
> couple of the guys with me had letters of credit and
> that took care of us all.
> 
> We ran into Major Fiorello LaGuardia, who was in

charge of the new Air Service flight training center in Foggia, Italy. This was the same man who was to become Mayor of New York City and the namesake of LaGuardia Airport.

LaGuardia selfishly arranged orders so that the misrouted Cadets were sent to his own school at Foggia. There, the instructors were mostly Italian, so the orphaned group dropped their French dictionaries and quickly picked up Italian ones. The training aircraft were French-built Farmans and three large, cumbersome Italian Capronis. Why three Caproni Ca. 2 three-engined, bomber-type aircraft, with wingspans of ninety-eight feet and fuselage lengths of forty-nine feet, were assigned to the primary training school in Foggia remains a mystery. The students were more than a little apprehensive about the strength and airworthiness of the Capronis. These fears were quickly dispelled when an Italian daredevil instructor, a Sergeant Simprini, actually looped one of these ungainly birds, proving its strength and airworthiness. Sergeant Simprini was immediately placed under arrest for doing such a "damned fool thing." As it turned out, a Caproni had never before been looped, and Simprini, despite his brief incarceration, became an instant hero among his charges. The Italian training was inconsistent. Some of the graduates wearing the Italian golden eagle wings were to discover that they flunked their dual training when sent to Issoudun and had to begin their basic training anew.

"They had the golden eagle wings of an Italian pilot," Red noted, "but not the essential French brevet." Red returned to Italy, to Civitavecchia, just north of Rome, for gunnery school, then spent some time as an instructor and a ferry pilot before joining the 49th at Gengoult Aerodrome near Toul.

For his Flight Commanders, Fisher wrote a directive on "How to Lead a Patrol," and drilled the strategies into Woolley, Buford, and Wentworth:

> In attacking bi-place machines, there are only two safe positions for the fighter plane, behind and below, or coming up under his tail; the other being from

above and on an angle three-quarters from his front, coming over the wing and *viraging* off over the other, always being in the blind spot of the gunner. The Germans' favorite monoplace formation is seven planes, three of which would split off as decoys under the other four. The upper four are the first to be attacked, and the attack should go no lower than the altitude of the decoy. German bi-place rarely fly in greater numbers than two together. Separate them and deal with them singly. Worry them with long fire and maneuver them into position. Try not to let the enemy get between you and your lines. The discretion and judgment of the Flight Commander as to when to attack and when to break is inviolate—he is in command.

Graham explained to me that:

A man going into a fight with the uppermost thought in his mind being that of saving his neck, is in greater danger of losing said portion than an aggressive fighter is. Just like in football. The harder you hit a man when tackling him, the less chance of your being hurt. This is the fact I know to be true. And in hitting hard you make a surer and better tackle.

In my mind you always wanted to go in hard in an air battle and to kill the enemy because you were madder than hell. Then you had the best chance of coming out with your life. If you attacked and hit too carefully, some other Boche would sneak up on your tail while you were being careful with the first. But if you tore in, shooting and twisting your machine all over in a mad manner, and then tore in at another angle, there was not much chance that any Boche could get a good shot in.

Combat was a game of skill and chance. Almost as if in a dance, every movement on the pilot's part, every dive, stall, or *vrille* elicited a move by the enemy. It was like a three-dimensional chess game, with flaming tracer bullets instead of pawns. Right side up, looping, banking, diving, the pilot squeezed the triggers of his guns during split-second moments of advantage, or jammed forward on the control stick in heart-stopping moments of disadvantage. Dogfights momentarily threw together dozens of planes, and just as quickly they were torn apart.

In August 1918, the Flight Commanders knew that there were only a limited number of principles they could teach their men on the ground. The 49th continually practiced teamwork in the air. Realizing that the Germans were flying larger and larger formations, the Flight Commanders adopted a similar approach. They practiced patrols in formations of nine, twelve, and fifteen aircraft, but found such large single flights were unwieldy. They then broke them down into groups of four or five machines, flying the classic "V" formation at varying altitudes to allow for quick attacks and providing protection from above. The work was taxing, but it was a welcome relief after periods of inactivity. "A squadron is just like a prep school," Sumner quaintly recalled. "If you have nothing to do, everyone just gets grumpy and things go along like a bumpy road."

On August 18 at 6:15 A.M., Ned Buford led two less experienced pilots on the first patrol of the 49th Aero Squadron. It was more like a sight-seeing mission to familiarize the pilots with the front. On the way to St. Mihiel, both new pilots experienced motor troubles and returned to Gengoult. Ned, feeling he had best take advantage of the early morning weather conditions, continued alone. At about 7:20 A.M. at 15,000 feet, he spied a German Rumpler observation aircraft trying to cross into Allied territory. Buford dove to the attack. The Rumpler immediately started to climb away, but the Spad was quicker than the two-seater. Buford forced the German down to 13,500 feet, got under the enemy's tail, fired a long burst at close range, and watched the Rumpler start to fall. It went into a *vrille*, straightened out into a steep dive, and crashed between Montsec and St. Mihiel. During the fight, Ned had been subjected to fierce Allied Archie fire from gunners who thought that both planes were German. Never mind, the 49th had drawn its first blood.

With its first victory scored, the squadron prepared to select their insignia. Flight Commander John Wentworth, the illustrator and architect, who had created the "Hat-in-the-Ring" insignia for the 94th, made a suggestion. They all knew the era of the individual lone fighter was over. Men now had to fight together like a pack of hungry wolves. Wentworth drew a sketch for the insignia: a finely detailed gray wolf's head with jaws wide apart and teeth bared against an orange-yellow background and surrounded by a dark blue circle. The squadron enthusiastically embraced the new insignia and the squadron painters were set to work at once decorating each of the Spads with a ferocious wolf's head snapping at the nasty Boche. Buford's crew painted a small black Maltese Cross between the wolf's open jaws, the mark of the Squadron's first victory. They knew there would be many more crosses to come. As they were flying from a well-settled section of France, the men could not find a live wolf for their mascot, so they settled for a feisty captured German Shepherd named Fritz.

A few days after the squadron's first victory, Hugh Bridgman led two others on a familiarization patrol down the lines. It was at 9:30 A.M. on a sparkling early autumn day, with not an enemy plane in sight. At the extremity of their patrol line, just as they were turning back, Hugh spotted two enemy Rumplers hard at work snooping and photographing on the American side of the lines. Without hesitation, he dove on the two-seaters 3,000 feet below. He was slightly to the left as he came down and was able to get within twenty feet where he opened fire from the side. He pulled back on the stick and rose almost vertically, then banked over and dove to attack again from the right. He tried this several more times in an attempt to separate the two, who were continuing to protect each other. With this apparent lack of success of separation, he singled out one, and with guns firing steadily, flew at him head on. It was a game of who would give way first. At the last moment, each broke, just before a collision, turning away from each other. Hugh pulled up and turned to rejoin the fray, and to his amazement, there was not a German in sight; they had both completely vanished. Bridgman's two charges, who had stayed above the fight, quickly resumed their assigned places in the formation, and home they flew.

Bridgman had experienced one of the unusual aspects of air fighting: the seemingly instantaneous change in the visual conditions of battle. One minute the pilot was one of three planes diving, twisting, turning, and firing at one another. The next minute, the sky was empty. How could this happen? Quite easily. Traveling at 120 to 140 miles per hour in opposite directions, aircraft could be as far as five miles apart after only one minute, leaving the pilot virtually alone in the sky.

On September 3, 1918, Woolley received orders to lead a patrol over the lines. It was a balloon-busting mission. As the Allied ground offensive had ripped gaping holes in the German positions, and Allied pilots had successfully denied the forward lines to German observation aircraft, the Boche were compelled to rely more heavily than ever on intelligence from their observation balloons. Standing in wicker baskets slung from the belly of these ungainly, hydrogen-filled "sausages," skilled observers were the eyes of the German army, reporting enemy artillery placements, troop movements, and aircraft activity via telephone to the ground. The Germans were keenly aware of the importance of the balloons and encircled their "nests" with a variety of defenses: machine guns on special antiaircraft mounts, rapid-firing, small-caliber cannon launching "flaming onion" projectiles, and Archie with its high explosive bursts.

Colt Firearms in Hartford, Connecticut, helped the Allies develop special balloon guns that increased the caliber of the Vickers machine guns from 7.7 mm to 11 mm. Although seemingly small, this increase in caliber added greatly to the effectiveness of the guns. One plane in every flight, including my father's, was equipped with two of these "balloon busters."

Woolley's mission on that clear autumn morning was to bring down a German balloon near Pont-à-Mousson. As he led his patrol into the air, he took the point, careful to keep Bridgman, Graham, and the others in a tight "V" formation behind him. It was no time for singular heroics. This was a wolf pack.

He adjusted the throttle, keeping his Spad at a moderate speed so that they could maintain a tight formation. He avoided any sudden maneuver that could lose his men. As his patrol gained altitude and proceeded to Pont-à-Mousson, they paralleled the front to avoid the enemy Archie fire that would attract enemy aircraft. He continued to survey the sky, looking for the black dots that could so quickly bring death. He knew that the younger pilots would not be able to help him in this. It took many hours in the air above the lines to learn to discern enemy aircraft. Many fresh pilots fell to their death without even being aware that German planes were nearby. He turned his head from side to side, his eyes searching the sky around him. There were no enemy aircraft to be seen in the area. The patrol could cross the lines safely.

He scanned the ground below. There it was! A sausage-shaped *drachen* floating behind enemy lines.

Woolley knew that he had to have every possible advantage to bring down the balloon. The gas-bags from which the wicker baskets hung with their observers were the eyes of the German army. Below, their "nests" were ringed with guns and were in direct telephone communication with fighter bases that could dispatch deadly Fokkers into the air at a moment's notice. He led his men upward, and positioned himself for the attack. He had good height, the sun was at his back, his formation was tight in line, the westerly wind was not strong enough to hamper his flight back over the lines, and there were no enemy planes in sight. Perfect.

Woolley moved the control stick of his Spad left and right, waggling his wings in the signal for attack. Two of the five planes kept their altitude as protective cover, while he, Bridgman, and Graham dove from 7,500 feet onto the target below. Bridgman and Graham watched my father's every move. He would signal to them when to break off the attack, when to reform again, and when to head for home. Signaling in the air was conducted by the simplest of maneuvers—a waggling of the wings or a redirection of the leader's flight path. He was the key to their survival.

With their Hispano-Suiza engines roaring and their flying wires shrieking, they sped down to the target. Seeing them, the observer parachuted to safety from his observation basket. This did not distract my father. Set fire to the balloon first, then shoot the observer on the end of his parachute if there is time. It seemed cold-blooded, but those were his orders.

A withering barrage of machine-gun, automatic-cannon, and Archie fire rose to meet the attackers. The thick, braided suspension cable banged and rattled as it wound onto the enormous drum, spun by a gas-powered winch that frantically hauled the balloon down to safety from its observation height. The German ground crew worked quickly, but not quite quickly enough.

The Americans closed in: 1,500 feet; 600 feet. At 300 feet my father pressed the trigger of his balloon guns, releasing a stream of 11 mm incendiary bullets into the rapidly descending target. He zoomed over the balloon, through the wall of enemy ground fire spraying up like Fourth of July exploding "flower pots," and pulled back on the stick to regain precious altitude. Looking back over his shoulder, he could see the other two attacking Spads repeating his every move. He slowed slightly to allow them to regroup. There would be no other runs at the target. The balloon was too low, the hail of projectiles from below was too dense, and without a doubt, the sky would quickly fill with enemy Fokkers.

The five Spads regrouped as one and headed back to the Allied lines. Flying in easy "S" curves, they were able to look back and see heavy black smoke rising from the vicinity of the balloon position. Dad felt certain that it was the burning target. Would they be credited with its destruction? Was it too far back for someone from the Allied lines to spot and provide confirmation? Never mind. He and his patrol had performed flawlessly, the enemy sausage was down, and they were returning safely. Mission accomplished.

Despite bad weather over the next few days, the 49th continued to fly a variety of patrols and protection missions. Each night about nine o'clock they read the squadron orders and the times of the patrols for the next day, which were posted on the door of the Operations Office. After they were read, a cheer would come from one corner of the dark barracks from the flight who had learned that their first patrol was not until 11 A.M.—while a groan from the other side testified that the other two flights left at daybreak. Despite the groan, these men were inwardly pleased. They knew that dawn was the best time to fly—the weather was calm, and the sun was at their backs.

Most orders were fairly routine—"Patrol the line of friendly balloons at 15,000 feet on lookout for enemy photo planes; patrol St. Mihiel–Bey at 10,000 feet; fly protection for Salmson aircraft No. 9 (20th Squadron) on a photographic mission." An hour or so before a patrol, the pilots would gather to plan what formations they would fly and what tactics they would follow.

Each patrol lasted about two hours and covered about two hundred miles. Two patrols a day were considered a day's work. It was about all that pilots and machines could bear. The flyers were, nevertheless, ordered to remain on alert for most of the daylight hours.

When they had spare time, the pilots often wandered back to the flight line, where they watched their three-man crews realigning sights, checking the machine guns, and making countless little performance-enhancing adjustments to their machines. If there was nothing else, there was always target practice with captured rifles and pistols. After all, marksmanship was the key to bringing down enemy aircraft.

On the morning of September 7, a protection patrol including Lieutenant Warren T. Kent departed at 8:00 A.M. Only four planes made it to the lines; the others withdrew with mechanical problems. Eight Fokkers jumped the patrol at 15,000 feet. One of the Fokkers left his formation and attacked Kent, who was last seen going down in a nosedive in the region of Thiaucourt. The Wolf Pack experienced its first casualty.

Kent's replacement, First Lieutenant Z. William Colson from McRae, Georgia, arrived two days later. Bill was a soft-spoken, slightly built Southern gentleman, quick-witted and impatient with senseless Army rules. I visited Bill in June of 1970 at his home in Methuen, Massachusetts, where he had retired after a career as a doctor. He had been fond of my father and wanted to assist me in any way he could. Not in good health, but with a bright twinkle in his eyes, he told me about his Great War experiences. While training at Issoudun, he and the other Cadets had grown frustrated watching others "take off and land and crash." There were too few airplanes to go around, and so much temptation outside the base, that the Commanding Officers tried to keep Cadets busy with digging latrines, shoveling gravel, and doing guard duty. When this did not keep the Cadets from leaving the field and going AWOL, Colson recalled with a smile, the Medical Officer "used a case of measles or mumps" to put the camp under close quarantine.

After a month or so of this inactivity, the normally teetotaling Bill Colson, from a good Baptist home, had had enough. One day, he slipped through the guard lines and enjoyed a sumptuous meal and a bottle of sparkling Burgundy at a local café:

> After the meal I felt greatly refreshed, and walked boldly back through the guard lines without challenge, and went directly to the flying field. An American captain was standing by one of the hangars watching a famous French test pilot bring a Nieuport to a three-point landing. Now, ordinarily, I, a Private First Class, gave Captains a wide berth, but on this occasion I walked up to him and in an easy and natural manner said, 'By god, Captain, that boy can certainly fly an airplane.' Just then the Frenchman, in a splendid grand opera–style uniform, jumped out of his plane and came over toward us. The captain told him I liked his flying, and he responded to my compliment in well-spoken English, and with a low bow. I bowed just as low myself, and said, 'Yes, Lieutenant, I have decided that you are the one to take me on my first joyride.' Thus, I was the first in my detachment to take to the air. We climbed into our places, and with a wide-open throttle, we darted toward the breeze. Suddenly the earth seemed to drop from us. The large canvas hangar behind us shrank in size. We had flown into Wonderland . . .

When Colson arrived at the 49th, the quartermaster measured him for his flight suit and noticed that he had about the same build as the pilot who had been replaced, so they reissued the injured pilot's equipment to Colson. Colson gingerly pulled on the "teddy bear," or flying suit, that the pilot had worn at the time of his crash. It smelled of benzene and was stained with blotches of blood. Colson took the "teddy bear" back to the quartermaster and said, "Hey, I'm not superstitious, but could I start out with something clean?" His request was granted.

Orders were posted on August 21: "Effective this date and until further orders planes will not cross the lines into enemy territory except in case of extreme necessity, such as during the course of combat, when affording protection, or when an enemy plane is sighted not more than one-half mile across enemy lines." Headquarters did not want to give the enemy any information as to the composition of the American forces by letting an American aircraft with its squadron identification markings fall into their hands. The pilots of the 49th knew that something big was in the offing.

The flyers of the 95th were also aware that something was in the wind. They had moved with the rest of the First Pursuit Group to Rembercourt, close to the front lines and the zone of the planned attack. The First Pursuit Group had the responsibility to clear the skies of German planes anywhere near the Allied depots and new aerodromes under preparation. One pursuit plane was in the air at all times over the aerodromes then in use. These high, solo patrols were flown at 17,000 feet for a duration of one hour and forty-five minutes and were not the most popular duty for pilots itching for action. For the most part, they were simply cold and uneventful.

Their purpose was to attack and bring down any enemy machine that might have broken through the defensive patrols, thereby denying the German High Command intelligence. The success of the action hinged on secrecy. The enemy must not realize that the Americans were preparing for their first big drive: the St. Mihiel offensive, which would attack the St. Mihiel salient. The Germans had captured St. Mihiel in 1914 in their first attempt to encircle and capture Verdun. The salient was twenty-five miles deep. The Allies hoped to push the Germans out of the salient to a forty-five-mile line stretching from Verdun to Pont-à-Mousson on the Moselle River.

At this time, after hospitalization from injuries in an accidental crash, Bill Taylor rejoined the 95th and was glad to be back in time for the offensive. He confided to his friend Heinrichs his deep affection for Hope, a nurse with whom, before his crash, he had fallen in love. Bill was convinced that she was also crazy about him, but Waldo knew that on occasion it was really Bill who was just plain crazy. It seemed that Hope enjoyed teasing the nineteen-year-old flyer, and he naively mistook her intentions for undying affection. Waldo listened kindly to the confessions of his young friend. The fighting would begin soon enough. That would take his mind off such foolishness.

On the evening of September 11, orders finally came down to all the American flyers awaiting the action: "The First Army attacks on the whole Front at 0500 hours September 12, 1918."

That night, a disgusted Heinrichs watched as many of his fellow officers in the 95th celebrated the eve of the first American offensive by getting gloriously drunk. "I don't see how these chaps expect to make a go of aviation with their heads under liquor," Heinrichs complained. "Here's the test."

# CHAPTER 14

# All-American Offensive

At five o'clock on the morning of September 12, 1918, the roar of artillery erupted in a violent cacophony, transforming the quiet American sector of the Western Front into the focal point of the war. The weather was uncooperative, with gusty winds, rain, low overcast skies, and visibility down to 15,000 feet. Still, American aviation was to be part of the big show.

The First Pursuit fighter pilots took off from the dark field at Rembercourt, the field illuminated by flares. Flying 500 feet above the ground, they could see the silhouettes of American foot soldiers advancing, backlit by exploding artillery shells ravaging the ground ahead of the Allied lines. The Spads shuddered in the air from the concussions caused by passing shells fired from the 16-inch naval guns, concussions that on the ground rattled doors and windows for ten miles around. The Spads were part of an armada of 1,480 aircraft—366 two-seater observation planes, 323 day bombers, 91 night bombers, and 700 fighter-pursuit planes—operating in the offensive under the command of Colonel Billy Mitchell. Forty percent of the aircraft and crews were American; the remainder were British, French, and Italian, all drawn together in coordinated support of the American push to reduce the St. Mihiel salient. It was, at last, the first American offensive of the Great War, the largest American military assault ever unleashed, the greatest fleet of military aircraft the world had ever seen. "You can't imagine what it was like," Woolley wrote to his mother. "The air fairly swarmed with planes. Thank goodness most of them were Allied planes."

Hugh Bridgman of the 49th, part of the great aerial armada, was also aloft early on the morning of the offensive. "The flashes from the guns we had massed on the lines looked like fireflies, twinkling constantly for a distance of fifteen or twenty miles up and down the line," he described to his parents. "The only things I saw were liaison planes, flying up to the lines following the infantry, then chasing back to report on their positions. Below I saw an attack taking place with small tanks. They moved at a ridiculously slow pace, as did the men behind them."

The American pursuit pilots flew a second patrol and then a third on that first eventful day of the offensive, flying up to 4,500 feet as the clouds lifted. They were the eyes of the American Expeditionary Force, charged with the task of constantly observing and reporting to Headquarters the progress of the battle, the extent of the American advance, and the position of the retreating German troops. As they flew from St. Mihiel across the Meuse River toward Verdun, the patrols saw flames engulfing the entire towns of Lavignéville, Chaillon, and Creué. They located the retreating Huns, observing from the air as they set fire to villages, haystacks, ammunition dumps, and supply depots. Extremely heavy shelling continued all along the line. The Americans were advancing, though from 4,500 feet in the air, it was sometimes hard to tell which troops were American in khaki and which were German in field gray.

Throughout the day, reports filtered back to Squadron Headquarters. The advance had progressed three-quarters of a mile without any resistance. An entire Austrian regiment of 2,200 had surrendered without a shot. A total of 8,000 prisoners had been taken. Back in 1914, the French had lost 30,000 men in an attack that had held the town of Montsec for just twenty-seven minutes. In this offensive, the Americans permanently took Montsec, as well as Thiaucourt and St. Mihiel, in a few days, with exceedingly low casualties. The doughboys had removed the St. Mihiel salient. Their attack had succeeded, driving the Germans into retreat, a retreat to their last defensive stronghold, the Hindenburg Line.

On the evening of the first day of the attack, the pilots of the 49th stood beside their hangars looking toward the lines where intermittent flashes lit the sky, followed soon after by what sounded like low thunder. Occasionally a searchlight beam roamed the sky, a lone finger of light searching for a night bombing plane. At what seemed to be clocklike intervals, strings of red, green, or white fiery balls would sail slowly upward from Bocheland, hesitate, then slowly fade out. What the hell were they? Signals of some kind? Now and then, parachute flares burst out in brilliant floods of light, then sank back toward earth. The entire front seemed to be on fire.

Assigned to an early-morning patrol, Woolley was delayed by the rough running of his sometimes unpredictable engine. He was able to have it smoothed out, but the problem caused him to leave the field fifteen minutes late. Searching an empty sky, he never did find his patrol, but he came upon another Spad and the two continued together. Constantly turning his head, peering up and down the front, he spotted antiaircraft bursts. They were white. Allied! A German plane was in that area. The antiaircraft guns were not always good at bringing down aircraft, but they were superb at drawing attention to the enemy.

The two Spads flew toward the location of the bursts. Sure enough, they spotted a German two-seat *réglage*, or artillery-spotting machine. They dove. Just as he attacked, my father glanced over his shoulder. It was a good thing he did. Five Fokkers were diving on him from the sun. Instinctively, he pulled back on the control stick, pushed the rudder bar to the left, and *viraged* off. As he climbed, he turned his Spad back toward the Fokkers who, along with his companion, had mysteriously departed. Damn. A great opportunity for combat and a possible victory gone. Scanning the sky, Woolley saw three Spads headed toward Toul. He moved his joystick to the left and then the right, waggling his wings, desperately trying to signal them to assist him in finding the elusive fighters. But to no avail. He knew he could not pursue five Fokkers alone, not unless he wanted to "go west." He turned back to Gengoult, landed, and made a brief official report of the action.

All pursuit aviation had been active during the opening of the American St. Mihiel offensive. As the Germans retreated, the pilots were repeatedly ordered to attack ground troops and to perform low-level aerial reconnaissance missions to keep Headquarters informed of the rapidly changing battle lines and troop positions. Sumner Sewall described the low-level work as "a wonderful party." "It's more fun than a farm," he wrote in a letter to his mother. "You go sliding along searching out town after town; sometimes you find an American patrol in it, and sometimes a Boche; then you cock your old machine up on its ear and pour a few rounds into them and watch them run. They always get a machine gun working pretty quickly, after which it is better to play elsewhere."

Patrolling low over some woods, Jim Knowles scored a remarkable *coup de main*. He spotted a Boche convoy moving along a road and dove on them with both guns blazing, sending horses and men in all directions in mad confusion. Several horses dropped, while others jumped up against wagons and trucks, snarling the whole convoy. Knowles then raced home, made his report, and a bombing squadron was immediately dispatched to the spot. A few well-placed bombs effectively stopped the entire convoy, most of which was soon captured by the advancing infantry.

Ted Curtis talked with me about how he flew low patrols during the St. Mihiel offensive. He described one frightful incident in particular:

> We caught a supply train and artillery retreating on a long road the second evening of the attack and stirred up the best stampede you ever saw with our machine guns. Most of the Germans took to a ditch, the horses ran wild, upsetting wagons, hurtling cannon from their carriages and generally destroying the entire train. Before our ammunition ran out, we killed scores of horses and men, which delayed their retreat for hours.

In the middle of the attack, engine failure suddenly forced Curtis to land in what he thought was still German territory. Fortunately, the Americans had retaken it a few hours before. Grinning dough-boys directed him to the 26th Division Brigade Headquarters, where he reported the conditions he had encountered to General Edwards. The General was so pleased to receive the valuable in-formation that in an expression of gratitude, he sent Curtis back to the squadron at Rembercourt in his personal limousine.

During the offensive, Sewall's low patrol work also managed to disrupt the German retreat on the ground:

> I was sailing along looking for anything I could see, when I suddenly spied a perfectly fine staff car rolling along and filled with men. Well, I dived on the darn thing to see for sure that it was French or American, when to my surprise five officers in long gray coats jumped out and threw themselves down in the ditch. By that time it was too late to shoot in that dive, so I pulled up and turned as if to go, while they slowly pulled themselves out of the ditch and started for their car. I then dived and opened up an awful burst of tracers and incendiaries and I wish you could have seen the beggars run. I chased a couple into a ditch and a couple more behind some trees. I stayed in the area for a long time chasing them around, but you would be surprised at how hard it is to hit a running man. At last I shot up the car a bit and left . . .
>
> On the way back I found a fine little German riding horseback, and I played with him a long time and scared his horse, so he was damn near thrown. Horses just go wild when they hear a machine gun rattling at their back.

On another low-altitude flight, Sewall thought that a particular line of trenches had been abandoned, until he noticed "that every turn and corner held a nice little dutchman. They looked so darn funny down there, just like rats in their holes. I just hap-pened to see them, for they were pretty well hidden. I dived on them a few times and they all ran into their *abris* [shelters]. Then they got a machine gun working pretty well, so I left for home. Really this little game of Hunt the Hun is the greatest game out."

The game turned deadly on the cool, clear morning of September 14. Sewall noted that it was the first "real blue sky" day since the beginning of the offensive. With the good weather came the Boche aircraft, droves of them, tumbling from all sides, out of the clouds, out of the sun, forever turning up where least expected.

Sewall wrote:

> Up to that time, we had the air pretty much to ourselves. But as we lifted our solid little Spads off the ground [and] the mist-covered Meuse passed below to the rear and the broad checkered plains around Lachaussee, bathed in a powerful morning sun, started to unfold to the Moselle and the East, things looked different, felt different, and when we squinted and strained our eyes up into that morning sun we learned that they were different. There, apparently hanging motionless in the sky at nearly 12,000 feet, were six chunky dots, our old friends the Fokkers, sitting and watching like six wise owls, harmless looking it is true, but with a pounce and a bite learned only by experience.
>
> We did the one thing possible—a tactful retreat to the safe limit of the Meuse followed by a half hour's strenuous climb to 15,000 feet and then another proud face to the lines to remove said reason of retreat. The trick worked well, for when we next picked up our six little spots they were six hundred feet below us with the two rear men lagging back on the tails of the 'V' like two ripe cherries ready to be plucked. We worked ourselves around into the sun to attack, for apparently we had not been seen. We scanned the whole sky and everything seemed fine; only a moment more—a dive, a squeezing of a trigger, a familiar rattle, and then the long straight drop of another black cross, and perhaps another leave to Paris.
>
> Whether this Universe progresses on a prearranged schedule, or is based on chance, or whether we may

even go so far as to wonder about the possible existence of a sixth sense, are of course philosophical
questions not to be bothered with here, but certainly
there are times when even the lightest and most stu-
pid of us cannot drive such thoughts from our minds.
At any rate, in that last moment before we dived, I
turned, God knows the reason, and there in the very
ball of the sun with its thick heavy axle practically
resting on my rudder hung the great silhouette of a
Fokker. How he had arrived there, where he had come
from, and why he had held his fire so long, did not
worry me in the slightest, for happily man is equipped
for just such a circumstance as this with a sort of in-
voluntary set of muscular reactions built around that
one great instinct of self-preservation.

I dived, there was a rattle, then a series of snaps,
and three of my most needed flying wires streamed
back completely severed. Once again I turned my head
to learn more of my predicament and was greeted by
seeing two most solemn Spandaus swinging into line,
then came again that awful rattle; long white pencils
of smoke went poking through the air just over my
head; a pipe above my motor kinked out, throwing a
deluge of water into my face and a clean little ironical
hole appeared in my windshield not six inches from
my nose. This last burst really rather discouraged me.

Discouraged or not, Sewall took immediate, violent evasive
action:

Pulling full my *manettes* [throttle], I went mad on the
controls. I dived, *vrilled,* and slipped one second on
my back and the next standing vertically on my nose.
My troubles seemed to disappear and it all became a
great game against wild odds, and I was sort of fascinated by what the next moment might bring. All the
time, that damnable rattle was clicking at my back
and [there was] the deadly snap of bullets as they
passed through some part of my plane . . .

The sound of a dull thud caused me to look over

the edge of my cockpit and there I learned the rather startling bit of news that a sheet of flame was bursting from my gas tank. As I recalled it later, it seemed that this last sight was but another hair on the camel's back, another great handicap in the game. I actually seemed to derive a sort of wild delight out of it, but that it impressed me at the time as being rather serious is borne out by the fact that I later realized I had thrown off my belt, evidently with the almost uncontrollable instinctive impulse all fliers have of jumping from a burning plane. The horrible mental picture of such a flaming coffin is not easily repressed.

Sewall continued to dive. A beautiful green field came up to greet him. He leveled off, and flew past a few telephone wires. There were a couple of bumps and then all was quiet. Sewall sat in a sort of stupor. He realized that he was sitting in his Spad uninjured on a field west of Hannonville, but he did not know what to do next:

> I was almost immediately awakened by a thud in the field nearby, and upon turning, was astounded to see one of my tires bouncing gaily around, having just completed a little landing of its own. I have since that day always been convinced that that tire had been shot off during the early part of the fight, for it had six bullet holes in it, and that in my hurry I had beaten it down. But I must admit that I was so vigorously blatted and howled at [by my friends] the first time I offered this theory, that for friendly purposes I have often let it pass as an hallucination, with myself as the fool.

Ted Curtis flew low over the wreckage to check on his friend's condition. Sewall climbed out of his plane and "proceeded to enter into all sorts of hideous calisthenics until finally I must have persuaded him of the proper functioning of my various limbs and organs, for he waved and flew away."

Then Sewall inspected his crumpled aircraft:

One glance told me the story of the flames. An explosive bullet had gone down through the back of my
seat, pierced the gas tank, which in a Spad forms the
bottom of the fuselage, and upon hitting the bottom
surface of this, had exploded, blowing out a hole as big
as one's head through which all the burning gasoline
poured out into the open air. Certainly, as explosive
bullets go, that was a most worthy one.

Worthy indeed. Sewall later learned that the Fokker had broken off his attack when the flames had appeared, thinking that
his adversary was done for. The fire spewing from his gas tank
had actually saved his life.

Sewall's squadron mate Waldo Heinrichs endeavored to take advantage of a spell of good weather and on September 14 took off on
a patrol with high hopes of action. After a few moments in the air,
he felt a terrific jolt. He turned his Spad back to the field. Just as his
machine touched down, the propeller flew completely off its hub.

His mechanics disassembled the engine and found that the
propeller reduction gear had somehow frozen, and two or three
teeth had literally broken off, jamming the entire mechanism.
The momentum of the spinning propeller itself then completely
sheared the gear. Heinrichs knew he was lucky to be alive, but he
cursed his rotten luck that once again faulty equipment had prohibited him from finding the action he craved.

In the 94th, Rickenbacker and Coolidge were tallying victories
at a furious pace. Rick had the most confirmed kills; Coolidge
was second, his score rising almost as quickly as Rickenbacker's.
They were both great pilots and highly successful, but they flew
with quite different styles. Ham, always a team player, scored his
kills when flying missions in the company of others. Rickenbacker liked to fly alone, high above the patrols for which he
was responsible, protecting their position, constantly searching
the skies for enemy aircraft. When not leading patrols, Rick flew
volunteer solo missions, focusing his entire energy on hunting
enemy aircraft.

Coolidge did his best to record his experiences for posterity
during the St. Mihiel offensive:

It's a little like trying to recall all that one sees from an express train window after the journey is over, only we have the added difficulty of having to pay considerable attention to our little express train itself. We are the engineers as well as the passengers.

We started down our lines just at their edge and every second came flashes and white puffs from our batteries. We were so close that every explosion rocked us about frantically and often threatened to dash us into the treetops. In fact, sometimes our little ships were almost unmanageable . . . I could see horses mounted by officers rushing to and fro on the roads, and trucks, wagons and men moving madly along, but dared not to fire on them for fear of their being Americans. You simply couldn't distinguish their uniforms.

While crossing back over the lines, Coolidge's motor died:

Down I went into a little valley and had a nasty time worming my way into a tiny patch of good ground, past telegraph wires, barbed wire entanglements, and shell holes. I came to rest not four feet from one of the last named. A Spad is heavy and lands fast, at best; so it's no fun to have forced landings.

He found his way to a French Divisional Headquarters, where the commanding General hosted Ham and another stranded American pilot at a lavish dinner, then returned the pilots to their airfield in his personal limousine. Coolidge observed, "These Frenchmen certainly beat the world for politeness."

On another sector of the front, Woolley, Bill Colson, and two other members of the 49th flew on a voluntary patrol north of Verdun. They had attained a perfect position in the sun from which they dove on a formation of four Fokkers. The Boche flew on unaware that they were about to be attacked. Colson picked his man, held his fire until he was confident he could not miss, then pulled the trigger of his machine guns. Bullets sprayed the Fokker. It dove instantly. Bill, thinking that the

German might be playing possum, kept his guns full on, sideslipping to follow the diving Fokker. When he noticed another German moving into position above and behind to help his comrade, Colson did not care. He held his guns to their original target.

Suddenly the Fokker above him opened fire. Tracers flashed by both sides of Bill's fuselage. He pulled his throttle wide open to gain altitude. His motor did not respond. Evidently, the long sideslip to attack the first Fokker had forced air into the main gas feed line. Unable to climb or dive to avoid the attacking Fokker, Colson turned to face the oncoming German, flying at him head-on. The Boche pulled up his nose to avoid a collision and gave Bill the chance to dive straight for the ground. By the time the Boche spotted Colson once more, Bill was hundreds of feet below, out of range. With his motor running smoothly once again, Colson had begun to climb for altitude when he noticed that one of his wing supports had been shot in half. With that in mind, he gingerly headed for home. Back at Gengoult, Colson inspected the damage. In addition to the severed wing support, there were six neat bullet holes through one side of the fuselage, three on either side of the pilot's seat. The German's marksmanship was excellent, but not excellent enough to hit the pilot; Bill had miraculously survived.

At the end of the first week of the St. Mihiel offensive, the American squadrons were ordered to replace the British Vickers machine guns on their Spads with new American-built Marlins. This switch made the pilots uneasy. The Vickers was jam prone and cantankerous, but at least it was a known entity. The Marlin was not.

Looking through the carefully written pages of Heinrichs' diary, I came to the entry for September 17, the first day that the 95th flew with the new guns. A note appeared in the diary: "The following entries are not in strict chronological order." Something had happened to the meticulous Waldo Heinrichs, the sober, disciplined YMCA man who had kept a detailed daily record for more than a year. As I read on, I understood exactly what that something was:

2:30 patrol September 17. My new Spad with new Marlin rifles on it in which I placed but little confidence. Mission was to set enemy balloons on fire. Seven Spads left on time . . . Sighted 7 Fokker D-7 biplanes near Lakes of Lachaussee flying South one far behind the rest. Mitchell [flight leader] gave signal to attack . . . [I] followed Mitchell down onto the last Fokker, who apparently was left behind as the other six Fokkers went on South. Mitchell pulled out of his attacking dive with his guns jammed . . . I followed him down onto the Fokker and fired 2 or 3 bursts with altitude on him before the other six Fokkers executed a sharp turn and came back on us. My guns jammed . . .

So did the new Marlin guns on all seven of the American Spads. Why? It was later determined that the crewmen back at the airfield had loaded the unfamiliar Marlin ammunition belts upside down. With their guns jammed, the Americans were flying unprotected in a dogfight with seven experienced German Fokker pilots.

As he struggled to clear the jam, Heinrichs fell into a *vrille*. He managed to pull out of it, but not until he had fallen beneath his opponent. The German pilot quickly switched from his defensive aerobatics and opened fire on Heinrichs:

> The other Fokkers were on me by now and one of them joined the attack on me; I headed for our lines but was cut off. I escaped one terrible burst [from] my first opponent and ran directly through the spider web of the tracers and explosives of the second. I shall never forget the rat-tat-tat of those two guns never jamming and firing in very rapid synchronization.
>
> I felt a bullet tear through my mouth and it felt as though my whole lower jaw were gone and my mouth became a gaping cavern. Remember spitting out teeth and blood and then turned again for our lines. Again ran into their fire and felt a terrible blow on my left arm. Tried to yank throttle wide open but got no more

speed out of it—seemed it wouldn't work. Looked down to see my arm hanging useless by my side— broken. Spat again as the blood was choking me and blood blew back in my face blinding me and covering my face and goggles.

Felt another bullet get me in left thigh between hip and knee underneath. Let go my stick for I saw the game was up, and threw my goggles up on my forehead and saw bullet-hole through my windshield, perhaps the same one that went through my mouth. Windshield was all cracked in fine spider web, and leather lining of cockpit was all spattered with explosive bullet bits.

My machine fell in fast nosedive straight for the woods below from 3,600 feet or so. Threw off throttle [cut power] with my right hand, liberated from stick and again saw left hand hanging useless. Grabbed stick again and pulled out of dive just at edge of woods not over 225 or 300 feet high . . . Saw telegraph wires appear directly in front of me, dove under them because I couldn't get over them and drove deliberately through a light pole beyond the wires with my right wing. Landing was a beauty and I stopped just on further edge of open field not more than 60 feet from edge of woods. Crowd of soldiers (German) one with rifle over his arm came running toward me so I stood up in cockpit and held up my right arm in token of surrender . . . Slid out of machine, staggered beyond end of left wing and lay down exhausted.

Heinrichs maintained consciousness as his captors dressed his wounds from a first aid kit, and after what seemed like an eternity, stretcher-bearers carried him to a field-dressing station. From there he was taken to a field hospital where he fell into a deep sleep, no longer caring what happened. Later, as a prisoner of war, he took an inventory of his various wounds. An explosive bullet had splattered bits of steel into the palm of his right hand. Fragments of another explosive bullet were in his right heel. Two explosive bullets that pierced his left elbow tore out a hunk of flesh and muscles as big as his hand. His left arm was fractured, three inches above the elbow. He had a deep flesh wound in his left thigh. An explosive bullet had torn through his left cheek into his mouth from the rear, splintering four front upper teeth and five front lower teeth. Though he was in terrible pain and remained a prisoner for the rest of the war, Heinrichs felt lucky to be alive.

When Bill Taylor learned that his closest friend had been shot down and was missing, he was devastated. Already despondent because Hope, the nurse with whom he had fallen in love, had just ended their relationship, Taylor fell into a deeper depression that quickly turned to anger. "The goddam Huns have killed Waldo," he thought to himself. "Now they are going to pay."

He went out on a voluntary patrol with the avowed intention of "getting one of the bastards for 'Heinie'." That was the last anyone saw of Bill. Denny Holden, out on a voluntary balloon raid, saw a flight of Fokkers heading away from the lines and noticed a plane burning on the ground. When Taylor did not return that evening, the squadron suspected the worst. Could the burning plane have been Bill's? The following afternoon, a newspaper correspondent reported he had witnessed a single Spad attack five Fokkers. The Spad was overpowered by the terrible odds and fell in flames. The time and the place of the action were correct; no others were missing. It had to be Bill.

As they collected his personal effects the next day, they all agreed that Taylor was an unusual, impulsive kid. There was a good chance, they believed, that Heinrichs was still alive, wounded and a prisoner, but still alive. There were, however, no more chances for twenty-year-old "Big Bill" Taylor.

Over at the Second Pursuit field, Woolley and the 49th continued to fly patrols on a regular schedule, reporting the progress of the advance, protecting Allied photographic planes, and trying to destroy or keep German balloons on the ground. On low patrols, they carried packages of cigarettes and newspapers carefully protected in wrapped bundles. Woolley and his flight flew low over the attacking Americans and tossed the bundles from their planes. An attached note told those on the ground that the Air Service was "right with" them and encouraged the doughboys to "keep going like Hell"—or words to that effect. The infantry was delighted when it saw American planes, and was even more delighted with the cigarettes and newspapers.

On a day grounded by bad weather, a small group of officers from the 49th set out in Fisher's gleaming Cadillac to explore some recently abandoned German positions. They found that the Germans had retreated in such haste that they had left their meals half eaten on china plates, their washing still hanging out to dry. The German quarters in the trenches were elaborate sunken, concrete structures complete with electric lighting, dry, clean rooms, ventilation, heating systems, and every imaginable device designed for their comfort.

In the woods not too far from the rear of the trenches were rest camps for their frontline troops complete with comfortable barracks, movie theaters, and bowling alleys. The pilots walked through the woods on winding footpaths, over rustic bridges spanning babbling brooks. They drove in the squadron Cadillac to the former German headquarters buildings, an old château. A low rustic railing and Verboten signs protected spacious, carefully tended flower beds. The officers' quarters were luxurious.

The visitors appropriated a few appealing trinkets left behind while taking care not to dislodge souvenirs that might be booby-trapped. There was not much left because the gang from the 95th had beaten them to the really choice material. They had cleaned out the German officers' quarters, loading up two large Dennison trucks with rifles, swords, helmets, and other military souvenirs, as well as pianos, carved chairs and tables, cupboards, beer steins, glassware, rugs, stoves, and mirrors. With the loot, the 95th decorated their tent quarters and the famous 95th bar, hanging a German sign that read *Zum Winkel Krug*, roughly translated as "The Corner Pub," over the entrance. Their only regret was that they had failed to get their hands on a peach of a little roadster left behind by a high-ranking German officer. Some infantry "brass hat" had taken it for himself.

There was a catch in their throats as they drove their Cadillac 8 through the villages of Vigneulles, Hannonville, and other small French towns recently freed in the St. Mihiel salient. It was as if the towns had burst into life after four years of German occupation. French flags flew from every window. Everywhere they drove, Frenchmen smiled, doffed their hats, and gallantly bowed to their American liberators. Women waved and smiled in gratitude.

As the salient continued to be reduced, the Pursuit Squadrons attempted to patrol the lines in large formations of fourteen or more aircraft. Often less than half the machines could actually complete these patrols without having to turn back because of mechanical problems with the Spads.

Pilots new to the front quickly learned that "the less experience, the greater the danger." Just sighting the enemy in the air was difficult, as Bill Colson explained to me many years later, describing his initial flight over the lines. Colson's engine was not performing up to par, but he continued on his mission as best he could, sailing along some 1,500 feet below his patrol. Before he knew what was happening, hundreds of black bursts of shrapnel filled the sky. Bill was sure that the entire squadron above him must have been destroyed. He waited—expecting to receive a shell under his seat at any instant. Later he admitted, "No college fraternity initiation could be half as unpleasant, or as thrilling."

On landing after this first mission, Woolley, the Flight Commander, asked Bill how many enemy planes he had seen. Bill replied, "Chas, it must have been a very quiet day over the lines, as I did not see one." He learned, much to his surprise, that there had been well over a dozen in their patrol area. He had been told that spotting the enemy in the air was difficult, an acquired and essential skill. He recalled Woolley's words: "What appears to be a speck in the distance in a moment can become a full-sized Fokker pouring tracers into your fuselage."

The Allied antiaircraft gunners either had a great deal of difficulty distinguishing between Allied and German aircraft or, as many aviators suspected, they just fired on anything in the air. Colson began to distinguish the proximity of the antiaircraft explosions by their sounds. A faint dull sound meant the Archies were harmless, bursting far away. When the Flight Commander heard this sound, he usually led his pilots in a series of tumbles through the sky, to confuse the gunners into thinking their fire was on target. A dull "oooh" meant the shells were bursting fairly close. A sharp barking "cr-cr-cr-cr" meant the Archie was bursting close indeed. When Colson heard this sound, he learned to gently, ever so gently, sideslip his Spad to evade the fire while not alerting the enemy gunners to its accuracy.

On September 23, the 49th moved to the Belraine Flying Field, about seven miles from Bar-le-Duc. As they flew to the new field, they noted that the roads going up toward Verdun were clogged with heavy Allied traffic. Something new and big was up!

They soon found out what that something was. The orders tacked to the operations door on the evening of September 25 were clear and succinct: "The First Army attacks along the entire front at 5 h 30 September 26, 1918." Once again, the American pilots would be called on to support the infantry with observation and strafing. Once again, it was going to be difficult and dangerous work.

# CHAPTER 15

# The Final Push

For the American Expeditionary Force, the St. Mihiel success was now a past glory. Pershing could not allow the two million men of his American army to rest on their laurels. General Foch, Commander-in-Chief of the Allied armies, was determined to end the war with one final push, an offensive along the entire Western Front. The Belgians at the English Channel, the British on their right, then the French, and finally the Americans, prepared for the massive attack of September 25. Logistically, Pershing was at a terrible disadvantage as he had to move his entire army from St. Mihiel across the Meuse River up to new positions above Verdun and across to the Argonne Forest. This was the most devastated section of the front. There were only two usable roads in the area of advance, and these were constantly exposed to German artillery fire. Though it was not large in area, the new American Front was hugely important. The A.E.F. was to take the railroad lines that supplied the southern half of the German army, an objective that was a key to victory. It would not be easy. The wooded and ridged terrain was defended by the Kriemhilde Line, a heavily fortified section of the Hindenburg Line, held and reinforced by the Germans since 1914.

At 11:00 P.M. on September 25, a signal flare soared into the night sky. American artillerymen yanked the lanyards of the

2,775 artillery pieces loaded for the attack, and the "million dollar barrage" began.

Woolley awoke at 4:15 A.M. The earthshaking Allied barrage continued. Pulling on his "teddy bear" and stepping out of the barracks, he walked stiffly in the predawn as he made his way to the Officers' Mess. He ate a satisfying breakfast—eggs, bread, butter, coffee—and smiled at the usual jokes: "Better make a meal of it, it'll probably be our last." That sort of thing.

At 5:30 A.M. the American First Army went over the top in a dense fog. An hour and a half later, Woolley was leading a patrol of the 49th at 9,000 feet just north of Verdun.

"A dream—a nightmare—a glimpse into Hell—or the morning of Judgment Day," that was how one American pilot described the battlefield. Along the twenty-two-mile front, exploding artillery rounds created a swelling roar of thumps, screeches, twangs, and ripping tears as Allied shells sought their targets. Bands of flame soared above No Man's Land, as both Allies and Germans filled the air with screaming shells and streams of green incendiaries, waving back and forth in a semicircle, like water from a ghostly fire hose.

Woolley's ship rocked and shivered with the artillery blasts. He could actually see shells flying by, sudden streaks or threads of pink in the morning sky. One American plane was actually hit by an Allied shell, but only one. Surprising, as high explosives seemed to fill the air.

Behind the German lines, a dense white mist still hung in the valleys. From the air, the patrol could discern burning towns. The Allied balloons were up, great gawky sausages, with the first morning rays of the sun reflected on their sides, still wet with fog and dew. They floated very close to the lines at an unusually high elevation. But there were no German Fokkers in sight, nor any enemy balloons. The morning of the great attack, the Americans completely ruled the air. Woolley dove his patrol down for a closer look. At this altitude they became an extension of the ground war, flying just slightly above the field of battle.

The patrol flew to Clermont, circled north of Placardelle, then headed back to Gengoult for refueling. In the afternoon, my father took off again to scout out progress on the ground and led a patrol of six over Brabant, Montfaucon, Sivry, and Chaumont. He noted in his reconnaissance report: "Two machines reached lines and made patrol slightly in advance of the line of battle. One biplace machine sighted very low and heading into enemy lines, N.W. of Dun-sur-Meuse. Too far away to attack. Dun-sur-Meuse burning in several places."

The Americans had taken 25,000 Boche prisoners and had advanced some six miles, but they, too, had sustained extremely heavy casualties. It was rumored that the Germans had known about the attack far in advance and, after the fog lifted, had unleashed thousands of hidden machine guns on the advancing doughboys. There was great confusion everywhere on the ground. French troops relieved from the forward trenches filled the two available roads, which slowed the Americans attempting to get to the front. The roads were so congested that even the ambulances could not get through to evacuate the wounded.

The American offensive continued the next day, as did the patrols. Woolley took off at 6:55 A.M. into a dark and rainy sky. Atmospheric conditions had deteriorated to the point that the patrol had to turn back. Further flying was impossible. The following day, they took off again, flying into dense clouds and rain at 1,000 feet. He could not see the other planes in his patrol, much less the ground. Once more they had to turn back.

It was apparent that unlike the St. Mihiel offensive, which had taken only four days, this one would not be as easy. It was hard, hand-to-hand fighting against a determined enemy. The Americans found themselves in the same predicament that the French and British had previously experienced, launching massive and costly ground assaults on strongly fortified defensive positions.

Pershing's army found it difficult to mount coordinated attacks, difficult to move up supplies, and difficult to get accurate intelligence, because the Air Service was unable to get into the air. Adding to the flyers' difficult task of dealing with the weather came a new directive from Air Service Headquarters. Headquarters Staff ordered the Second Pursuit Group to arm each *chasse* plane with two twenty-five-pound bombs to be dropped during ground-strafing attacks. The flyers, sensing the difficulties

involved, complained bitterly: "Some real bright non-flying officer had to have thought this up."

They were all in accord. Carrying bombs on the Spad XIII was
not a brilliant idea. Fifty pounds might not seem like a lot to an
officer behind a desk, but in the air, an extra fifty pounds would
cut down drastically on the speed and maneuverability of the
Spad, which had an already-heavy takeoff weight of more than
1,800 pounds. It was risky enough to fly low over the trenches,
avoiding Archie and machine-gun fire in order to strafe the
enemy. But turning the Spad *chasse* planes into bombers simply
made no sense. Unfortunately, as impractical as it was, there was
no choice. Orders were to be obeyed.

At 4:00 on the afternoon following the initial order to carry
bombs, twelve pilots of the 49th, burdened with this extra load,
took off on patrol. Just as Woolley had feared, his Spad could not
climb as well with the added weight of the bombs. Even the takeoff had been long, slow, and tricky. Still, the patrol struggled into
the air and made it to their target, the town of Romagne. As my
father flew over the town, he searched for the designated target.
When he found it and came within range, he pulled the wire to
release his two twenty-five-pound bombs. To observe the results,
he looked below, but could see no bombs fall, or any explosions.
As he watched the other pilots reach the target, he saw bombs
fall from only three aircraft. What had gone wrong? Maneuvering
his plane to look beneath the other Spads, he discovered the answer. The bombs were still hanging there, somehow caught in the
support wires of the landing gear. What to do now? Could anyone land safely with bombs dangling from the underside of his
aircraft?

Woolley signaled the patrol to return to the field. One after
another, his pilots gingerly landed their now dangerous Spads.
Thankfully none of the bombs fell or exploded during the landing—
they remained immobile, hung in the wires beneath the aircraft.
Relieved but furious, Woolley climbed out of his aircraft and
looked under the wings. It took only a glance to understand the
problem. The untrained mechanics had unwittingly installed the
bombs in the bomb release mechanism backward!

When the advance bogged down, the Air Service responded

to the now static conditions by sending out groups of ever-increasing numbers of Spads, often combining two squadrons on the same mission. These were "wolf pack" tactics, unrelenting low-level attacks on ground targets, attacks on anything in *feldgrau,* or field gray, that moved. Smaller patrols were also mounted, with the single intent to destroy and clear the skies of German reconnaissance and artillery-spotting two-seaters.

On September 29, the entire 49th flew as a squadron on a troop-strafing mission. They were ordered to hit a concentration of enemy troops located on a road three or four miles behind the German lines. They set out in several formations and climbed through light clouds from 1,800 to 6,000 feet. As they approached the targeted road, they attempted to use the clouds as cover, but found the ground and the target completely hidden from view. Leading one of the formations, Woolley took them on a wide sweeping turn, found a hole in the overcast, dove through, and raced toward their objective.

The road that they were ordered to strafe was empty of enemy troops or any other Boche transport activity. He then picked out a village known to be still in enemy hands, and with his wings, signaled the group to follow. They dropped their unwelcome burden of bombs from a height of 900 feet. This time, the release mechanisms worked. Still, the bombs seemed to do little damage, at least as far as any of the pilots could see.

Later strafing patrols were more successful at finding their targets. To the pilots, flying at 900 feet instead of 9,000 made it seem as though they were racing at breakneck speed across the ground, especially when they dropped as low as 150 feet. At this level, it seemed as if everything in the world not tied down came shooting up at their machines—explosive bullets went off around them like electric sparks, and "flaming onions" streaked by them in fiery strings.

Ham Coolidge wrote about a strafing mission in which he took part:

> Little glimpses were all I could catch before I was by [the target]. Another turn and down the line again. I had a vague confused picture of streaming fire, of

rearing horses, falling men, running men, a general mess. Turn again and back upon them. This time I clearly saw two men shot off the seat of a wagon, then more awful mess. A fourth time I turned and came back. One gun stuck, but the [my] incendiaries still blazed on. Horses rearing on fallen men; wagons cross-wise in the road; men again dashing for the gutter. I craned my neck to see more and to be sure not to run into trees or houses beyond.

Suddenly a ra-ta-ta-ta and a series of whacks like the crack of a whip broke loose. I knew only too well that the bullets [from machine guns on the ground] were coming very close to crack that way! I rocked and swung and turned and the rattle died away be-hind. I found myself trembling with excitement and overawed at being a cold-blooded murderer, but a sense of keen satisfaction came too. It was only the sort of thing our poor Doughboys have suffered so often.

In stark contrast to wolf pack tactics, special orders were is-sued at the same time to fly solo missions to locate and destroy a specific balloon at a very specific location. The pilots undertook these assignments with mixed emotions. If they were success-ful and the balloon flamed, instant confirmation of the kill was forthcoming. On the other hand, the Germans protected these vital sources of intelligence with maximum firepower. Machine guns, 77 mm Archie guns, and rapid-firing small-bore cannon that hurled deadly "flaming onions" ringed each balloon. Attack-ing Spads had to fly through that veritable curtain of fire and then deal with the possibility of the target violently exploding di-rectly in their path of flight. Adding a bit more zest to the party was the possibility of a pack of Fokkers sitting in the sky above, waiting to pounce on the hapless attacker as he emerged from the withering ground fire at the end of his run.

These single, specifically targeted missions often turned into something of a much more varied nature, as Alex McLanahan was to discover. On one solo flight, Alex repeatedly searched the designated area for the offending *drachen*. He could not find the balloon, but he did spy a vulnerable Rumpler. The two-seater was sneaking along the north bank of the Meuse River looking for an opportunity to dash across the forward lines, snap a few quick photos of the Allied troop and equipment concentrations, and then run for home with precious intelligence about the enemy.

McLanahan was not about to allow this to happen, and from a distance began to fire at the enemy plane. The effect was immediate, and back into Hunland the Boche flew. Then without warning, Alex heard the rattle of machine guns behind him. Turning his head, he saw a Fokker practically sitting on his tail, ready for a sure and easy victory. In an immediate reflex action, Alex stood his Spad on its tail and looped over the Fokker, and the attacker immediately became the attacked. McLanahan fired two fifty-round bursts into his brightly painted adversary, who, after the second burst, went into a steep dive and headed for the Meuse. Alex watched him descend until he disappeared into the heavy ground mist below.

Low on fuel, he then turned south and was headed back for home at Rembercourt, when he spotted an ascending balloon. It was not the balloon he had originally been ordered to destroy, but it was an opportune target nevertheless. "What the hell!" he said to himself, and dove at the "sausage," which was by then being rapidly winched back to earth. Disregarding his dangerously low fuel supply, he poured machine-gun fire into the balloon until both guns jammed. At this point, he realized that this was a signal to head for his side of the lines. Turning and looking back, Alex saw no Fokkers ready to end his day, but he did see a decidedly welcome black plume of smoke ascending from the ground beneath his recent combat location. Not bad for a solo mission: one Fokker down and out of control; one flamed balloon; and one pilot more than a little delighted with his skills and his results—especially when both victories were later confirmed.

The men of the 49th also had mixed emotions about such balloon assignments. Flying at low altitudes over German lines, there was no room for error. If their motors failed or if they were disabled by ground fire, it was almost certain that they would land in enemy territory.

Bill Colson was considerably relieved after he had survived

two strafing patrols in one morning. Assuming that his work was over for the day, he responded enthusiastically when the Officers' Mess Sergeant, a prolific scrounger, offered him samples from a newly located supply of beer. After several liberal samples, Colson swaggered away from the mess feeling delighted with the world, and headed for the operations tent to see what was being planned for later in the day.

Approaching his "C Flight" lineup of planes, he noticed the engine of his Spad slowly ticking over. Knowing that the motor had been performing flawlessly, he asked his Flight Sergeant what was going on. The Sergeant informed Colson that the Flight had been ordered up for an immediate strafing expedition. The objective was a column of ammunition trucks on a road northeast of Romagne.

Bill's first impulse was to go to Woolley, his Flight Commander, or some other higher authority, and say that he was not sure that he could fly his tricky Spad after his enthusiastic sampling of the new beer. On second thought, he worried that this might be taken as an indication that First Lieutenant Z. William Colson was getting "yellow," and he decided that killing himself on this mission would be preferable. After donning his flying suit, his body temperature rose considerably and he felt the effects of the strong beer all the more. After climbing into the cockpit, where one of his mechanics carefully adjusted his safety straps, and with the whirling propeller serving as a fan cooling his face, he turned his Spad into the wind and made a particularly snappy takeoff. For the first and the only time, Bill thoroughly looked forward to ground strafing. On a road north of Romagne, he spotted two Germans retreating in a truck, and dove on them with his guns chattering full on. Quick as a flash, they stopped, bounced out of the truck, and disappeared. He never knew where they went.

At that instant, heavy machine-gun fire rose from the ground, directed specifically at him. He laughed out loud, thinking how comical it would be if he should get a bullet right through the middle of his stomach. He would be just like a tall beer barrel, with spigots spouting beer front and back. Sobering slightly as he neared the Aerodrome, he realized that his final and most severe test would be the landing. He had heard so much about the dulling effect of alcohol that he dreaded what was to come next. Flying low over the ground, he gauged his distance closely, and brought his Spad down in one of the neatest landings he had ever made. He had never felt better in the air, but it was a performance he never wished to repeat.

George Fisher, the Squadron Commanding Officer, believed that consuming alcohol in moderation after a day's flying was good for his men. He felt that the men were going to drink anyway, and that it was better for them to drink on the field rather than in bars in the nearby town of Bar-le-Duc. The Officers' Mess provided whatever alcoholic beverages the pilots desired that the resourceful Mess Sergeants could provide. Officers paid for their drinks through a system of chits, which were added to the individual's mess bill. Many of the pilots believed that those who drank, at least in moderation, had a better chance of holding up to the taxing pace and stress of combat flying than those teetotalers who found it difficult to relax and forget the strain. Bill Colson preferred port wine, which he drank "until the conversation of the dullest man in the squadron sounded brilliant." At this point, he would promptly return to his billet, sleep like a baby, and be ready the next morning for any eventuality.

As October progressed, the Allied offensive regained momentum. Romagne was captured, and the British on their front retook Lens for the first time since the start of the war.

There was confusion in the air. Patrols from one squadron often did not know what missions the patrols from other squadrons were ordered to perform, or where they would be performing them. On more than one occasion, our pilots, outnumbered and locked in vicious combat, saw other American planes flying in another direction, apparently unaware of the predicament of those outnumbered. Why did they not come and help? Often the other flyers did not see the combat, or mistook a real battle for a mock battle often staged by German Fokkers to lure in inexperienced Allied flyers.

Most of the senior officers in Air Service Headquarters who issued the orders for the various squadrons had never flown. Few, if any, American ground staff officers had any firsthand knowledge of flying. Ordering fighter aircraft to fly bombing missions was bad enough. The squadrons laughed at other classic senseless Kiwi orders. One ground officer, after noting that planes usually bounced several times on landing, ordered:

> Hereafter pilots must refrain from hopping their planes on landing like birds from place to place. They will place their tires firmly on the ground and make them run smoothly and without taking off again to a steady landing straight ahead.

Another classic: "Effective this date, there will be no more forced landings."

It was outdated regulations, however, that most infuriated the pilots. The regulation United States Army officer's tunic, dating back to the nineteenth century, was made of wool with a stiff, high-standing collar. This design was fine for one looking straight ahead in parades, but a disaster in the air. Pilots who for self-preservation had to constantly twist and turn their heads, looking for their positions relative to the ground, the whereabouts of patrol mates, and the "Hun in the Sun," soon found that the American regulation uniforms chafed their necks raw. British aviators wore their reasonable regulation open-collared tunics with a cotton shirt and tie. These tunics were not only comfortable, but also dashing in appearance when worn with shining aviator's wings, light-tan whipcord breeches, and highly polished, custom-made boots.

At the moment the first American pilots received their commissions in France, they traveled to Paris, located a fine tailor, and ordered British-style uniforms. They felt that since they were aviators, United States Army regulations did not apply to them. As the ever-growing numbers of regulation-minded, strait-laced Army officials observed more and more aviators wearing snappy, non-regulation uniforms, the inevitable happened. Printed orders tacked on the bulletin boards of every American squadron warned flyers that if they were caught outside the aerodrome in an open-collared blouse, they would be placed under arrest for being "out of uniform." Billy Mitchell came to the rescue, authorizing a reasonable compromise. The open-collared tunics could be worn while flying, but regulation high-collared tunics must be worn when aviators were off the airfield and subject to the scrutiny of inflexible senior officers.

Even more ridiculous in the eyes of the flyers were the regulations requiring commanding officers of Air Service squadrons to wear spurs during parades. The flyers thought, "How can we win this war if headquarters is back in the nineteenth century preparing for a cavalry charge?" Unfortunately, many of the Allied leaders really did believe that the horse cavalry was a more important fighting tool than the aircraft squadrons, including British Commander Sir Douglas Haig, a former cavalry officer who stated in his old-school way that bullets had "little stopping power against the horse."

When foul weather kept the American pilots from the air, they had the opportunity to take a late breakfast at "easy nine" (9:00 A.M.) and visit with old and close friends from other squadrons. Many felt a bit uncomfortable talking about their combat experiences; still, there was so much to learn from the good and bad experiences of other pilots. Every shred of information regarding combat was useful, and reliving lifesaving aerial maneuvers was not only informative, but also damned entertaining.

Ham Coolidge related in his letters some of the experiences he had encountered early in the big American push along the Meuse River. During one flight he came upon a Halberstadt two-seater lazily taking photographs of American positions on the Allied side of the lines. Ham immediately attacked. Although furious about the immediate jamming of his guns, he did not break off the fight, but continued maneuvering around the German aircraft. Seven Spads soon arrived as reinforcements. Together, the Americans tried to cut off the German's retreat and force him to land at an American airfield. Coolidge looked down on the roads below and saw autos stopping and people gawking, open-mouthed, as the German passed only fifty feet over their heads with eight angry Spads on its tail. The Boche refused to cooperate and land, so one impatient American pilot fired a burst of incendiaries into the Halberstadt. Down he went in flames, well behind the Allied lines. The following day Ham felt it had been "the most thrilling day" of his life, and it came within a hair of being his last:

> Two of us attacked enemy balloons six miles behind their lines at 4:35 P.M. I hardly had time to think of 'archie' fire and streams of machine gun bullets that flew by as I dove on my balloon. I could see my incendiaries pour into the old gasbag, and the observer jump out in his parachute. A few seconds later the flames burst out, and down it went.
>
> My companion [Walter Avery of the 95th] was ahead of me and about to attack another balloon, when I suddenly saw a formation of seven Fokkers above. My heart stood still. He never saw them; it was hideous. My shriek of 'Look out Walter!' never got beyond my mouth because of the roaring exhaust. In a second they were upon him. Just a glimpse of the poor boy in the midst of those devils was all I could catch before the whole mess went circling toward the ground.

Coolidge learned later that Avery had survived the crash with bullet wounds and a broken jaw. The man who shot down the German ace Carl Menckhoff spent the balance of the war in several unpleasant German prison camps. Coolidge further recalled:

> When I reached the spot, they were careening around like a flock of buzzards over a freshly killed prey. I was so mad I saw red, and dove upon the nearest German. He didn't see me, so I waited till I was close upon him, then just riddled him with bullets. At that very second I heard that awful whip-cracking sound and saw and felt bullets flying by my head. I was completely surrounded, but my situation was so futile that I was strangely cool. I turned and flew head on towards my attackers. I was beginning to wonder what sort of a funeral the Germans would give me, when a Spad flashed down from the sky above, and another and another! The protection, six Spads, had arrived.

I almost wept for joy—but suddenly realized that the fireworks weren't over yet. For fifteen minutes we milled together, rolling and tumbling—Spad, Fokker, Fokker, Spad—in the wildest, most confused whirling mass I ever hope to see. The air was just streaked in every direction with the smoke of the tracer bullets.

We all have little photographic impressions of different moments in that fight. I remember looking back once only to see one Fokker on my tail and another from the side, shooting streams of bullets at me. A second later it might be entirely different. Things happened too fast and changed too often to enable any of us to retain anything but a confused impression of that awful combat. Gradually we edged toward our lines and finally crossed them with the Fokkers in hot pursuit. They turned back together, however, when we finally did reach the lines. It is unhealthy for them to come over our side of the fence.

The day was not over yet, however. After the main bunch had gone home, a few of us were still out on the lines. The Boche evidently thought we had *all* gone, for they sent an observation plane sneaking over to do some quick reconnaissance work. Three of us almost simultaneously spotted him a few miles behind our lines. We raced at him together and ten seconds later he was in flames. He sailed on a little, at about two hundred feet above the ground, then tottered and crashed in a final burst of flames!

He was delighted with the results of his work, but uncomfortable with the prospect of ever being feted as one of America's leading aces:

There are a few millions of other men in the war doing just as hard and dangerous work, much of which is never known about or 'noised abroad.' It's much nicer just to sit tight and be humble and thankful to the Almighty for His great goodness. The feeling I have on looking back on three victories in an hour is not one of triumphant power. It is rather a feeling, stronger than ever, that we mortals are mere specks of dust in the wind, blown about at His pleasure, and I realize as never before, that it was due to no cleverness or bravado on my part that I scored those victories; it was simply His will that I should live through it, and mere chance brought me the successes.

When the terrible weather finally cleared, the 49th was deeply engaged in the American offensive that came to be known as the Meuse-Argonne Campaign. My father and his men prowled over enemy lines, concentrating on low-altitude work, reconnaissance, and strafing. On one occasion they were sent out to investigate a report of four tanks operating in the area. Were they enemy or Allied? What was the troop activity in that immediate vicinity? In his Spad, Woolley skimmed just above the ground, straining to see the progress of the attack. His field of vision from the cramped cockpit was limited by the machine guns in front of him and the wings below. Traveling at 120 miles an hour, rocking and tossing his Spad, about to avoid shrapnel and bullets—it was hard to see anything clearly, much less visually isolate a hidden machine gun or determine the nationality of four smoke-belching tanks. He finally concluded they were American, and held his fire.

Perhaps the most unusual relationship a pilot experienced was with his sometime cantankerous flying machine. His life depended on his machine, which was a source of pride and often frustration, the difference between victory and defeat. Pilots lovingly named their aircraft, or adorned them with names of others significant to them, modified them, pampered them, and, most important, were forced to entrust them with their lives.

Coolidge revealed his feelings on the subject after a fierce combat in October: "My poor, dear Spad, No. 22, is so badly shot up that it will have to be replaced by a horrid new one. It's strange what affection you can develop for an inanimate object, but my old Spad, stained in oil and smoke and even cold sweat from my brow, was like a trusted horse to me." Ham cut the painted-linen Hat-in-the-Ring insignia and his number "22" from the fuselage of his retired aircraft and sent them home as souvenirs of the plane that had served him so well. This insignia survives today in an air museum in Washington State.

Not long after the demise of "Old 22," Ham returned to Rembercourt from a well-earned leave to Paris, where he had purchased, in anticipation of cold weather ahead, new boots and warm woolen scarves, mittens, and sweaters to augment his government-issued flying gear.

He spent one night of his leave with his old friends the Normants at Romorantin, where he and Quentin had previously spent such happy weekends. This visit reminded Ham of his own family and his younger brother, Roger, who was studying at Groton, the prep school from which he had graduated less than three years before. It seemed a lifetime ago. Quentin had edited Groton's literary magazine, while Ham had practiced pass plays on the Groton gridiron. Ham wrote to Roger: "Get husky and wise at Groton this year, old boy. And remember that even if your old brother isn't there to cuss you out all the time, he's thinking of you often."

Upon his return to Rembercourt, Coolidge was pleased to find that Eddie Rickenbacker had at last been awarded the Distinguished Service Cross with not one, but four oak leaves, justly recognizing five of his many acts of bravery. Captain Coolidge continued to be frustrated by the fact that Rick, a First Lieutenant, his Commanding Officer and the leading American ace, had not yet been promoted to Major, or even Captain, the ranks enjoyed by the commanding officers of every other squadron in the Air Service.

Coolidge was annoyed to learn that while he was on leave, a rather clumsy friend had borrowed his new Spad and landed it so violently that the landing gear had been damaged. Ham's mechanics assured him that any ill effects had been repaired, and that the ship was as good as new. Without checking the plane himself, Ham took his mechanics at their word and departed on a patrol with two others. They soon came upon a German two-seater and maneuvered, unseen, into a favorable position to attack. Coolidge, in the lead, dove first. Suddenly his Spad gave a terrible lurch, snapping him forward into his safety harness. Aware that something was dreadfully wrong, he immediately broke off the fight, and, followed by his two companions, headed for home, leaving one bewildered and thankful Boche in peaceful retreat.

Coddling his plane back to the field, he was able to land safely, and discovered that his friend's bad landing had internally snapped and broken his vertical stabilizer, or rudder. The fierce air pressure incurred in his sharp dive had nearly torn it off. This condition made the Spad unmanageable until he slowed down, the air pressure lessened, and the rudder returned to its original position. Even though his mechanics had always been extremely careful and conscientious before, this was a clear case of an inadequate inspection. Ham in all probability used the Lord's name in vain more than once when he roundly chewed out his crew for this potentially lethal lack of attention.

Woolley's spirits were up, and he continued writing casual and cheery letters back home:

> There is much joy to be had out of sitting behind a 220 hp eight-cylinder V-type motor, wide open, with the exhaust pipes shooting out on each side of your seat and just listening to her purr at 2200 rpm. It is nearly as lively as a winter drive in our Hudson roadster down Winchester's Highland Avenue through snowdrifts. I'd rather play snowplow, though, I'm sure. While plowing snow, one doesn't have to peer over one's shoulder continuously looking for Boche, nor dodge shrapnel, either.

On the other side of the lines, the German air commanders had to work continuously to boost the morale of their disillusioned pilots. Ernst Udet, Hermann Göring, and other seasoned pilots of the depleted Richthofen Circus had discovered that the Americans were much more formidable adversaries than they had anticipated. The Yanks flew far more aggressively than the French or British, and their sometimes unorthodox and unpredictable individual maneuvers confused and disrupted the Germans' highly disciplined style of aerial combat. More important, the Yankees had an inexhaustible will to fight and to win; the will that the German commanders felt was draining from their own discouraged pilots after four grueling years of war. And as important as their skills as flyers were, the Americans also had vast resources—fresh pilots to fill the ranks, an abundance of fuel, aircraft spares, and aircraft supplies. The Boche supply of essential rubber was practically nonexistent; brass, copper, and aluminum were in short supply, causing long delays in aircraft production. The scant aviation fuel available from German petrol depots was deliberately diluted with water in an effort to increase the supply. All it did was hamper the performance of their aircraft.

Orders to the German flying units were clear. The High Command had been forced to throw a large portion of its depleted fighter assets against the big push of the American Army. The Jasta commanders were ordered to make every attempt to regain air superiority—no matter what the cost. They had to do it by attacking the Allies with Jastas sorely lacking in trained pilots and badly supported by dwindling spare parts. The goal of the entire German Imperial Air Service was to make the inevitable Allied aerial victory as costly as possible. And costly they made it, for the Allies and for themselves.

# CHAPTER 16

# The Meuse-Argonne with the Wolf Pack

As the Battle of the Meuse-Argonne continued, the Air Service discovered it was up against the most experienced German air fighters of the war. In the operations tents, notices were posted that listed the names of these leading German aviators, the distinctive markings on their planes, the number of victories to their credit, and, if known, their style of air fighting. The greatest element of strength shown by all the German Jastas was their teamwork; perfect, well-trained, and well-oiled teamwork.

In addition to their teamwork in battle, the Germans employed tactics to lure unsuspecting Allied airmen into carefully laid traps. On a morning patrol, Hugh Bridgman spotted three Fokkers flying very low and very slowly. An easy target, he thought. He dove down 6,000 feet to the attack, and followed the German machines into enemy territory. Shortly before he was in range, Bridgman was startled by the sound of machine-gun fire from four more Fokkers diving on him. The low-flying patrol had been a decoy. He had foolishly taken the bait, and now he was about to be caught in the trap. In desperation, Hugh let off a long-range burst with his incendiary bullets. Miraculously, one of the Fokkers caught fire.

Bridgman then pulled straight up to avoid the attacking aircraft. To his disgust, his motor chose that moment to stop. Diving again, he desperately worked the engine controls. It suddenly burst into life, and he raced for home, zigzagging violently to avoid enemy fire from the air as well as from the ground. He had somehow survived the trap! A few days later the youngest pilot in the 49th received a wonderful gift. The telephone rang at the Operations office, and the caller gave confirmation of Hugh's victory, a victory that he had earned just two days before his twenty-first birthday.

Bill Colson encountered another German trick. Colson was flying on a high patrol and positioned in the left tail of the "V" formation. Woolley was the Flight Commander. Looking below, Colson saw what he thought to be a flight of Fokkers in a vulnerable position. Colson dove to attack. As he was about to open fire, he noticed that the plane he was attacking did not have a black cross on its wings. Instead it had what appeared to be a red-white-and-blue cocard on the side of the fuselage, and a red cross on its rudder, markings similar to an English aircraft.

Appalled at how close he had come to downing an Allied plane, Colson pulled away and headed off to the wild scramble of planes going on to his right. As he did so, the man he had taken for an "Englishman" nosed his plane up toward Colson and fired a short burst from his guns. Confused, Colson fought a purely defensive fight, pulled up above him, then dropped down, riding on his tail, spending a full five minutes maneuvering behind the mystery ship—a very long time considering the fact that most aerial engagements could be counted in seconds.

To Bill's relief, the stranger finally tired of the close maneuvering, dove off, and disappeared. When Colson reported the incident to his commanding officer, George Fisher, Fisher told him that there had been no Englishman in the area. The pilot he had spared was in fact a German, flying a Fokker decorated with Imperial colors of red, white, and black cocards to confuse his opponents. "Colson," Fisher snorted, "we will count you as already lost! A man who will make a purely defensive fight in close quarters with a Fokker, which is so much more maneuverable than a Spad, is done for! Any day that you live now, anything that you may be able to accomplish, will count as so much extra!"

Laughing a little at himself, Bill told me of sitting a few months later at Maxim's in Paris, toying with a mess of snails and listening to the conversation of a group of aviators at a nearby table. One described for all to hear "that fool Colson's first combat with an 'Englishman.' " Colson sat silently undetected while the aviator recalled the incident in detail. "Now boys," the flyer said in conclusion, "if any of us should go into Germany in later years, we should make a tour of the institutions for the insane and in one of the most violent wards, we will find a German aviator shaking the bars crying. 'Why didn't he shoot—*Mein Gott*, why didn't he shoot?' "

As the Meuse-Argonne offensive progressed, the Allied commanders planned to increase the level of bombing, which they felt might be the key to bringing the retreating Germans to their knees. Germany had bombed Paris and London with the giant Gotha bombers and the "lighter than air" ships designed by Count Zeppelin. The raids themselves had inflicted little physical damage on the cities, but had had a pronounced impact on home-front morale; the Allies hoped a similar impact would be made on the war-weary German military. The raids also had specific military targets. The rail marshaling yards and ammunition dumps were of the highest priority.

The squadrons of the American First Day Bombardment Group were constantly in the air raining bombs down on these important targets, but at the same time they suffered heavy losses at the hands of the Boche fighters. In mid-October, Woolley was leading a protection patrol of seven Spads near Doulcon, a town located on the Meuse, upriver from Verdun, when white bursts of friendly Archie fire just to the north signaled the presence of enemy aircraft. He swung his patrol in the direction of the Archie puffs and immediately spotted six Fokkers. On a prearranged signal, the patrol split up, with Dad leading three Spads in the attack, while the other three Spads hovered above for protection. The first four plunged down after the six Germans below. In a flash other Fokkers that had been hiding in the sun dove down on the attackers.

From above, Bill Colson watched the fight unfold and quickly led the trio providing cover protection down into the fray. Within seconds tracer rounds were sizzling in all directions. The Americans and the Germans were in a classic aerial dogfight: circling, diving, climbing, maneuvering, and firing in short bursts when they gained a momentary advantage over their opponent. Spads in their somber green, brown, and beige camouflaged plumage fought in wild, whirling, twisting individual jousts with red, yellow, and green striped Fokkers. To the combatants, the fight seemed to last a lifetime, but in reality it was over in less than five minutes. Suddenly the sky was empty of the enemy. Woolley's group reformed and headed back for the field at Belraine.

As each plane landed, First Lieutenant Ed Casey, the Operations and Intelligence Officer, took the reports and victory claims from the returning pilots. There were eleven confirmations requested! Of those requests, seven were confirmed. Five pilots were credited with victories and two with doubles, but the other two members of the seven-man flight received no confirmations. Woolley and Colson, although leading their sections and orchestrating the fight, would not be officially credited with their victories. One member of the patrol, First Lieutenant Clair A. Kinney, did not return; no information was ever gained as to his fate. One other casualty of the 49th's largest single fight to date, this one minor, was a Spad disabled by a bullet through its oil tank. The plane and pilot landed safely, but with an unlubricated engine frozen beyond repair. Reviewing the statistics of this engagement, it seems almost unimaginable that the pilots of the 49th—some with hardly any experience, and some with just a few months of air fighting—were knocking off Germany's best at a ratio of seven to one.

In October the 49th was operating from a rough, unimproved, temporary field at Belraine, a bit northeast from the 95th's field at Rembercourt. Both fields were muddy and contained few permanent buildings, only lines of tents to quarter officers and men. The pilots longed for the return of the "good old days" at Toul, the comforts of the Gengoult Aerodrome, and the comparative serenity of the old front.

On October 18, Woolley led a small afternoon mission, carrying bombs. They circled the designated target at 1,000 feet, but could see neither troops nor trains. Then Woolley located an alternate target and signaled the others, and at 15:30 the squadron dropped their small bombs on Remonville. Just as each released two twenty-five-pound bombs, two German biplace machines attacked the mission from a distance. Woolley signaled to his patrol, circled, and tried to climb to the enemy's altitude, but the Rumplers climbed even higher and escaped. Heading back toward the lines, the patrol reformed and encountered four Fokkers, which they engaged. Eight additional Fokkers immediately dove into the fray, and it was time for the 49th to withdraw. Escaping from the twelve enemy planes, they attacked two additional Rumplers. Suddenly a swarm of twenty Fokkers appeared as protection for the two-seaters. Not at all satisfied with these new odds, Woolley led the Spads back to the safety of Belraine.

I am sure that my father, who had been at the front just about as long as any other pilot in the American Air Service, yearned for his first "official" victory. To this end he flew many voluntary patrols in which he was able to attack enemy aircraft, but never seemed to be able to find the right combination to shoot one down and have it be confirmed by Allied observers.

There was a conspicuous coward in the Air Service. First Lieutenant Oscar J. Gude was one of the original members of the 94th. He had been in the air at the time of the tragic death of Raoul Lufbery; he had fired off all his ammunition at the enemy, then fled back to Toul. Following that incident, he did everything in his power to avoid being in the air, usually by refusing to fly with what he continued to claim was faulty equipment. After Lufbery's death, Gude's name did not appear in a single 94th mission report, but three months later his name surfaced. Gude had been assigned as a Flight Commander for the new 93rd Aero Squadron of the Second Pursuit Group, commanded by none other than Major John W. F. M. Huffer. There had been no details entered into his service record as to his lack of performance in the past—or his obvious lack of courage. Upon arrival at the 93rd, Gude was assigned a brand-new Spad, serial #15129. Reports of the 93rd Engineering Section show 15129 as "out of commission" for every single day of the first five weeks of its service, due to mechanical problems reported by its pilot; therefore, there was no flying for Gude. After five weeks he was assigned another new Spad which, in turn, quickly fell victim to one mechanical failure after another. On October 13, his name was stricken from the rolls as "Flight Commander" and squadron records show he continued this practice of quitting patrols with ever-present "motor trouble."

After weeks of Gude's refusing to fly, an exasperated Huffer ordered him to participate, without excuses, in an offensive patrol, and furthermore, to fly Huffer's own Spad, which he knew to be in "perfect flying condition."

Gude took off with a patrol of eight planes that proceeded to fly into a fierce rainstorm. The official history of the 93rd Squadron reported the results of his participation in the patrol as follows:

> The leader observed an enemy plane coming out of Germany which he, First Lieutenant Chester Wright, and two others engaged in combat. This fight took place in a teeming rainstorm, and when the patrol arrived back at the aerodrome, wet and happy [with its results], Lieutenant Gude failed to return from the mission. When last seen he was flying toward Germany.

Not only did Gude fly toward Germany, he also flew *into* Germany, landing at Mars-la-Tour on the airfield of Jasta 65. On the ground, he told his surprised captors that he had become lost and had run out of gas. The Germans were rather indifferent about Gude, but were delighted with a nearly new Spad painted in the personal colors of the 93rd's Commanding Officer, and, as a bonus, more than half a tank of pure gasoline, which for the Germans was in short supply.

Huffer was incensed when he learned that Gude had deserted to become a prisoner of war and avoid further danger, and he was deeply concerned that he himself would be held accountable for this additional act of cowardice on Gude's part. He was not; upon investigation the record clearly demonstrated to Headquarters that Oscar Gude could play a mean ukulele and shoot winning rolls of dice, but that he lacked the courage to be a fighter pilot.

This was the only known instance in the entire war of an Air Service pilot's intentional surrender. Other pilots who had an uncontrollable fear of combat were sent to the rear as ferry pilots or instructors, but no one else ever deserted. Gude survived imprisonment, and after repatriation returned to New York City. Jim Knowles commented to me that Gude had approached a fellow member of the 94th on a New York street, but the man had refused to acknowledge the cowardly pilot in any way.

Assignments and action for the 49th at Belraine continued at a fevered pitch. On the afternoon of October 22, the squadron was called out on a mission to furnish protection for the 96th Aero Squadron's Breguet 14 B2 bombers, which were returning from one of the larger raids into Germany ordered by the Allied command. These raids were intended to further disrupt the flow of ammunition and supplies to the front and to wreak havoc on the enemy rail system. The slow-flying bombers were subject to attack both entering and returning from German territory, in a manner quite similar to that encountered by the Army Air Corps' Eighth Air Force B-17s and B-24s in World War II. The heaviest attacks by the Boche fighters were made close to the lines, because that was the area most populated by the airfields of their Jastas. If the American pursuit protection patrols could time it effectively, they could meet the lumbering returning bombers still within German lines and, by protecting them, reduce the terrible losses being inflicted by the lethal Fokkers.

Woolley, leading the patrol, easily located the returning elements of the 96th and escorted them safely back over Allied lines. The Spads still had a good supply of fuel in their tanks, so he decided to continue in the air and work back and forth over the sector just vacated by the returning bombers. To the north, they spotted twelve Fokkers in three formations that had obviously been searching for the returning bombers, but at this point the Germans had no intention of mixing it up with the Spads, and retired deeper into their territory. Within minutes the patrol encountered four more Fokkers at a closer range, flying at an altitude of 7,500 feet. Woolley led the patrol to within 600 feet of the enemy, and in the company of two of his men, attacked, each firing about 150 rounds. A spirited dogfight ensued, during which the weather rapidly deteriorated; the combat then had to be fought in heavy rain and clouds; the same rain and clouds encountered by the 93rd slightly down the line at the time Gude ran to the enemy.

During this fight one Fokker was reported to have gone down in a straight nosedive from which it never recovered; the other three beat a hasty retreat into their own territory. The downed Fokker was never confirmed.

On the following day, October 23, the 49th encountered its heaviest fighting of the entire war while flying with two other squadrons, the 22nd and 139th of the Second Pursuit Group. First Lieutenant Dave Backus of the 49th left the hangars at Belraine alone, under orders to reinforce a protection patrol of the 22nd Aero. He joined the patrol at 14,000 feet, taking the fifth or last position, called "tail-end Charlie." At that moment he saw the 22nd Flight Leader signal by waggling his wings and beginning a dive. Backus, as high man at the rear of the formation, remained for a moment to make sure there were no enemy planes waiting to pounce on the formation below.

Finding no enemy in sight, he spiraled down to join the others, who were by then hotly engaged in combat. As he drew closer to the action, he saw two enemy two-seaters leaving the fight and heading for Germany. With an advantage of about 1,200 feet of altitude he dove on them, firing sixty rounds into the rear man, who immediately went into a vertical nosedive and spiraled down out of control. He fired a few rounds at the other, who was by then out of range. Backus then turned back to the original fight, which had now drifted more than four miles to the north and into German territory. Suddenly, flying from the west, came another two-seater. Backus dove on it, firing sixty to seventy rounds that seemed to have no effect other than to induce the Boche pilot to notch-up his throttle a bit further and continue his race for home.

The intrepid Dave once again headed back to the main fight, when he sighted two Fokkers heading directly at him. They apparently were unaware of his presence, as they made no attempt to maneuver or to fire their guns. Without a doubt, they were watching behind, not ahead and above where Backus had positioned his Spad. As the Boche passed below, about one hundred feet away, he *viraged* behind them and opened fire. One pulled up into a *chandelle*, an abrupt climbing turn, about seventy-five feet away, and Backus fired a burst that evidently killed the pilot instantly. His head disappeared into the cockpit; the Fokker seemed to hesitate just for a moment, then slowly fell off on one wing, leveled out into a nosedive, and vanished. In the meantime, the other German had pulled off to the right. Backus zoomed, then *viraged* and came down on the tail of the Fokker. He poured a hundred rounds into the hapless enemy machine, which went down in a spin and was last seen three hundred feet from the ground.

Just as Dave pulled away from the second Fokker, he watched the first hit the ground in an orange-red splash of flames. Well into German territory, Backus now decided to head back to his lines while taking a few more shots at yet another two-seater traveling northwest. The Spad's motor was now missing badly, and with the engine temperature needle off the gauge, he headed for Souilly airfield just south of Verdun. From 11:45 A.M. until 12:10 P.M., Backus had, in a space of twenty-five minutes from takeoff to landing, scored a hat trick—three victories, all to be confirmed. Backus and Ham Coolidge were the only two American-trained pilots to attain this distinction. Backus was awarded an oak-leaf cluster for his Distinguished Service Cross for exceptional gallantry.

The official commendation read:

> Backus, David H. First Lieutenant pilot, 49th Aero Squadron, Air Service. A bronze oak-leaf for extraordinary heroism in action in the region of Landreville, France, Oct. 23, 1918. A patrol of American monoplace planes attacked an enemy formation of superior number. Flying rear position, he maneuvered above the attack to prevent other enemy planes from assisting their companions. In the midst of the combat he saw three planes escaping from battle. He immediately gave chase and attacked and shot down all three of the enemy.

Not exactly the way it happened, but without question, Backus had been victorious over three Germans.

On that same morning, Dad prepared for combat in the way he had done so often over the past seven months. He pulled on a wool khaki shirt, a uniform jacket with a turned-down collar, tight-woven gabardine trousers, and finally his "teddy bear" flight suit. Woolen mittens inside specially made leather gauntlets helped keep his hands warm, but at high altitudes his fingers still seemed to freeze in the open cockpit. To prevent frostbite, some pilots smeared their faces with whale oil or donned windproof facemasks made of Chinese Nuchwang dogskin or wolverine hide. He did not bother. The masks cut down on his ability to see the enemy, and turning up the high fleece collar of his flight suit worked well enough for him.

Woolley climbed into the cockpit of his Spad and lowered himself into the small seat situated directly above the gas tank. He motioned to his mechanic to start the motor.

"*Coupez,*" the mechanic called.

"*Coupez,*" Woolley answered, holding the ignition switch in the "off" position. The mechanic turned the propeller four times and stood back.

"Contact," he yelled.

"Contact," Woolley called back and flipped the ignition switch. The mechanic swung the propeller with a swift downward stroke. The engine caught and roared with all eight cylinders firing perfectly. Woolley checked his gauges. RPMs. Oil pressure. Temperature. Fuel. Everything was fine. His crew released the straining aircraft and he taxied onto the muddy field. He opened the throttle, sped a short way over the mire, pulled back on the control stick, and the Spad took to the air.

A few minutes later, the three other men of his patrol were on his wing. He checked his watch: 10:58. He had enough fuel to stay airborne until about 1:00.

In search of the enemy, he first led the patrol two miles up into the numbing cold air. Keeping the sun at their backs, they twisted and turned, continuing to climb, alternately raising and lowering the noses of the planes, continuously scanning the skies. They all felt the discomfort always experienced at high altitude, felt their breathing deepen in the ever-thinning atmosphere. To warm their hands, they clenched and unclenched fists; they rubbed their cheeks to keep the circulation going in their faces. The physical strain of a two-hour patrol at 20,000 feet, almost four miles, was equivalent to a two-hour climb on Mt. Everest— with no oxygen and in primitive climbing gear!

The Spads had an operational ceiling of 21,800 feet, but were not equipped with oxygen-breathing equipment or electrically heated clothing, which was enjoyed by the German two-seaters that constantly operated at extreme altitudes.

As the patrol cruised, the sun at their backs threw brilliant rainbow haloes around the shadows of their aircraft on the white clouds below. From the bone-chilling 20,000 feet, the patrol dropped down below 5,000 feet and continued on, constantly scanning the skies for enemy aircraft.

Near Doulcon over the Meuse, Woolley looked above, and there! A formation of four Fokkers was waiting to pounce upon any attackers. My father glanced at his watch: 11:45. He had a favorable position, 1,000 feet above and behind the enemy formation with the sun at his back. The odds were good. He moved the stick back and forth, rolling his Spad slightly, the signal for attack. Then he dove on the lower formation with Bill Colson and two other Spads at his side, the wind howling through their flying wires. They dove as fast as their Spads would carry them. They were to make one pass and *virage* away before the upper formation could attack. Emerging through wispy clouds, they pulled within shooting range. Woolley squeezed the trigger of his machine guns, releasing seventy-five rounds. He could see the tracers penetrating the body of the Fokker until . . . his guns jammed. Dad *viraged* away, out of the action. Fighting the wind, he frantically worked the cocking lever of the guns with his right hand as he struggled to clear the jam. With his left hand alone, he strained to keep control of the careening aircraft. Finally, a sharp click. The guns were clear.

He looked through the web of tracer bullets stretched across the sky. The upper Fokkers had attacked. It was a free-for-all of twelve spinning, cartwheeling fighters. All sense of time, direction, and speed were lost. The only real things were the black cross insignias of a Fokker framed in his sights and the goggled face of a German pilot, a face distorted by the 200-mile-per-hour wind. Alerted by instinct, Woolley saw a Fokker diving in attack on squadron plane number five. That was Colson. He *piqued* and fired, but was he close enough to do any damage? The German broke off his attack. Out of the corner of his eye, Woolley noticed a smoking Fokker spinning down in a *vrille*, the first one he had attacked. The air was filled with fighter planes continuing to attack each other from all sides, rocketing out of the clouds, down from the sun, appearing and disappearing literally in the blink of an eye.

Another member of the patrol appeared at Woolley's side. They dove and together fired 350 rounds at a lone Fokker. The other pilot's guns jammed, and he *viraged* away. Woolley's guns were now working to perfection, and he watched with satisfaction as his tracers streamed into the fuselage of the brightly painted German. The Fokker, when last seen, was in a spiraling vertical nosedive.

"None of the pilots in this combat had time to see the final results," Woolley later wrote in his combat report, "because eight other Fokkers attacked our smaller patrols."

At Belraine, "C" Flight, all smiles, landed and taxied up to the flight line by their large canvas hangars. My father climbed out of his aircraft, pulled off his goggles and his leather flying helmet, wiped the oil from his blackened face, and was met by Captain George Fisher, who grabbed his hand and shook it vigorously in congratulations for a job well done.

Fisher had already received confirmations from a forward observation post. Dad had at last scored not one, but two official victories in a single mission. With Backus' triple, Woolley's double, and three other single victories, it was the 49th's finest hour, their finest performance: eight victories in a single day with no losses except one overheated and frozen engine in Backus' Spad. My father's previous disappointments—after so many fights with victories but none confirmed—were forgotten. He now had two "officials," and there would be time for more. He was confident; his well-trained Flight could depend on one another and fought superbly as a well-coached team. They had beaten the best the

Germans had. They had emerged the victors. After eighteen months in France, and more than a year in the Air Service, First Lieutenant Charles H. Woolley had performed extraordinarily well in this, his most successful day in aerial combat. At this moment he was on top of the world, a most happy warrior.

# CHAPTER 17

# Costly Victory

Ham Coolidge, despite his mounting victories and the positive direction of the war, was becoming somewhat withdrawn, and to the others seemed almost morose. In reading Ham's letters of the last few weeks, one fear seems to grip him more tightly than any other. Archie! Time and again he mentions Archie and to him its startling effects. He mentions seeing the "puffs" when daydreaming on the beach while on leave at Deauville. He describes "barrages of Archies and flaming onions" while participating in balloon raids, and how he "had an empty feeling in his tummy which a sudden burst of Archie only accentuated." Was he, after the strain of combat and the loss of his best friend, experiencing some form of combat fatigue, or was this some strange premonition?

As October drew to a close, a period of continuing poor weather with almost zero visibility curtailed flying. The morning of the 27th, Coolidge attempted to lead a five-plane patrol out into a dense fog. He returned in less than an hour; nothing could be seen. The weather slowly improved, and by 2:30 that afternoon, Ham and Eddie Rickenbacker were able to jointly lead an eleven-plane protection patrol, serving as cover for Allied bombers returning from another large raid deep into enemy territory. Twenty-five minutes into the mission, the patrol spotted the bombers. They were under attack from a formation of Fokkers.

Immediately, Coolidge flew to their defense. At the end of the mission, patrol member First Lieutenant Sam Kaye filed his official report:

> In the region north of Grand Pré, just across the river [Meuse], an anti-aircraft shell made a direct hit on Captain Coolidge's machine, blowing both right wings off and sending it down in flames. Time, about 14h 55. Altitude 1,700 feet. Captain Coolidge was leading the patrol at the time . . .

Where Coolidge had been flying moments earlier, his companions could see nothing but lingering wisps of white smoke. Not the black smoke of the German antiaircraft guns, but the white smoke from the guns of the Allies.

All fighter pilots at the front were stunned when they heard about Coolidge's incomprehensible death. No one ever got hit by Archie. No one. Especially not a seasoned pilot like Coolidge. And to be killed by friendly fire—it was too tragic to contemplate.

Joe Eastman confided to his diary:

> We like to think he was killed instantly by the explosive. He was the one man I've seen in the Army who made an evening practice of kneeling by his cot in prayer. His scoreboard showed seven or eight confirmed victories, which he described to me in detail not so many evenings ago, always giving them as illustrations of the conviction that it's all a matter of 'pure chance happening' . . .

Ham had always tried to encourage Eastman not to be concerned about his lack of confidence, his lack of victories, or his continued problems with reluctant airplanes. "Pure good chance" would happen. Ham personally exhibited to Joe the leadership and compassion that made him not only a team captain on the athletic fields of Groton and Harvard, but a loved, respected, and admired Flight Commander of the 94th.

Hamilton Coolidge was buried where he fell, three hundred

yards northwest of Chevières, a small village near Grand Pré. Coolidge rests today in the same place, the grave beautifully appointed and lovingly tended by a French family whose grandparents were hired to care for the site in 1919. A trust established in France by the Coolidge family continues today to support the perpetual care of their hero's grave.

During the first week of November, the weather further deteriorated, and rumors flew. The Kaiser had accepted the Allied peace plan. The doughboys in the trenches had received orders to slow the attack. From over all the aerodromes came the remarks, "Are you all packed yet?" or "I'm glad I didn't buy that new uniform after all!"

Despite the rumors, pockets of fierce fighting continued. Even as Germany reeled back in retreat, he gamely fought on. The fighter planes of the Air Service relentlessly continued to strafe, bomb, and attack. Still, those that flew the Spads knew fighters had no business carrying those pesky and ineffective bombs. Fisher requested that Woolley and the members of his Flight draft a joint memorandum outlining the problem. The memorandum that was sent up the chain of command to Colonel Billy Mitchell read:

> When bombs are carried on high patrols, they not only decrease the speed of climb greatly, and so shorten the effective time of the patrol, but they also put an extra strain on the motors. Bombs cannot be dropped with any degree of accuracy from high altitude from a pursuit plane. Although it should take but an instant to release the bombs, that instant is very likely to be the deciding factor when pursuit planes carrying bombs are attacked at a low altitude. When bombs fail to release in such a situation, the result is sure to be fatal to the unlucky plane. Therefore, it is felt that a strong protection patrol should always fly over a low strafing patrol which carries bombs.

Early in November, the American airmen vigorously continued to press the attack against the remaining stubborn units of the Prussian Imperial Air Service. Vicious and deadly combat was fought whenever weather conditions allowed. In 1970, as I was conducting my research at the National Archives, I came across a copy of a memorandum dated "3 December 1918" addressed to "Chief of Decorations Section." The subject was "Report on trip to investigate and receive recommendations for Medals of Honor from the Air Service." Among the names recommended for the nation's highest award was that of First Lieutenant William H. Vail, 95th Aero Squadron. A copy of this long-buried memorandum was made at the Archives to share with Bill Vail, whom I had grown to know in the course of my research on the 95th. Also named in the document was First Lieutenant Frank Luke, the man Luke Air Force Base, about twenty miles outside of Phoenix, was named for.

Among air historians, Frank Luke's story is well known. He was "the Arizona Balloon Buster," and had flown with the 27th Squadron of the First Pursuit Group. In less than two months, Luke officially shot down fourteen balloons and four aircraft. After German fighters brought down his best friend and flying companion, Lieutenant Joe Werner, Luke, seeking revenge, started flying unauthorized solo patrols, and during one on September 29, 1918, he was shot down. But what of Vail?

When I first located Bill Vail, he was retired and living in California. In 1918, he had been recognized as a crack shot, one of the best in the Air Service. Much to his dismay, that ability to shoot well had actually kept him from the front, as he was assigned to work as an instructor at the Cazeaux gunnery school. Pulling every string he could find, he was finally released from Cazeaux and assigned to the 95th at the end of September. On November 6, eager for action, he volunteered with another Chicagoan, First Lieutenant Josiah "Josh" Pegues, to fly an afternoon two-man patrol.

A short time after I had sent Vail a copy of the forgotten memorandum recommending him for the Medal of Honor, Bill wrote back and for the first time ever described in detail what had happened on that fateful November 6 afternoon:

> I was on patrol with Lieutenant Josiah Pegues, when
> he and I spotted a German two-seater observation

plane. Pegues was in the lead, and dove on the machine. Both of us were so intent on attacking the German two-seater that we did not see that there were nine enemy planes above us, under which the enemy two-seater observation plane was drawing us. I even fired a few bursts as near as I dared toward Pegues' ship, but to no avail in those few seconds. I then had three options: to go with Pegues and let the outnumbering enemy strike at us from above; to put my nose down and retreat with every ounce of speed in my Spad (something we both should have done had Pegues been aware of the overwhelming odds about to reach us in seconds); or to pull up the nose of my Spad and meet the nine down-diving enemy planes head on. This [last] I did . . .

As Vail took on four Fokkers to protect his friend, five more Fokkers dove on him from above. The four Germans who were after Pegues turned to attack Vail. One Spad, flown by one incredibly brave man, was then flying against nine hostile Fokkers. Odds of nine to one were not odds. It was a death sentence.

Bill Vail continued in his letter:

[I] was officially credited with one victory before the Boche shut off my engine with their machine gun fire, then shot off my left leg. My foot simply dropped off the rudder bar as the burst of machine gun fire tore out the bones in my leg above the left knee.

I then attempted a diversionary effort from the enemy plane gunfire as I came toward the earth with a dead engine and dead stick. I operated the plane with one foot—my right on the rudder bar in the foot clip with which I could pull back for left rudder since my left foot was gone. My Spad was riddled with enemy gunshots. The wing wires cut. One engine panel strut shot out in front of my face.

Knowing they had a "kill," the Germans followed Vail down, continuing to pour fire into his rapidly disintegrating plane. On several occasions Bill, in spite of his terrible wounds, pulled up his crippled Spad and fired at his attackers:

> I was so intent on looking backward to make myself as poor a target for the Hun airmen as possible, that I did not know that I was so near the earth until the last moment. I pulled up, but it was too late, and I went into the earth practically in a vertical dive. Oh, what a terrible crash . . . Having no engine power and the soft mud of France there in the Argonne, saved me from death.

The Spad turned over on the ground, cruelly pinning Vail under the wreckage. Some American doughboys found Vail lying beneath his crumpled aircraft, his head caught beneath the wing, driven into the soft mud by the 220-horsepower Hispano-Suiza engine. Vail, writing to me more than fifty years after the incident, related:

> Both [my] arms were disabled from the desperate, frantic effort on my part to lift the weight—an impossibility when directly under an Hispano-Suiza V-eight airplane engine. [A] brave guy [an American soldier] who was right at hand managed to get leverage on the wing in some manner, [managed] to lift the weight of the engine holding my head buried face upward—with [the] wing stretched over my face cutting off [my] breathing. I was completely blinded at the moment, but had enough consciousness to tell him what to do, and when the weight was lifted by his efforts from the end of the upturned wing, [I managed] to work my smashed-up head out of the mud and pulled forward with my one functioning limb—my right leg—a few inches before my savior let the weight down again.

Doughboys removed Bill Vail from the field and carried him in a blanket used as a stretcher. It was fourteen long hours before he reached Mobile Hospital No. 1, where surgeons amputated his right foot, removed a bullet from his arm, and bandaged his slightly fractured skull.

Bill Vail concluded his letter to me with the following: "This is the most I have ever written about it, Charlie. Perhaps had I done so years ago (I didn't seem capable), that Medal of Honor mentioned in the memorandum to Chief of Decorations Section, 3rd December 1918, might have been awarded me. Ever the very best to you. William H. H. Vail."

What pleasure it brought me to be the one to inform Bill that after fifty-two years, his act of valor and personal sacrifice to save the life of his companion had not gone unnoticed; he *had* been recommended for the nation's highest honor. To be sure, he was awarded in 1919 the Distinguished Service Cross in the War Department General Orders Number 37, but without question the Medal of Honor should also have been his.

Vail's great act of heroism in saving the life of Pegues was to be one of the last feats of bravery performed during the Great War in the air. Poor flying conditions returned again in the days following Vail's dramatic fight. There were more balloon missions flown by the squadrons of both Pursuit Groups with few successes. The German defensive line collapsed. Bulgaria, Turkey, and Austria-Hungary capitulated to the Allies. Communists revolted against the Kaiser in Berlin and Munich. German sailors mutinied. A German delegation met with Allied leaders in the personal railway carriage of Supreme Allied Commander Ferdinand Foch to work out the details of the Armistice. On November 9, Kaiser Wilhelm II abdicated and fled to Holland. Thousands of German soldiers lay down their arms and simply walked away from the war.

Just prior to the Armistice, Alex McLanahan, Ted Curtis, and Sumner Sewall were "on alert" at an "advanced field" close to the lines near Verdun, when they saw a plane, unannounced, line up for a landing. It was a Fokker! They stood watching in amazement as the German aircraft landed gracefully on the tiny American airfield and came to a halt. Sumner and the others drew their automatics and ran to the enemy. The German climbed awkwardly from the cockpit, raised his hands, and explained that he was lost and had landed on the American airfield by mistake.

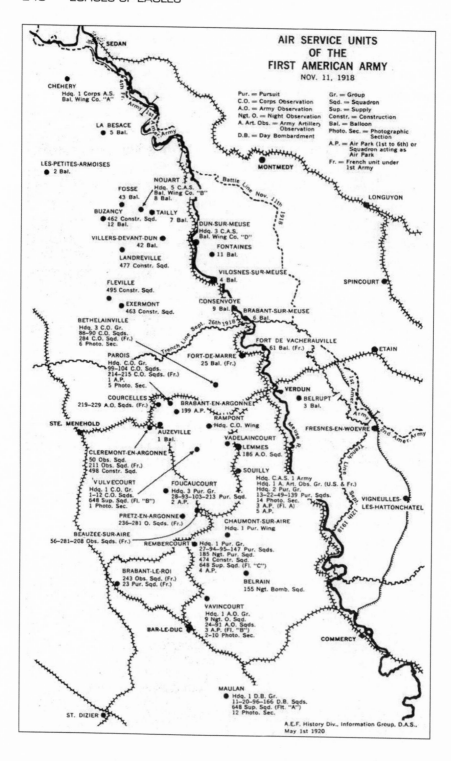

**AIR SERVICE UNITS**
**OF THE**
**FIRST AMERICAN ARMY**
NOV. 11, 1918

Pur. = Pursuit
C.O. = Corps Observation
A.O. = Army Observation
Ngt. O. = Night Observation
A. Art. Obs. = Army Artillery
Observation
D.B. = Day Bombardment

Gr. = Group
Sqd. = Squadron
Sup. = Supply
Constr. = Construction
Bal. = Balloon
Photo. Sec. = Photographic
Section
A.P. = Air Park (1st to 6th) or
Squadron acting as
Air Park
Fr. = French unit under
1st Army

SEDAN

CHEHERY
Hdq. 1 Corps A.S.
Bal. Wing Co. "A"

LA BESACE
5 Bal.

LES-PETITES-ARMOISES
2 Bal.

MONTMEDY

LONGUYON

NOUART
Hdq. 5 C.A.S.
Bal. Wing Co. "B"
8 Bal.

FOSSE
43 Bal.

BUZANCY
462 Constr. Sqd.
12 Bal.

TAILLY
7 Bal.

DUN-SUR-MEUSE
Hdq. 3 C.A.S.
Bal. Wing Co. "D"

VILLERS-DEVANT-DUN
42 Bal.

FONTAINES
11 Bal.

LANDREVILLE
477 Constr. Sqd.

VILOSNES-SUR-MEUSE
4 Bal.

FLEVILLE
495 Constr. Sqd.

SPINCOURT

EXERMONT
463 Constr. Sqd.

CONSENVOYE
9 Bal.

BRABANT-SUR-MEUSE
6 Bal.

BETHELAINVILLE
Hdq. 3 C.O. Gr.
88–90 C.O. Sqds.
284 C.O. Sqd. (Fr.)
6 Photo. Sec.

FORT DE VACHERAUVILLE
61 Bal. (Fr.)

ETAIN

PAROIS
Hdq. C.O. Gr.
99–104 C.O. Sqds.
214–215 C.O. Sqds. (Fr.)
1 A.P.
5 Photo. Sec.

FORT-DE-MARRE
25 Bal. (Fr.)

VERDUN

COURCELLES
219–229 A.O. Sqds. (Fr.)

BRABANT-EN-ARGONNE
199 A.P.

BELRUPT
3 Bal.

STE. MENEHOLD

RAMPONT
Hdq. C.O. Wing

FRESNES-EN-WOEVRE

AUZEVILLE
1 Bal.

VADELAINCOURT

CLEREMONT-EN-ARGONNE
50 Obs. Sqd.
211 Obs. Sqd. (Fr.)
498 Constr. Sqd.

LEMMES
186 A.O. Sqd.

SOUILLY
Hdq. C.A.S. 1 Army
Hdq. 1 A. Art. Obs. Gr. (U.S. & Fr.)
Hdq. 2 Pur. Gr.
13–22–49–139 Pur. Sqds.
14 Photo. Sec.
3 A.P. (Fl. A)
5 A.P.

VULVECOURT
Hdq. 1 C.O. Gr.
1–12 C.O. Sqds.
648 Sup. Sqd. (Fl. "B")
1 Photo. Sec.

FOUCAUCOURT
Hdq. 3 Pur. Gr.
28–93–103–213 Pur. Sqd.
2 A.P.

PRETZ-EN-ARGONNE
236–281 O. Sqds. (Fr.)

VIGNEULLES-
LES-HATTONCHATEL

CHAUMONT-SUR-AIRE
Hdq. 1 Pur. Wing

BEAUZEE-SUR-AIRE
56–281–208 Obs. Sqds. (Fr.)

REMBERCOURT
Hdq. 1 Pur. Wing
27–94–95–147 Pur. Sqds.
185 Ngt. Pur. Sqd.
474 Constr. Sqd.
648 Sup. Sqd. (Fl. "C")
4 A.P.

BRABANT-LE-ROI
243 Obs. Sqd. (Fr.)
23 Pur. Sqd. (Fr.)

BELRAIN
155 Ngt. Bomb. Sqd.

VAVINCOURT
Hdq. 1 A.O. Gr.
9 Ngt. O. Sqd.
24–91 A.O. Sqds.
3 A.P. (Fl. "B")
2–10 Photo. Sec.

BAR-LE-DUC

COMMERCY

MAULAN
Hdq. 1 D.B. Gr.
11–20–96–166 D.B. Sqds.
648 Sup. Sqd. (Flt. "A")
12 Photo. Sec.

ST. DIZIER

A.E.F. History Div., Information Group, D.A.S.,
May 1st 1920

Their captive was Leutnant Heinz Beaulieu-Marconnay of Jasta 65. He had marked his Fokker "U.10," the same designation used to brand horses and equipment of *Ulan Regiment Nr. 10*, his former cavalry regiment.

Later, Beaulieu-Marconnay confided to his American captors that he was not greatly upset about his mistake. He had recently lost his brother, Oliver, a twenty-five-victory ace and commander of Jasta 19; he had been killed in action. He was sick of the war. "Too damn much Hohenzollern," he said, referring to the family of the Kaiser. "The war will soon be over anyway."

The German pilot was correct. As the German defenses crumbled, the 49th moved even closer to the fast-retreating front, to a field at Souilly. On November 10, Woolley led a patrol of seven Spads from 13:05 to 15:01 at 3,000 to 4,500 feet. Six Fokkers were sighted flying above them nine miles behind German lines. Slowed by the bombs they were forced to carry, pursuit of the Fokkers was out of the question. They ineffectively dropped their bombs on Autreville and, in frustration, returned to their new field.

Earlier that morning, Major Maxwell Kirby had departed from the 94th's field at Rembercourt on a voluntary solo patrol. Kirby, who had been a qualified Army aviator before the war, had been mired in non-flying duties since his arrival in France. Frustrated, he finally persuaded Billy Mitchell to give him a crack at combat flying. Assigned to the 94th on October 15 to gain frontline combat experience, he took every possible opportunity to be in the air, but as yet, he had engaged in no combats.

This voluntary patrol was to be the exception. His first and only combat report read:

> In the region of Maucourt at about 10h 50 when emerging from a low cloudbank, I suddenly came upon a Fokker monoplace at an altitude of 150 feet. I fired a burst into him at very close range (45 feet) and pulled away. He went down in a steep dive into the side of a hill and crashed. Confirmation Requested—1 Fokker.

Confirmed it was, and twenty-four hours and ten minutes before the Armistice was put into effect, Kirby had scored the last aerial victory of the war.

At 10:00 P.M. on November 10, 1918, word was out. The rumors were true. Armistice! *Poilus*, Tommies, doughboys, as well as German foot soldiers, began celebrations on both sides of No Man's Land. The festivities stretched from Dunkirk to the Swiss border, from Palestine to the Italian Alps.

At Rembercourt Aerodrome, home of the First Pursuit Group, a great clamor began. Joe Eastman, ready to retire, was rolling up his puttees (woolen leg-wraps worn over the lower leg in lieu of polished boots), when he heard an unbelievable din outside his barracks. He rushed to the door and watched a parade of enlisted men sloshing through the mud, ignoring the mire, drumming on an assortment of pots and pans, blowing bugles, and cheering wildly.

A highly excited Jimmy Meissner then burst into the barracks, straight from the Headquarters of the 147th. "They've signed an Armistice!" he shouted. "Official wire received up at Operations from the Commander, Air Service! All hostilities to cease tomorrow at eleven hundred hours! Everyone over to the 95th's bar!"

The flyers broke out bottles from every imaginable hiding place and passed them from hand to hand. The usually restrained 94th howled with joy, bottles held high, and set off for the pleasure palace of the Kicking Mules. By the time the advance contingent of the 94th reached their goal, slipping and sliding over the greasy field, all hell had broken loose. Up from the darkened hangars that surrounded the field came a steady stream of landing flares and signal rockets—red, green, and dazzling phosphorus white.

Over by the 95th barracks, someone no doubt inspired by the cowboy yells, revolver shots, and general pandemonium commandeered a machine gun and joyfully rattled off a belt of ammunition over the heads of the merrymakers. A few alarmed shouts in his direction questioned his parenthood and ordered him to shoot in another direction. Leaping over puddles, sometimes not quite over, the pilots congregated at the 95th bar and proceeded to try to drink it dry. Outside, the din of singing, cheering, and banging on anything that could resound continued unabated.

As the toasts became more obscure and more slurred inside the bar, a fine diversion was created outside its flimsy walls. It was Captain Rankin's band! He had formed this band for parades and other semiofficial ceremonies, but on the night of November 10 they did not play Sousa marches. In fact, it sounded more like Bourbon Street at Mardi Gras. The crowd poured out from the bar, and at the head was Captain Eddie Rickenbacker. With the machine gun again rattling and Rankin's band playing, Rick led a serpentine, single-file parade through the darkened field, intermittently illuminated by the last of the flares. "The parade" shortly turned into a free-for-all wrestling match—a match made all the more exuberant by the liberal number of mud puddles that were quickly filled with jubilant, wrestling aviators.

Things were no less jubilant at the 49th field at Souilly. Amid toasts, hectic, playful wrestling, and joyous shouting came profound relief, relief from the terrible strain. It was finally over. Dad thought of those with whom he had flown—Sumner Sewall, Ted Curtis, Jim Knowles, now all aces; Johnny Mitchell, Alex McLanahan, close friends; Heinrichs, Avery, both seriously wounded; "Big Bill" Taylor, Ham Coolidge, Quentin Roosevelt, and so many others, all gone west. He had fought over Toul, Château Thierry, St. Mihiel and the Meuse-Argonne territories. For victories, he had received two official confirmations, and had scored enough unofficial victories to qualify as an ace. In less than three months of action, the Wolf Pack, the 49th Aero Squadron, had accounted for twenty-five enemy planes, and suffered only six casualties.

His role as Flight Commander had played a significant part in his squadron's success. "Hell," he said aloud, looking around at his fellow pilots. "We lived through the bloody war. It is *over*."

# CHAPTER 18

# Post-War Progress

The 49th received orders on December 6 to proceed to the First Air Depot at Colombey-les-Belles to prepare for demobilization and the journey back home. The airfield had formerly been the distribution point for planes bought from the French manufacturers and flown to the front. On December 14, Woolley flew his Spad No. 24, now an old and trusted friend, to Colombey, where he sadly turned it in, along with his other government-issued equipment.

The living accommodations at Colombey were really quite pleasant. Woolley spent a great deal of time in Sanger Hall, a building named for an American flyer, a Captain Sanger who was killed accidentally at Colombey. In Sanger's memory, his wife had paid for the construction of the building and had hired Parisian interior designers to make the building as attractive as possible for the in-transit American officers. Two large public rooms featured open fireplaces, a piano, a phonograph, magazine tables, sumptuous sofas, comfortable lounge chairs, and curtains of striking emerald green.

It had taken the United States a year and a half to create and transport an army of two million men across the Atlantic. Now the big questions were: How and when are we going to get them home? Slowly, it seemed, at least in most cases.

Captain George Fisher, the 49th's Commander, was ordered back to the United States in early December, and First Lieutenant Woolley was appointed as his replacement. Hugh Bridgman did not mind the delay. "I look at it this way," Bridgman stated. "If we wait until the initial rush is over, we'll be able to enjoy the trip back home crossing in first-class accommodations."

During the wait, the pilots of the 49th and the other squadrons on their way home spent much of their time playing bridge, reading, and swapping stories with old friends passing through Colombey. News had it that Rickenbacker was back in the States doing Liberty Bond tours, and the 94th, which had replaced most of the original pilots, had been ordered to Germany as part of the Allied Army of Occupation. While on occupation duty, the 94th outdid the colorful paint schemes of the wartime Flying Circuses of Germany by turning their Spads into the gaudiest aircraft that ever flew the skies over Europe. Their machines—covered with shamrocks and stripes in brilliant green; orange lightning bolts on black; red-white-and-blue polka dots; and stars and stripes bursting across fuselages in a torrent of brilliant color—dazzled the Third Army of Occupation at an air carnival in the skies over Coblenz. When they were ordered home, the 94th turned over most of these dazzling aircraft to the 138th Aero Squadron, which was to remain in Germany.

Woolley, during his brief trips into Paris, enjoyed making the rounds to his wartime haunts and meeting up with old friends. At Henri's Bar he ran into Bill Casgrain, Jim Knowles, Johnny Mitchell, and others of the "Villeneuve gang." Casgrain had spent the months of June through November as a prisoner of war. When his old pals belatedly presented him with his French *Croix de Guerre*, Casgrain snorted, "What the hell is this, the booby prize?"

Other released American prisoners of war drifted into Paris. My father joined Peter Puryear and Harold Willis at a festive reunion party at the Crillon Bar. Puryear told of his escapes from prisoner of war camps. From Baden, a camp in Germany, he had managed to break out of the camp with a French aviator and was headed toward a German airfield to steal an airplane, when, exhausted from exposure, they were recaptured by an alert sentry. After his recapture he was moved from camp to camp.

Finally, Puryear found himself in a camp at Villingen, not far from the Swiss border. There he teamed up with seven other prisoners, including my boyhood hero, Harold Willis of the Lafayette Escadrille, and put together a complex escape plan that included short-circuiting the entire camp's electrical system, donning disguises as prison guards, and simultaneously breaking out from three separate locations of the prison. It worked! Five days later Puryear swam the Rhine to safety, while Willis and the others successfully swam the same river from other locations. Willis told me about his part of the adventure twenty-three years later, during one of his many visits to our wartime home in Washington, D.C.

Waldo Heinrichs, who returned from another prisoner of war camp, had survived his terrible wounds and was receiving medical care and convalescing in Paris, his jaw crumpled, his arm still in a sling. Ted Curtis had visited him at the hospital, and Sumner Sewall had delivered his *Croix de Guerre avec Palme*, along with some new warm socks. "Heinie was proud of the medal, but the socks were more useful," Sewall joked after the award had been delivered.

In December Heinrichs was well enough to be sent home, and an account of his arrival in the United States appeared in the January 26, 1919 edition of *The New York Herald*. The captain of the liner transporting Heinrichs and other wounded Americans home had celebrated New Year's Eve, the ship's last night at sea, a little too enthusiastically. He misjudged the entrance to New York harbor, and on New Year's morning ran the liner aground on Long Island. The article's headline blared, "Luckiest Man in War, Wounded Many Times, Tells of his Escape."

"Even on his arrival here," the story explained. "Heinrichs played true to form, for he made his landing on American soil dangling from a cable stretched from Fire Island Beach to the rigging of the S.S. *Northern Pacific*."

All in France had heard about the death of Hobey Baker, the celebrated Princeton hockey star and gridiron hero, one of the best known collegiate athletes to fly in the Air Service. Baker, in early October, had been given command of the new 141st Aero Squadron. The squadron's Spad aircraft were not available, however, until the last week of October. Baker had somehow managed to attain three confirmed kills, but he was not satisfied in the least with his performance. In addition, the twenty-seven-year-old former athletic sensation was reported to be low on funds, and heartbroken. His fiancée, Mimi Scott, a New York debutante doing hospital work in France, had just broken their engagement. Baker felt he had no reason to hurry home.

After he received orders to leave France on December 21, Baker walked out onto his squadron's airfield near Toul. His friends tried to discourage him. They were concerned about him, concerned about his distraught state of mind. There was nothing but potential trouble when taking "one last flight." Baker ignored their warnings. He was flying an unfamiliar aircraft. He climbed aboard an available Spad that had just undergone carburetor repair. Baker took off in a light drizzle, pulled the machine up in a right *chandelle*, or rising turn, and leveled off at 600 feet. The engine died! Baker did exactly the wrong thing. Instead of holding his course in a straight line, he, like a novice, tried to turn the aircraft back to the field—and violently crashed. A few minutes later, he died in an ambulance, resting in the arms of the Squadron Armament Officer, a man who had once been his football coach at Princeton.

During a war-end cleanup of paperwork, a legal officer came across forgotten charges filed against Major J. W. F. M. Huffer. The charges had been brought by Major Davenport Johnson; yes, the same "Jam" Johnson who had been commanding officer of the 95th, and later the Second Pursuit Group. A Judge Advocate reviewed the charges and decided that the matter should be brought to trial.

What a trial it was. It certainly tried the "patience" of those who were at all familiar with the affair! The charge was "Violation of the 95th Article of War." Specifically:

In that Major J. W. F. M. Huffer A. S. Sig. R. C., did while in uniform at Gengoult Airdrome, France on or

about the 22nd day of June 1918, well knowing that a
woman known as Marcelle Collas was a commonplace
prostitute, cause her to be present at a dance at which
other officers of the U.S. Army and civilians were present; and in their presence did openly and publicly as-
sociate with her at said dance.

No one could believe that such a ridiculous court-martial was
actually going to be held. While plans for peace and the fate of
Germany were being decided by the world's diplomats in Paris,
the U.S. Army was going to charge a Major for going to a dance in
the company of a suspected prostitute. Most knew why Johnson
had brought the court-martial charge. He was a "by the book"
West Pointer who resented Huffer's loose command style and
French manners. But more to the point, Huffer was the one who
had reported Johnson for an infraction of the Air Service rules to
then-Colonel Billy Mitchell. Johnson's court-martial charges were
brought more in revenge for this blemish to his own record than
in any quest for justice.

Nevertheless, the trial began on December 2 at First Army Artillery Headquarters, Souilly, France. The witness list for the
defense read like a "Who's Who" of America's aviation heroes:
Eddie Rickenbacker, Jimmy Meissner, Reed Chambers, and at
the top of the list, Brigadier General Billy Mitchell.

The prosecution had to prove that Collas was a prostitute, and
that Huffer had known she was a prostitute when he brought
her to the dance. When asked how he knew Marcelle was a prostitute, Johnson responded, "Other officers knew she was a prostitute and told me. She was painted up more than an ordinary
virtuous woman would paint, and from her looks you would
know who she was." Other officers testified that they indeed did
*not* believe that the fair Marcelle was a prostitute.

The prosecutor introduced two documents that Johnson had
obtained from the *Commissaire de Police* in the city of Nancy.
One document said that a certain woman was a *fille qui se livre
au libertinage*, a "woman who lives the life of a libertine." The
other document was a *Notice de Renseignements*, identifying a
woman as a prostitute; two photos were attached.

Unfortunately for the prosecution, the names on the documents were Maria Honorine Collas, not Marcelle Collas. Witnesses who knew Marcelle Collas and who had been present at the party testified that the photos on the document in evidence were not photos of Marcelle. Since the prosecution was unable to prove that Marcelle was a prostitute or that Huffer even suspected that she was a prostitute, Huffer was acquitted, and the leaders of America's military aviation turned their attention to matters of greater importance.

On March 8, 1919, First Lieutenant Charles H. Woolley was in command of the 49th Aero Squadron as it began its journey across the Atlantic. The trip home was not the first-class luxury voyage that Bridgman had hoped for. The liner was jammed. There were few deck chairs available, so members of the squadron spent most of their time standing on the spray-covered deck, slightly chilled, but enjoying the smell of the fresh salt air as the ship rolled with the swells of the Atlantic. After arrival in New York, Woolley closed the squadron down. He oversaw the reams of paperwork, the distribution of travel vouchers, and the doling out of final pay. He then gave each squadron member a copy of his service record, shook his hand, and sent him home.

The final tally revealed that more than 1,000 American airmen had died in the Great War. One hundred sixty-four were killed in combat, 319 died in accidents, 335 died from diseases and other causes, and 200 were missing in action.

Dad and his squadron mates came home to a changed country, one that was about to finally give women the right to vote and one that had voted in Prohibition, outlawing the manufacture and sale of alcoholic beverages. Opponents of Prohibition cried out in another play on President Wilson's words: "They're trying to make the world *dry* for Democracy! Did we fight the war for this?"

Many returning combat pilots found it difficult to make the transition from wartime flying adventures to peacetime. The French ace, Jean Navarre, was an extreme example. After the Armistice, an unsettled Navarre shocked Parisians by stripping in fashionable nightclubs, finally killing himself while practicing to fly through the Arc de Triomphe in a future victory parade. Other pilots from the Allied countries left for Poland or Siberia to fly against the Bolsheviks. German pilots formed small squadrons for the Freikorps, a volunteer force raised to eliminate the communists who were threatening to take over a shattered Germany.

In 1919, Woolley, then twenty-five, was among those who were to formulate the future of American aviation. Before the war, he had never flown in an airplane. After the war, he could not imagine life without flying. But continuing to fly after the war was not a simple thing to do.

Many former military pilots flew in competitions, attempting to set records for speed, height, or long-distance flying. Major Harold Hartney retired from the Air Service and became a professional air racer after the war. In 1919 he flew a captured Fokker D VII in the first "Path Finding New York to San Francisco Reliability Tests." Hartney took first place in his class, completing the grueling flight to the West Coast and back. During the course of the race, nine other pilots were killed. Other veteran pilots flew for the embryonic U.S. Airmail Service, joining colorful characters like Leon "Bonehead" Smith, who was so tough that he survived a blow on the head from a spinning propeller.

There was no post-war aircraft-manufacturing boom in the United States. Most automakers had stopped their involvement in the aerial business and had gone back to what they new best: building automobiles, churning out axles, transmissions, and headlights. The U.S. Army sold a few DH-4s and surplus captured German airplanes to stunt flyers, and burned the rest!

Many, however, refused to give up on aviation. Brigadier General Billy Mitchell was America's outspoken proponent of military air power. In 1921, after months of highly publicized controversy, he organized a demonstration to prove the value of military air power, in which Air Service bombers sank the decommissioned German battleship *Ostfriesland* in twenty-one minutes. In 1925, Mitchell was unfairly court-martialed for insubordination, convicted, and stripped of his rank. A broken man, he died in 1936.

Woolley shared Mitchell's conviction that aviation was the key to America's military might, but he had an entirely different political style and agenda. Unable to indulge in high-level public confrontations, he, together with Jim Knowles, Harold Willis, Gardiner Fiske, Chester Wright, and other combat veteran pilots in the Boston area, founded the Aero Club of Boston and began to promote the values of aviation by appealing directly to the public. When it was announced in the spring of 1921 that the United States was going to approve National Air Guards, they set out to organize the first one to be approved. Federally recognized in November 1921 as the 101st Observation Squadron, it adopted as its motto *Omnis Vir Tigris*, "every man a tiger." It was a great victory for those instrumental in the organization of the first American National Air Guard to be recognized by the Federal government. The Great War, hopefully, was to be the war to end all wars, but even so, it was necessary for America to prepare for the possibility of future wars—and for the possibility that future wars would be fought from the air.

With the establishment of the 101st Observation Squadron, which began operations from a grass field in Natick, Massachusetts, it soon became apparent that a first-class modern airfield was needed. In 1921, there were only a handful of up-to-date airfields in the entire United States. It was going to be a tough battle to convince the city of Boston that there was a need to create an air-transportation facility close to an urban area that was bordered on one side by the Atlantic Ocean. Further contacts with Washington uncovered the fact that Federal funds could be available to assist in the creation of a suitable airfield for Boston.

A committee of men with aviation backgrounds was formed to study possible locations in the area. The site selected was known as Commonwealth Flats at Jeffries Point in East Boston. The State had improved the area shortly before by bringing in enormous quantities of fill, and only a few small residences would require relocation. My father and Jim Knowles, acting for the 101st, introduced legislation at the state level to support the construction of a modern air facility at Jeffries Point. Their legislation suggested that the city lease the land at a nominal rent to the state. In return, the $35,000 already-appropriated Port of Boston fund could be directed to build runways and erect hangars and maintenance facilities for both military and commercial use. All that was needed was to attain state legislative approval and, through a strong publicity campaign, prove the need. "Boston: Air Guard and Air Port," read the headline of the February 4, 1922 *Boston Evening Transcript*. "The Proposed Airdrome in East Boston Would Be Not Only a Vital Factor in New England's Scheme of Defense from Enemy Attack, but Also the Focus of Many Commercial Passenger Lines."

After a heated debate, the Massachusetts legislature passed the bill to support construction of the airport, although it cut the requested appropriation by $15,000. The Minutemen of the Boston Chamber of Commerce, the members of the Aero Club of Massachusetts, and the Massachusetts National Air Guard all personally solicited local businessmen and raised the necessary additional funds. On September 8, 1923, some 50,000 spectators thrilled to an air meet held at the newly opened East Boston Airport, hailed as "probably the best in the country in its proximity to the business section" of a city. The airport my father helped create is today one of America's busiest: Logan International Airport.

Jim Knowles was appointed as the first Commander of the 101st Observation Squadron. When he moved away from the area to pursue business interests in St. Louis, Woolley was selected to command the unit, a command he kept for five years, the imposed statutory limit. Photos and clippings portray him as an aviation booster, doing anything and everything to promote the cause of flying. He joined his enlisted men at evening lectures in Boston's Old South Armory to discuss the design, construction, and care of aerial machines, and flew with his pilots every weekend. He was an honored guest at the fourth annual ball of the Aero Club of Massachusetts, as were Mrs. J. Randolph Coolidge, Ham Coolidge's mother, and other prominent Bostonians. He continued fund-raising. "Speaking for the officers and enlisted men of our Squadron," Woolley told the press, "I hope an amount will be realized sufficient to establish a fund which can be used in emergency for special tools, parts, and equipment necessary for use in flying, but not covered by State or Federal appropriations."

Piloting a Curtiss JN-4 from the new East Boston Airport, Major Charles H. Woolley flew Massachusetts Governor Channing Cox on his first flight. Special care was taken to provide photo opportunities for the *Boston Herald* news photographers who flew alongside. Later, posing in an aviator coat, leather cap and goggles, the Governor declared, "From now on, I am a confirmed aviator."

During the 1920s, Woolley continued to promote civil as well as military aviation. When the Worcester Airport opened in 1927, he was an honored guest and was presented with an engraved silver cigarette case (although his name was misspelled as "Wooley"); the case survives today in the possession of his grandson, Charles H. Woolley, II. Woolley was also involved with improving the airfield at Squantum in Quincy, Massachusetts, where he had witnessed, in 1910, the first Harvard Aero Meet.

My father became acquainted with Harold T. Dennison, a young Boston architect with an interest in the creation of a commercial airport, and a young aviatrix named Amelia Earhart. Earhart, originally from the Boston area, had learned to fly in California and had purchased her first plane from aircraft designer and entrepreneur Bert Kinner. In 1927, returning to Massachusetts, she was employed as a social worker at Denison House, Boston's oldest settlement home. She flew in the company of local pilots, joined the Boston chapter of the National Aeronautics Association, and became a regular in the *Boston Globe* newspaper columns, which described her as "one of the best women pilots in the United States."

Earhart invested with Dennison and Kinner in the Dennison Airport, which opened near Quincy Shore Reservation Boulevard at Squantum. Woolley was invited to sit on the board of Dennison Airport and Dennison Aircraft Corporation, serving as an advisor to Earhart and her partners when they opened a flying school, operated an air taxi service, and offered for sale the Kinner "Canary" and other civilian aircraft.

No one was aware that quiet preparations were under way for a history-making flight from Boston in the spring of 1928. In the corner of a large hangar at the East Boston Airport, mechanics were busily fitting pontoons to a trimotor Fokker aircraft owned by the Honorable Mrs. Frederick Guest of London, and recently the property of the explorer Commander Richard E. Byrd. Mrs. Guest, formerly Miss Amy Phipps of Pittsburgh, Pennsylvania, who had originally planned to make the flight across the Atlantic herself, financed the entire program. The group assisting Mrs. Guest, who was unable to make the trip, included George Putnam, a publisher as well as a producer of adventure films. This group had approached Amelia Earhart regarding the flight. After she had been interviewed in New York, the group unanimously selected Earhart to fly in the trimotor Fokker, named *Friendship,* and thus become the first woman to make a non-stop air crossing of the Atlantic. The *Friendship* was piloted by Wilmer Stultz; the flight mechanic was Lou Gordon.

Though she was only a passenger on the flight from Newfoundland to the coast of Wales, when *Friendship* landed, Amelia instantly became the world's most celebrated aviatrix, and one of the great celebrities of her time. Earhart recalled Woolley's contribution to the historic flight in her book *20 Hrs., 40 Min.*, published by George Putnam in 1928:

> I'm told it's interesting to know exactly what the outfit included. Just my old flying clothes, comfortably, if not elegantly, battered and worn. High laced boots, brown broadcloth breeks, white silk blouse with a red necktie (rather antiquated!) and a companionably ancient leather coat, rather long, with plenty of pockets and a snug buttoning collar. A homely brown sweater accompanied it. A light leather flying helmet and goggles completed the picture, such as it was. A single elegance was a brown and white silk scarf.
>
> When it was cold I wore—as did the men—a heavy fur-lined flying suit which covers one completely from head to toe, shoes and all. Mine was lent to me by my friend Major Charles H. Woolley of Boston, who, by the way, had no idea when he lent it what it was to be used for. He suspected, I think, that I intended to do some high [altitude] flying.

Major Charles H. Woolley served as Amelia's official escort on her triumphant return to Boston, guiding the world's most celebrated female flyer and her mother through cheering downtown crowds, and then to a formal dinner at the Ritz in her honor. He was the perfect companion for Earhart for this occasion—handsome, gray-haired, and attired in his sharply pressed and bemedaled uniform. She was "Lady Lindy," whose looks and demeanor made her a female version of America's favorite male celebrity, Charles Lindbergh. Earhart was later to marry her publisher, promoter, and most ardent admirer, George Putnam.

My father's minor brush with the celebrity world, and his involvement in aviation affairs—even his position as Commander of America's first National Air Guard—did not, however, pay the bills. His father, naturally, had hoped he would take over the family laundry business, but this was not to be. War had changed him. He had left Boston a twenty-three-year-old student and had returned a seasoned combat pilot.

William Woolley Brooks, a distant cousin in the investment business, introduced my father to the firm of Baker Young & Company, a Boston firm specializing in investment sales. With the urging of the president, Mr. Young, Woolley joined the firm. Focusing on bond trading, he quickly became successful. Though he enjoyed the world of finance, it was not a totally fulfilling world. His ample income allowed him to fly, and to follow other pursuits, which included driving fast and sporty automobiles. Another pursuit at that time was a woman named Alice Spicer.

Spicer, an artist, was part of a circle that swirled from Boston to New York and Paris in the flamboyant post-war years. She was a free spirit—so free, in fact, that it was rumored that after she had first married, she had fallen in love with her brother-in-law and caused the breakup of both their marriages. The Spicer family and the Senior Woolleys were contemporaries and good friends. After her divorce, Alice and my father met through their parents. For several years they carried on a transatlantic romance that brought him occasionally into contact with the Paris avant-garde of the 1920s, including the dancer Isadora Duncan and the F. Scott Fitzgeralds.

Spicer and her world intrigued my father, and during one summer visit, he presented her with a shiny new Fiat roadster in which they toured the south of France. But as much as he thought he cared for the artistic American expatriate, he, himself, was definitely not a member of the "lost generation." Moreover, he did not feel entirely comfortable in Alice Spicer's world. The affair came to an end, which proved to be for the best.

# CHAPTER 19

# Boom, Bust, and Back to the Air

**M**y mother, now ninety-five, lives alone in her town house near the gates of Wellesley College. She is as bright and almost as active today as she was seventy-six years ago, when her friends in Boston told her, "Oh, there's someone we want you to meet. He's a great guy by the name of Charles Woolley, and you two would get along well . . ."

My mother loves to tell the story of going to a party at the well-appointed Beacon Hill apartment of socialite Bobby Winslow. "Charles arrived, having just finished a game of squash, one of his favorite pastimes. The door opened and I can see him now," my mother recounts with a sparkle in her eyes. "He stood there with Bobby and looked around. Then he walked directly over to me and said, 'You're good. Where'd they ever find you?' " That was the beginning of a love affair that was to endure for thirty-five years.

At the time of their meeting, Gloria Grilley was a vivacious nineteen-year-old with fine features and a slim figure. By all reports she was a beauty and a charmer, headstrong and highly independent. She was also the product of a devout Christian Science family.

My grandmother was not enthusiastic about the entrance into her daughter's life of the older, more sophisticated Charles. Gloria had been dating a nice sensible boy from MIT whom Grand-mother had fancied. She had hoped they would marry.

When they first began to see each other, my father was log-ging a number of flying hours on a regular basis. These hours were required to sustain his flying skills, skills essential to main-taining his position as Commander of the 101st Observation Squadron. One day he invited Gloria to join him in a flight. She jumped at the chance to sit behind Charles in the open cock-pit of a Curtiss Jenny. It was her first flight. As they landed, he hit a soft spot in the cinder runway. The next thing she knew, the plane had flipped up on its nose. When she came home, my worried grandmother said, "Gloria, I have enough trouble keep-ing up with you on the ground. You go out with that Charles Woolley and you come home with half a propeller from an air-plane wreck!" It took Gloria a little while after that event to get back into a plane. In fact, for the rest of her life, she was never really fond of flying.

Dad was impressed by Gloria's wit and her good sense, and he was attracted by her thoughtfulness and honesty. Still, my father insisted that he had no intention of marrying. He was a confirmed bachelor.

As reported in the Boston papers, Major Charles Woolley mar-ried Miss Gloria Grilley in a simple ceremony on June 8, 1929.

As newlyweds, they lived in the bachelor apartment on Chest-nut Street in Boston that Charles had previously shared with Sumner Sewall. There, among Charles' friends, Gloria met Amelia Earhart. After chatting easily together for some time, the famed aviatrix asked the young wife of her friend, "What did Charles ever do with his flying suit that I wore across the Atlantic?"

"He returned it to his squadron," she replied. "He felt it was important enough for them to have it as a keepsake."

"Well, I'm awfully disappointed," Amelia confided. "I hoped that he'd keep it for himself."

Charles later owned a fast speedboat similar in shape to an aircraft pontoon, built by the Pigeon Hollow Spar Company of East Boston. Honoring his famous friend, he christened it *Yel-low Peril*, after Amelia's bright yellow Kissell roadster of the same name.

Charles felt it was the right time to leave the investment business and embark on a career with an aviation company. He was generally risk averse, but everything about the economy looked bright. Jim Knowles was climbing the ladder of success in the pharmaceutical industry; Reed Chambers from the 94th was a leader in a new business, aviation insurance. German flyer Ernst Udet and Harold Buckley followed each other into Hollywood and the entertainment business. Buckley wrote screenplays; Udet, after becoming one of Europe's best stunt pilots, traveled to California to continue that profession. Ted Curtis was successful at Eastman Kodak selling movie film to his old wartime flying friend Marion Cooper, who had become a cinema studio head.

In the early days, commercial aviation was considered a risky business. It was said that "Fear and Fare" were the two things that kept Americans from flying. Aeromarine West Indies Airlines, the first American scheduled passenger airline, flew passengers from Key West to Havana, as well as from Miami or Palm Beach to Bimini and Nassau. Called the "Highball Express," it was popular with passengers who were eager to leave American Prohibition laws behind. There seemed to be good reason to fear, especially after two highly publicized crashes. One crash plunged partying passengers into the Gulf Stream near Bimini, where five lives were lost. Another plane crashed into the waters twenty miles from Havana, killing four. Following these crashes, Aeromarine promptly closed its doors in 1923. Aeromarine founder Inglis M. Uppercu noted after its demise that "the one thing sorely lacking by the airlines was backing from Wall Street and large banks. You cannot get one nickel [from Wall Street] for commercial flying."

Unlike European governments, the U.S. Federal Government did little to subsidize the airline industry, but the Post Office Department provided the first financial boost to the industry when it auctioned off airmail routes to private interests in 1925. Juan Trippe, a politically well-connected Wall Streeter who helped engineer congressional passage of the bill authorizing the route allocation by the Post Office Department, headed one of the groups that bid for the first "Air Mail Route No. 1, New York—Boston." Another group from Boston called Colonial Air Transport also bid for that route. The bids were almost identical, so the Post Office told Trippe to combine his interests with Colonial. The two groups merged and won the right to carry mail from Boston to New York at the rate of three dollars per pound of mail carried 1,000 miles. Colonial started operating airmail service between New York and Boston on June 18, 1926. Trippe pushed for passenger service from the beginning and wanted to expand to the Chicago–New York link. The other board members balked at such ambition and bought out Trippe's shares. Trippe left Colonial and went on to found Pan American World Airways, for many years America's only international airline.

In 1926, Sumner Sewall was the New England Traffic Manager for Colonial. One year later, a former mail pilot named Charles Lindbergh climbed aboard the *Spirit of St. Louis*, departed from Roosevelt Field on Long Island, New York, on May 20, 1927, and thirty-three hours later landed at Le Bourget in Paris. The first solo crossing of the Atlantic made Lindbergh an international celebrity, one of the great American heroes of the twentieth century.

Lucky Lindy's crossing, followed by that of Amelia Earhart, did a great deal to convince the public that flying was safe. In 1928, there were only 60,000 passengers, but in 1929 more than 160,000 flew. Investment dollars in airlines grew at an equally astonishing rate. At United Aircraft and Transport, not to be confused with United Airlines, an executive saw his $40 cash investment made in 1926 blossom in three years to more than $3 million. United Aircraft's president, Fred Rentschler, invested $253, which by the spring of 1929 was worth $35.6 million. Investment dollars flooded into the aviation industry.

Sewall and Woolley hoped to enjoy some of the same success. The airline business seemed like a winning proposition. Colonial had one of the most active routes in the country and was a leader in the air passenger business.

Admittedly, there were kinks to be worked out in Colonial's passenger and mail services. Over a six-month period, Colonial had 116 forced landings. When pilots experienced bad weather or mechanical trouble, the mail and passengers had to be delivered by train to their destination. After a trouble-free Boston to

New York (via New Jersey) flight, the short trip from the New Jersey landing strip across the Hudson River to Manhattan often took longer than the Boston to New Jersey leg of flight had taken!

In an effort to increase sales for Colonial, Sumner Sewall introduced some innovative promotions. One was to offer wives free tickets when they flew with their husbands. The promotion was so successful that a grateful Colonial sent out letters of thanks to all the wives who had flown with the airline. Angry letters poured into the office. As it turned out, many of the "wives" had not actually been wives. Sewall cancelled the promotion.

To perform his duties as New England Traffic Manager, Sewall personally welcomed passengers at the East Boston runway and ushered them into the airline offices, which were housed in a building not much more than a shack. The reservation and ticketing system consisted of a telephone and a typewriter with carbon-copy tickets that Sumner pecked out on the ancient Underwood. He then led passengers to their seats in Colonial's three-engine Keystone Patrician aircraft. With fourteen seats, it was the largest passenger plane then operating.

During one flight from Boston to New York, a plane carrying Sewall and other passengers had climbed to about one hundred feet when an engine cut out. The pilot tried to return to the airstrip, but a horse and cart were cutting across the runway. To avoid hitting them, the pilot sideslipped and crashed into a hangar. Slightly shaken, Sumner looked out from the window of the crumpled aircraft and noticed liquid dripping down from the upper wing—gasoline. He also noticed that a corpulent businessman, one of the passengers, was puffing mightily on a lighted cigar.

"Put that out!" Sewall shouted.

"What shall I do with it?" the businessman asked.

Sewall roared, "Swallow it!"

The cigar was somehow safely extinguished and the passengers were transferred to another aircraft without mishap. One passenger asked Sumner, "Are all flights as exciting as this one?"

In 1928 Sewall left his position as Traffic Manager in Boston to become General Traffic Manager in New York for all Colonial services. Woolley left his job as head of the bond department for

Baker Young & Company and signed on as Vice President and Director of Schools for the Colonial Flying Service.

For a few months, he commuted from Boston to New York and worked at the company offices at 270 Madison Avenue. Mother would occasionally take the train to New York for the weekend, or Dad would fly to Boston.

In the fall of 1929, Mother joined my father in Bronxville, New York, the village where I was born on June 6, 1930. I was named *just* Charles Woolley, no middle name, not junior, just plain Charles. My father thought life would be simpler for me with no extra names or initials. Little did he know that twenty years later, the U.S. Air Force would give me three: N.M.I., standing for "no middle initial."

Typical of his sense of humor, Dad loved to tell people, "My son was born the sixth of June, and Gloria and I were married the eighth." Mother recalls, "I always had to explain, 'Yes, but it was the sixth of June of the following year!' "

Their joy with their new baby was tempered by the crumbling of their economic future. Shortly after Charles moved to New York to join Sumner in their new aerial adventure, the stock market collapsed. The airline stock bubble also burst. The industry rapidly consolidated. W. Averill Harriman and Robert Lehman, founders of the Aviation Corporation, a large airline holding company, acquired Colonial and rolled it into a larger entity— American Airways. Amelia Earhart was announced as vice president in charge of publicity and advertising. With the merger, Sumner Sewall was out of a job. A Boston newspaper story reported that:

> Sewall refused to be 'fired' and in a week or ten days was appointed to the American Airways with a somewhat general portfolio. For a month or more he was in charge of disposing of surplus equipment for the whole collection of airlines belonging to the Aviation Corporation . . . As weeks passed and American Airways changed president two times, Sewall found himself with a job but no work to do, and tired of the situation . . . Sewall decided to go down to [his home

in] Maine for the summer . . . Another Bostonian who was left somewhat suspended in the air by the vicissitudes which have marked the Aviation Corporation's history in the past eight months is Charles Woolley, head of Colonial Flying Services. . . . The Aviation Corporation decided to eliminate that phase of operations [with] the result that Woolley too left for Maine . . .

Sumner Sewall began a new career, a career in politics, when he was elected Alderman in his hometown of Bath, Maine, in 1933. From 1934 to 1936 he served as a State Representative, and was then elected State Senator in 1936, serving in that post until 1940. He served as President of the Senate from 1939 to 1940. In 1941 Sumner was elected Governor of Maine, thus preventing him from joining his old pals from the 95th as they donned their uniforms to once again serve in the military. Sewall left the Governor's office on January 3, 1945. In 1946, the U.S. Government sent him to Germany as the Military Governor of Württemberg-Baden.

As for the Woolleys, the three of us spent the summer in South Harpswell, Maine, at the fifty-acre family saltwater farm on the coast that had been purchased in 1928 by my grandparents as their vacation home. That summer on the rocky coast of Maine, unemployed, my father must have thought long and hard about the future. His dreams of a career in the airline business had been shattered, although he was confident he could return to the bond department at Baker Young. He now had a wife and son and needed a place for his family to live. His father had passed away in January of 1930, and his mother offered us the opportunity to move into the large family home in Winchester, the home with room for everyone.

Mother later explained to me, "Your grandmother had the large house in Winchester where, recently widowed, she felt lost and lonely, and she was eager for us to be with her. It meant a great deal to her to have you, her grandson, there in her home. She was a wonderful woman and I was very close to her."

Dad did go back to work at Baker Young, and he began to

make a few small investments. One was in a banana import business that, unfortunately, failed when a large shipment of bananas froze on the Boston docks. He kept his hand in aviation, and served as chairman of the committee to redesign and expand the cinder-covered field at East Boston Airport to accommodate additional passenger flights.

Some of my first childhood memories are of that home at 5 Fells Road in Winchester. The house, which still stands, is a large, three-story structure that was built around the turn of the century. I remember the living room, dining room, pantries, and huge kitchen on the first floor. There were four bedrooms and two baths on the second. And on the third floor, there were two more bedrooms—one for me and one for the housekeeper/cook—and two storage rooms jammed with family "treasures" and trunks of things not in use. I would wander from room to room in this house, and, as boys will do, explore and examine everything.

This house is where my interest in things military began. I recall opening my father's uniform trunk in the attic. Inside were his World War I uniforms, goggles, flying helmet, and beautiful Paris-made boots. I remember picking out of the trunk a strange mask with two isinglass eyepieces, attachment straps at the back of the headpiece, and a gauze nose and mouth covering. It had a strange medicinal, acrid smell about it. I learned later that it was my father's primitive gas mask from his days as an ambulance driver in France.

When I was about five years old, I explored the upper drawers of my father's tall highboy. There I found his war medals and his large, bone-handled folding knife, the knife he had asked his parents to send to him when he was with the ambulance service. Early one evening, not long after the discovery, a tangled knot in one of my shoelaces confronted me. I remembered the knife. I removed it from the drawer, opened it up, bent over, and started to cut my shoelace. The shoelace gave way suddenly, and the knife plunged into my right eye. My mother was not at home. She had gone to the railroad commuter station to pick up my father. My grandmother heard my cries, ran upstairs, picked me up, and carried me into her bedroom and cradled me in her lap. I remember looking out from the window in her second-floor bedroom down over the town of Winchester. It was dark. "Can you see the lights?" my grandmother asked. I still remember the sight of them twinkling in the distance. The wound quickly healed, but my sight in that eye slowly faded, first to a hazy, clouded view, then to just vague light, and finally, to total darkness. I was unaware then that I would never be able to follow my father into the air. I would never be able to see well enough to become a military aviator.

A few years after the incident with the knife, another of my father's wartime souvenirs touched my life once again. It was a Luger, a German officer's pistol that Dad had brought back from the Great War and presented to his younger brother, Jim. The pistol was in the Winchester house; Uncle Jim kept it hidden in a drawer. He had, however, shown me the gun, and in my prowling, I had discovered its hiding place. One day, surrounded by several of my friends, I demonstrated to them how the pistol worked. BANG! It went off—making a very neat hole in the window of my uncle's bedroom! To this day I don't know who was more terrified—me, when I did it, or my uncle, when he found out what had happened. Soon after that incident, my parents, then living in Washington, realized that I needed somewhat closer supervision, and I was unceremoniously shipped to my new home, the house that my parents had recently rented near the National Cathedral.

By the end of the thirties, the veteran aviators sensed that a new war was on the way. They desperately wanted to serve their country in the face of this new threat. In the fall of 1940, there was the annual meeting of the Archie Club, the club of flyers from the Boston area who had actually flown over the lines in France and who had been exposed to Archie. Many members felt that it was once again time to volunteer their services to the Army Air Corps, as they had to the Air Service twenty-three years before. As reservists, it was their duty. And flying and the military were what they loved.

# CHAPTER 20

# Full Circle

I was disappointed when my father started to land the AT6 at Bolling Field, Maryland, in early 1942. The short flight we had taken together had made me realize why he had devoted his life to flying. For me it was a joy, a thrill never to be forgotten. I was sad that our ride together was ending. We were at war. We all had to make sacrifices, even twelve-year-old boys.

I started to lift my goggles from my eyes as we touched the ground. But then, my father accelerated the plane and took to the air once again. What was going on? The engine roared, and the aircraft climbed above our nation's capital. To my amazement and joy, we were airborne once again. "Philadelphia," I heard my father mention through the headphones as he filed a new flight plan. We banked away from Washington and headed north. I was ecstatic. My father and I were still flying together, if only for another precious hour.

Life in wartime Washington was exciting. Each day, I returned home from junior high school, not knowing which of my father's friends would be there having cocktails and talking of men and machines, of wars past and present. Our house in Washington was small, but we did have a guest room. My father's friends often could not find lodging in the overcrowded hotels, so we had that little guest room filled most of the time. My father constantly brought people home, unannounced, for dinner, and poor Mother had to stretch the creamed dried beef or whatever was on the menu. Sometimes friends called trying to locate my father. Mother would invite them to the house for cocktails. On many evenings, when returning from his office, Charles had to ask, "Who is going to be here for dinner tonight?" Among the dinner guests were Harold Buckley, Harold Willis, Waldo Heinrichs, Ted Curtis, and even "Jam" Johnson.

Harold Buckley, now a forty-seven-year-old Hollywood script-writer, returned to the U.S. Army Air Force as an intelligence officer. Promoted to Lieutenant Colonel, he was assigned to the Burma Front in charge of intelligence for a fighter group of P-40s. His wife, Isabel—who, incidentally, founded the first Montessori schools in California—noted, "I could tell from his letters that he was much happier than he had ever been writing screenplays. He wrote me frequently that he had at last found work that completely absorbed him . . . the very tone of his letters disclosed his contentment and deep pleasure over the work he was doing." Jim Knowles told me that it was a good thing for Buckley that he got to Burma. The impulsive Harold had gotten into a fight over a fare with a Washington cab driver. When Buckley landed a solid punch, the cab driver's head hit the curb, and he subsequently died. No charges were filed.

The indefatigable Harold Willis had volunteered once again in 1940 for the American Field Service. He found himself driving ambulances in the deserts of North Africa in support of the British Eighth Army as they struggled with the famed German General Erwin Rommel, the "Desert Fox." Over dinner he enjoyed telling us about his time in the desert. He had the opportunity to visit the French Foreign Legion headquarters and found that he was listed among those Legionnaires who had died in the First World War! Now, in 1942 and out of the Ambulance Service, he was commissioned a Colonel in the Army Air Corps.

Waldo Heinrichs had left his job as a professor of Contemporary Civilization at Middlebury College in Vermont to serve in the U.S. Army Air Corps as an intelligence officer for the Eighth Air Force; while serving he compiled the official history of the 66th Fighter Wing. Ted Curtis became a two-star General with the Eighth Air Force. Career officer Davenport "Jam" Johnson also rose to the rank of General.

In Germany, veteran aviators from World War I led the rapidly expanding Luftwaffe. Second to Adolf Hitler in the Nazi hierarchy was Hermann Göring, a flyer who had scored twenty-two aerial victories in the First World War. Rudolf Hess, another high-ranking Nazi official had been another leading German ace. Ernst Udet, second only to von Richthofen in aerial victories, was finally persuaded in 1939 to join the Luftwaffe as a General. He rapidly became disenchanted with the Nazi political in-fighting and mismanagement and was devastated by the direction of the war. On September 17, 1941, using an old Mexican revolver that was given to him during his movie stunt-flying days in Hollywood, he took his own life.

The principles of air fighting remained the same, but the second air war over Europe was conducted on a much grander scale. Never again would airborne warriors fight on the intimate terms experienced by the adversaries of 1918. Never again would a fighter pilot be able to lock eyes with his opponent or be splattered in mid-air by the enemy's blood. Never again would combatants who dipped their wings and waved at their opposites fight aerial duels. With the deepest respect, von Richthofen, the greatest German ace, had been buried by Australian troops with full military honors.

The principles of the aircraft industry had changed dramatically. The American defense industry of 1918, which had had such difficulty producing aircraft built from spruce, linen, and wire, was in full swing by 1942. It produced for the USAAF thousands of B-17s, B-24s, and B-25s, the most complex metal structures ever built. The next challenge was the logistics necessary to get these thousands of planes and their spare parts overseas and into the hands of America's fighting forces.

To this end, my father found himself working with Major Arthur Richmond, civilians Sam Pryor, Juan Trippe, and other air-route planners. Many of these men, whom he had known earlier, were now involved with Pan American Airlines. As a group they spent most of their time in Central and South America, the Azores, and Africa, preparing routes and airfields for moving aircraft, freight, and personnel to the African and, later, southern Italian theaters of war.

During my father's long absences, Gloria Woolley also donned a uniform as a member of the American Women's Voluntary Services. One of her jobs was to serve as the telephone communications operator at Blair House. An imposing structure directly across the street from the White House, Blair House served as a guest facility for visiting dignitaries from around the world. At one point, General Charles de Gaulle entered Blair House and saluted her. My mother was thrilled. "For a little girl from Boston," she has told me many times, "it was a very exciting experience."

My teen years were spent in Washington, attending local schools and then college. At the height of the Korean Conflict, in January of 1951, I enlisted in the United States Air Force, but was not physically eligible to fly. I was touched when my father attended my swearing-in ceremony wearing his uniform of Colonel in the U.S. Air Force. Thirty-four years after his first enlistment, my father was still serving his country and, through hard work, still keeping up his flying status.

His last assignment for the military returned him to Paris, the city he loved. He was chosen to work closely with the French government and contractors to build a series of housing units for the American military still stationed in France. My mother, as a family dependent, joined him in Paris. They moved into an apartment owned for many years by a president of the Bank of France and maintained for his Jewish mistress. During the war, after the Gestapo had arrested her, he closed the apartment, leaving it as she had decorated it. It was a small apartment, lavishly decorated, full of Oriental antiques and elegant furnishings.

This time in Paris was to be the honeymoon my parents never had. Living in Paris was a delight for my mother. While her Charles was working, she spent hours wandering through Paris's many museums, antique shops, and the stalls along the Left Bank. On weekends, they dined together in the finest restaurants, visited the flower markets, and traveled to the places where Charles had lived and fought those many years before. At that time, my father owned a new DeSoto sedan that the government had shipped to France. The DeSoto was enormous in comparison to the French Renault Deux Chevaux. My father enjoyed cruising majestically with my mother through the streets of Paris, being careful to avoid eye contact with aggressive French drivers. They drove from Paris to villages throughout Europe, from Nancy to Wiesbaden, from Bordeaux to Rome, revisiting many of the places he had known during the Great War.

In 1954, Dad retired as a full Colonel, with over twenty years of active military service. Decorated with the Silver Star for bravery in the First World War, he received the Legion of Merit and later, an oak-leaf cluster for his outstanding service performed during World War II.

For their retirement, my parents chose to settle at the family summer home they now owned, the eighteenth-century saltwater farm in South Harpswell, Maine. They carefully restored and modernized the center-chimney farmhouse, tastefully furnishing it with family antiques and unusual European treasures they had collected during their years in France. Among the family possessions hanging prominently in their home was the treasured portrait by Sir Joshua Reynolds of the English sea captain Charles Woolley, which for 150 years had been passed down through generations of Woolleys.

After completing the restoration of the house, one of the oldest in southern Maine, my father turned his attention to forty acres of untended woods that were part of the family property. With assistance from two local woodsmen, he turned the unkempt forest into an officially recognized tree farm. Working in the woods, and spending hours with several of the local boatbuilders as they crafted wooden lobster boats so essential to the livelihood of coastal Maine, brought him an inner peace. He had spun through the clouds in a Spad fighter plane. He had led a squadron of Curtiss Jennys in the 1920s. He had found success in the world of finance. He had walked across the island of Cozumel, staking out its first airfield. He had loved the world of aviators and flying machines, but South Harpswell was his new world of comparative quiet and contentment. Those with whom he came in contact in this rural community respectfully called him "Colonel." Of course, if one had not been born on the coast of Maine, one would always be considered a "highlander"—an "outsider." But somehow my parents were different; they were accepted and not thought of by locals as "summer complaints," as seasonal residents were sometimes called.

My mother did miss the glamorous active life they had led in the world capitals of Washington and Paris, but she was aware that this was the new life her Charles craved. Still, there was entertainment to be had. They stayed in touch with the Sewalls, who lived in nearby Bath, and Ted Curtis and his wife, who summered at Small Point, just down the Kennebec River from Bath, often visiting their friends during the warm months, traveling back and forth across Casco Bay by boat, a shorter trip than by land. Mother pursued her passion for collecting antique jewelry, which kept her busy, but she did recollect: "After our life in Paris, moving to an isolated rural coastal community in Maine was a great adjustment. I had loved the excitement of living in Paris, and I felt I was too young for retirement, but it was time— Maine was the one place that Charles really wanted to be."

Seven years after retiring, Dad's health began to fail. After extended treatment for heart and circulatory problems, he passed away in June 1962 at the nearby Brunswick Naval Air Station Hospital. In the weeks following my father's death, Mother was filled with indecision about her future. Still a relatively young woman, she felt she should probably leave the isolation of South Harpswell, but she could not bear to leave the home she had created with Charles, the home that contained everything they had loved. On an August evening, two months after my father's death, while dining with friends and discussing her future, a violent thunderstorm passed over South Harpswell. Lightning struck her home, and it burned to the ground. The house had stood for two hundred years, and lightning had never before come close to it!

Everything Mother owned had been destroyed—her home, and the collections of a lifetime; in fact, of many lifetimes. After the fire, Mother returned to Paris for several months, visiting with her many French friends. Returning to Boston, she found a small attractive apartment on Beacon Hill. Her old friend Priscilla Kidder, the owner of Priscilla of Boston, the famed bridal business, offered Mother the opportunity to manage her Newbury Street shop. She enjoyed the work because she loved fashion as well as the happy atmosphere of bridal planning. She remarried and moved to Wellesley, where she lives to this day. "It's been a funny, peculiar life," she loves to say, "but it's never been dull."

Many traces of things that touched my father's life are preserved today. The 101st Observation Squadron, Massachusetts Air Guard, still flies, known now as the 102nd Fighter Wing. At the stylishly appointed offices and archives of the American Field Service in New York City, some of my father's letters are carefully preserved. The students who are sent overseas today by the A.F.S. go not to learn how to change tires on a Model T ambulance and evacuate gagging *poilu* from gas attacks, but to study languages, arts, and economics.

In the National Air and Space Museum stands a Fokker D VII with the characters "U-10" painted on its sides. It is the very machine that surrendered to Sumner Sewall, Alex McLanahan, and Ted Curtis more than eighty years ago. At the United States Air Force Museum at Wright Patterson Air Force Base in Ohio, there is a piece of stiff linen painted with the 95th's kicking mule insignia, which was donated to the museum by Waldo Heinrichs' son. Also on display is the steering column of an early Wright Brothers airplane that I presented to the museum in my father's memory.

Sepia-colored photographs of First Lieutenant Charles H. Woolley stand proudly in our home next to a frame of his pilot's wings, medals, and insignia—mementos my mother had given me soon after my father's death. These bits of metal and cloth are testimony to Dad's life with the military, that part of his life he loved so well.

The name at the end of a long e-mail that arrived late in November 2001 was unfamiliar. The text revealed that it was from a fellow aviation historian, Lee Branch. He was assisting a German researcher, Hannes Taeger, who was searching for information regarding the last fight of Hauptmann Carl Menckhoff, the famous thirty-nine-victory German ace who had been downed by First Lieutenant Walter Avery of the 95th Aero, then captured by the French. Taeger was looking for official combat reports regarding the incident. Branch also mentioned that he was in contact with Menckhoff's son, Gerhard, who worked for World Bank and currently lived in Washington, D.C. Of particular interest to me was to learn that Gerhard was in possession of his father's unpublished wartime memoirs.

I contacted the younger Menckhoff regarding a future meeting, and a few months later, I found myself standing before a lovely brick home some seven blocks away from where I had lived during World War II. I rang the doorbell, and a tall, slender, handsome man opened the door. Gerhard Menckhoff, the only son of the German ace, was about my age and bore a close resemblance to the photograph I had seen of his famous father. He welcomed me into his home, introducing me to his lovely and charming wife, Patti, and Hannes Taeger, the researcher from Dresden. Together, we spent the balance of the day and well into the evening sharing stories and recollections and comparing the lives of our fathers.

Despite the obvious differences, the two great aviators had much in common. Born in Westphalia in 1883, Menckhoff was older than my father. He was a strong-willed, independent character, a maverick of sorts—particularly when it came to military etiquette and discipline. After the war, very much like my father, he found it difficult to give up flying. He had begun an airline that grew to ten aircraft, but then failed during the deep economic depression in Germany. Menckhoff moved on to the world of industrial engineering, and he built a successful commercial-heating design firm that conducted business throughout Western Europe. A man of deep convictions, he had no use for the Nazi movement as it rolled over Germany. In 1938, upon returning from a business trip to Switzerland, Menckhoff was arrested by the Gestapo on charges of bringing unapproved quantities of Swiss francs into Germany. After serving a year of his prison sentence, he was released, and he moved permanently to Switzerland, leaving Nazi Germany behind.

During my stay in Washington, Gerhard proudly showed me his father's photos and medals, furniture, antiques, and paintings brought from the family home in Switzerland to the United States. As I knew, his father had written his wartime memoirs while in prison. Gerhard presented me with a typewritten copy translated into English for my benefit. His memoirs revealed him to be a strong leader, a man of humor, determination, and courage, the very qualities that made him a superb Squadron Commander and thirty-nine-victory ace.

I, in turn, presented Gerhard with my gift; a piece of fabric cut from his father's Fokker, fabric that had been given to me by the man who had removed it, Walter Avery, the American who shot down this famous German flyer. On the last night of my visit, I fell asleep in what I was told was Carl Menckhoff's own bed. I suspect the stern German ace would have been pleased that his son and I had met and had quickly developed a warm affection for each other. Our fathers had been enemies; we were the sons of adversaries, but we were comrades in the search for our common history.

Today, as I stand by my father's grave in South Harpswell, Maine, I am reminded of my flight with him from Washington to Philadelphia. On the way, he performed some gentle aerobatics for my amusement. I was proud of his ability, confident of his skill, thrilled to be his son. After we landed, he gave me a conspiratorial wink and said that the Philadelphia leg of the trip had been an "unofficial" bonus. We were bending what seemed to be unimportant regulations together, just as he and his squadron mates had done in the Great War.

I was reluctant to shed the fleece-lined flight suit, headphones, and parachute, all of which had made me feel so close to my father, so much a part of his world. As the years have passed, I have come to realize how much of the modern world of aviation was created by my father and his comrades, the young men who first traveled to fly in France in 1917.

Over the past forty years it has been a privilege for me to have heard these echoes of eagles and to have been able to record them for future generations. Yes, the eagles have gone, but their brave cries will never be forgotten. Their legacy lives on.

# Descriptions and Diagrams
## of Aerial Maneuvers

All written descriptions were given by First Lieutenant Norman Archibald, 95th Aero Squadron, in his book *Heaven High, Hell Deep*.

## Vrille

This is a diving maneuver to quickly evade an enemy on your tail. Power to the engine is decreased. The nose drops, but is held up by gradually pulling back on the stick. When the plane is about ready to go into a stall, the left rudder pedal is given a quick kick and held there. At the same time, the stick is pulled over and back to the right. The nose then points down, the plane spins rapidly, and altitude is quickly lost. The rudder is then straightened and the stick is put in a neutral and slightly forward position, causing the plane to stop spinning and come out into a glide. Power to the engine is then increased, the stick is pulled back, and normal flight is resumed.

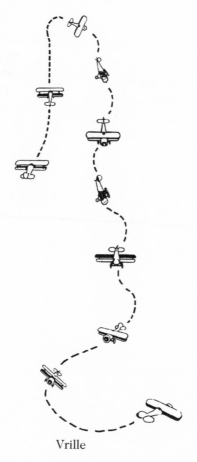

Vrille

## Vertical Virage

This is a maneuver to quickly change the line of flight to the opposite direction. When the control stick is put hard to the left (or
right), the plane is put on its side in a vertical position. When the
stick is pulled back in a circular motion to its original position,
the plane turns and due to its speed and with the engine still under full power, does so without slipping. The *virage* is a quick, effective movement without loss of altitude.

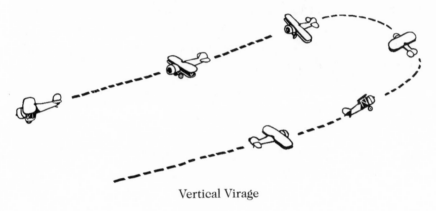

Vertical Virage

## Renversement

This is a more skillful maneuver than a *vrille* and a quicker way of changing direction than a *virage*. At 3,000 feet or more on a level flight with full power, the stick is given a short jerk backward. The nose of the plane quickly rises, the rudder is immediately given a sharp kick, either left or right, and the plane turns over on its back. Power to the engine is decreased and the nose drops. The stick is pushed forward and the plane comes out in a dive. When the stick is pulled back and full power is returned, the plane will be flying in the opposite direction.

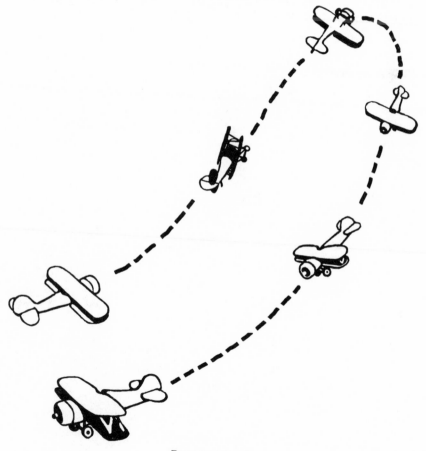

Renversement

## Vertical Side Slip

This is another evasive maneuver used when under attack. Power to the engine is decreased and the stick is slowly moved to the right, causing the plane to turn on its side. In this position the elevator acts as the rudder and the rudder acts as the elevator. As the plane continues to fall, "top rudder" must be given to keep the nose from falling. With the rudder pushed to its limit and the stick forward and over as far as possible, the wings, being perpendicular rather than parallel, give no support and the plane drops in a violent slip. Quickly pulling back on the stick in a circular motion to the position of a normal glide, the plane is brought out of the slip in a spiral. When all controls are returned to a neutral position, straight level flight is attained.

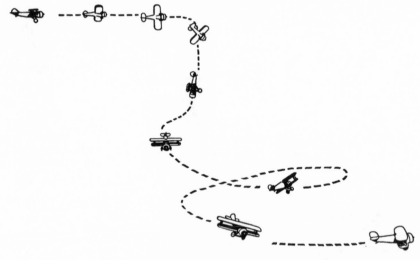

Vertical Side Slip

# Glossary of French, German, Aviation Terms, and WWI Slang

*40 hommes-8 chevaux:* (French) 40 men-8 horses, designation of the load limit for certain military French rail transport cars.

*abri:* (French) A dugout, bombproof shelter.

*ambulance:* (French) A field hospital. *Ambulance* came to designate a vehicle used to transport injured individuals after the work of the American Ambulance Field Service, later the American Field Service.

*Albatros:* German biplanes, reconnaissance and pursuit, manufactured by Albatros Werke GmbH and subcontractors. The Albatros D.Va was one of the most popular German pursuit aircraft.

*Archie:* A derisive term for antiaircraft fire. Archie referred to a London music hall refrain in which a woman fended off an ardent lover with the words, "Archibald, certainly not!"

*Armée de l'Air:* (French) The French aviation branch, also known as *Aviation Française.*

*AT6:* An American aircraft manufactured by North American and introduced in the late 1930s as an advanced trainer and all-purpose aircraft.

*B-17:* Along with the B-24, the most heavily used American bomber in World War II.

*B-24:* See B-17.

*barrel roll:* An aerobatic maneuver in which the aircraft rolls over and over as if flying inside a barrel.

*blessé:* (French) A wounded individual.

*biplace:* A two-seater aircraft

*biplane:* An aircraft with two wings, one above the other. A monoplane has one wing. A triplane has three wings.

*Boche:* Popular name for a German during World War I. Most probably derived from *alboche,* a French slang term for "Allemand," or German.

*bougie:* (French) Spark plug.

*brancardier:* (French) Stretcher-bearer.

*brevet:* (French) Term referring to a pilot who had passed his initial training and had won his wings, but had not necessarily been commissioned as an officer.

*Camel:* The Sopwith Camel, a British pursuit biplane manufactured by The Sopwith Aviation Co. Ltd. and subcontractors. Though difficult to fly, the Camel was extremely maneuverable. Camels destroyed, 1,294 enemy aircraft, more than any other Allied type.

*camion:* (French) Truck.

*Carnet d'Emploi du Temps:* (French) Logbook, used by American pilots to record their training exercises and later flights.

*carnet:* (French) See *Carnet d'Emploi du Temps.*

*Caudron:* French bombing, reconnaissance, and training biplanes manufactured by the Caudron Brothers Company and other contractors. Models included the Caudron G3, Caudron G4, Caudron G6, and the Caudron R11, which was the first three-place twin-engine fighter aircraft deployed by the Allies in World War I.

*chandelle:* (French) An aerobatic maneuver, a corkscrew climb.

*chasse:* (French) Hunting or pursuing an enemy vessel, the term originally used by the French and Americans for pursuit, later termed fighter aircraft.

*Cherchez le Boche!:* (French) "Chase the German!"

*cheval de bois:* (French) Phrase used to describe the bucking and overturning of an aircraft while landing.

*cocarde:* (French) Meaning a small knot or button of ribbons of the national colors, the term applies to wing insignias that displayed national colors. The French cocarde was a circle of blue, then white and red. The English cocarde was a circle of red at the center, then white and blue. The American cocarde had a white center, surrounded by red, then blue.

*Compte-Rendu:* (French) Daily report of military action for the French air service.

*contact:* The term shouted by pilots to warn the mechanic when the ignition switch of an aircraft was turned on as part of the starting procedure.

*coup de main:* (French) Raid for the purposes of reconnoitering.

*Coupez!:* (French) Cut! Warning shouted during aircraft starting procedure when ignition was cut so that the mechanic could turn the propeller by hand and prime the engine. Also used after landing to notify the mechanic that the ignition was switched off.

*Croix de Guerre:* (French) French War Cross established in 1915 and awarded for bravery. When awarded by a regimental, brigade, divisional, or corps commander, it was presented *avec étoile,* with a star; when presented by an army commander, it was presented *avec palme,* with a palm branch.

*Curtiss:* American manufactured biplanes. Models included the JN-3 and the JN-4, also known as the "Jenny." Curtiss JNs were not flown overseas.

*deflection:* Deflection shooting is the aiming of one's fire in aerial gunnery beyond a moving target, to compensate for the movement of both aircraft.

*deHavilland:* Manufactured by the Aircraft Manufacturing Company Ltd. The English-designed DH-4 was the best daylight bomber of the war. U.S. manufacturers produced 3,227 DH-4s fitted with the American Liberty engine. It was the only American-built aircraft to see service in Europe in World War I, 1,885 of which were dispatched to France.

*Dicta Boelcke:* (German) The air fighting rules of the German ace Oswald Boelcke.

*dogfight:* An air combat involving numerous machines operating at very close quarters.

*drachen:* (German) Dragon, the term commonly used for an observation kite balloon.

*dreadnought:* A class of battleship armed primarily with 12-inch to 18-inch heavy guns. Named after the English battleship HMS *Dreadnought*, launched in 1906, which was the first launched of this class.

*dum-dum:* An illegal hollow-nosed bullet, named after the town of Dum Dum near Calcutta, India, where this type of ammunition was first manufactured.

*éclat:* (French) Fragment or splinter of exploded shells.

*essence:* (French) Gasoline.

*Ecole Tir Arien de Cazeaux:* (French) The Aerial Gunnery School at Cazeaux.

*en repos:* (French) In rest billets behind the lines.

*escadrille:* (French) A squadron.

*feldgrau:* (German) Field-gray, referring to the color of German uniforms.

*flaming onion:* A type of antiaircraft artillery shells that, when exploding, looked like a string of onions.

*flight:* In the American air service, a unit of six planes. A squadron was normally composed of three flights, usually designated A, B, and C.

*Fokker:* German pursuit biplanes, monoplanes, and triplanes designed and built for the Germans by the Dutchman, Anthony Fokker. The Fokker D VII, a biplane which appeared at the front in the spring of 1918, is considered to be one of the most effective pursuit aircraft of World War I.

*G 3 or G III:* See Caudron.

*Gnome:* A French-built rotary engine.

*grand blessé:* (French) A seriously wounded individual.

*grillé:* (French) Broiled or burned up; used to describe an overheated engine.

*Halberstadt:* German reconnaissance biplace biplanes. The model C V saw extensive service over the Western Front in the summer and fall of 1918.

*hauteur:* (French) Height, a term used to refer to the altitude test for pilots in training.

*Hispano-Suiza:* The French V-8 engine that powered Spad VII, XI, XII, XIII, and XVI fighters.

*Immelmann turn:* An aerobatic maneuver in which a plane

changes direction rapidly by zooming up and turning on its side. Credited to German ace Max Immelmann, although some claim that the maneuver was in use before the outbreak of the war.

*interrupter gear:* Mechanism attached to a machine gun when mounted just behind the propeller to enable its firing to be timed, or interrupted, to avoid shooting off the aircraft's propeller.

*jagdstaffel:* (German) A German fighter squadron.

*jasta:* (German) An abbreviation of *jagdstaffel*.

*Jenny:* See Curtiss.

*joystick:* Slang term for the control stick in the cockpit of an aircraft.

*kiwi:* Slang term for a non-flying officer, from the flightless New Zealand bird, the kiwi.

*Légion d'Honneur:* (French) A high-level civil and military order instituted by Napoleon in 1802.

*Lewis Gun:* An aircraft and ground machine gun designed by an American, Colonel Lewis, but produced primarily in Great Britain for their use.

*Liberty:* A 12-cylinder, water-cooled aircraft engine developed and manufactured late in the war by a consortium of American companies.

*ligne de vol:* (French) Line of flight.

*manette:* (French) Throttle lever.

*maréchal:* (French) Marshal of cavalry.

*Marlin Gun:* An American aircraft machine gun developed late in the war.

*mauvais pilote:* (French) A bad pilot.

*Maxim Gun:* The German aircraft and ground machine gun invented by Hiram Maxim from the state of Maine. Refused by the American Ordnance Department, but eagerly accepted by the Germans and other European countries.

*mécanicien:* (French) Engine mechanic, or airframe rigger.

*Médaille Militaire:* Instituted by Napoleon III in 1852 and awarded to enlisted men in the French army for bravery.

*mitrailleuse:* (French) Machine gun.

*moniteur:* (French) Instructor.

*nacelle:* (French) Engine covering.

*Nieuport:* A long line of French aircraft built by Société Anonyme des Etablissements Nieuport. The Nieuport 28, the last of the production models, was the first pursuit aircraft piloted by the American 94th and 95th Aero Squadrons in combat.

*Notice de Renseignements:* (French) A police document, or dossier.

*panne de château:* (French) Emergency landing near an estate, used derisively to refer to pilots who managed to have mechanical problems causing them to come to earth in comfortable locations.

*permissionaire:* (French) A soldier on furlough.

*petit voyage:* (French) A short journey, referring to the cross-country test that was part of pilot training.

*petites voitures:* (French) Little vehicles, referring to the Ford Model T ambulances driven by members of the American Field Service.

*pinard:* (French) Slang for the red wine that was part of the French soldier's regular rations.

*pique:* (French) A maneuver placing the aircraft in a vertical nosedive.

*piste central:* (French) Central field of an aerodrome.

*poilu:* (French) Hairy or unshorn, the popular term for a French soldier during World War I.

*Pour le Mérite:* A German decoration instituted by Friedrich II (Frederick the Great), who was so enamored of all things French that he named the medal in French. Popularly known as the "Blue Max," it was the highest decoration awarded to German pilots.

*radial engine:* An aviation engine in which the cylinders are arranged in a circle around a master crankshaft. The cylinders are stationary and the crankshaft revolves.

*réglage:* (French) Adjustment of artillery fire through observation.

*renversement:* (French) Reversing, term used to describe an aerobatic maneuver in which the pilot rapidly reverses direction.

*rotary engine:* A single-valve aircraft engine on which the cylinders are arranged radially around a fixed crankshaft; the cylinders and propeller revolve.

*rouleur:* (French) A short-winged training aircraft, also called a Penguin, that could only taxi and not become airborne.

*Rumpler:* A series of German reconnaissance two-seat biplanes. The Rumpler C IV appeared at the front in February 1917, and the C VII appeared in the winter of 1917. Because of their ability to attain great altitudes, the Rumplers were among the most difficult German aircraft to bring down.

*Salmson:* A French biplace reconnaissance plane built by the Société des Moteurs Salmson. Nine squadrons of the U.S. Army Air Service flew the Salmson 2A2 model. Seven hundred five Salmsons were delivered to the Americans starting in April 1918.

*singe:* (French) Monkey meat, French soldiers' slang for canned beef rations.

*soixante-quinze:* (French) Seventy-five, the famous French seventy-five millimeter artillery piece.

*sous-chef:* (French) Under chief, or assistant leader of a volunteer ambulance section.

*Spad:* A French aircraft manufacturer, Société Anonyme pour l'Aviation et ses Dérives. The Spad XIII was the pursuit plane flown in combat by most American fighter squadrons at the end of the war.

*SSU:* (French) Section Sanitaire [Etats-] Unis, the official designation of an American ambulance section serving with the French army. "U" was used as an abbreviation for United States or American to avoid confusion with SSA denoting an English (Anglaise) ambulance section.

*TMU:* Transport de Matériel [Etats-] Unis, the official designation of an American section serving in the Automobile Service of the French army involved with the transportation of munitions and supplies.

*tracer:* A bullet spaced intermittently among the other rounds in a belt of ammunition that leaves a smoke trail to show the direction of one's line of fire.

*vertical side slip:* An aerobatic maneuver in which an aircraft rapidly loses altitude in a side slip.

*Vickers Gun:* An English machine gun used both on the ground and on aircraft.

*virage:* (French) Turning, or tacking a ship, an aerobatic maneuver in which the aircraft rapidly changes direction.

*vrille:* (French) A spin, an aerobatic maneuver in which an aircraft rapidly loses altitude in a tailspin.

# Sources and Suggestions
# for Further Reading

**Periodicals:**

Air Service Information Circular, Heavier Than Air, *Enemy Aircraft Destroyed by U.S. Army Air Service.* (Washington, D.C.: Director of Air Service, February 7, 1920.)

Ball, Charles H. *The Men Who Flew the Crates.* Boston Traveler, Nov. 15, 1963.

*Boston Herald* undated clipping. *Boston Flier in Africa Learns He Died with Escadrille in 1917.*

*Cross and Cockade Journal, The Society of World War I Aero Historians.* Vols 1–25.

LeShane, Albert A. *Colonial Air Transport, Inc. Part 2* Journal American Aviation Historical Society, Spring 1974.

*Over The Front, The League of World War I Aviation Historians.* Vols 1–17.


**Books:**

Allen, Oliver E. *The Airline Builders.* (Alexandria, Va.: Time-Life Books, 1981.)

Archibald, Norman. *Heaven High, Hell Deep, 1917–1918.* (New York: Albert & Charles Boni, Inc., 1935.)

Blodgett, Mabel Fuller. *Richard Ashley Blodgett, An Appreciation by His Mother.* (Boston, Mass.: Privately Printed McDonald and Evans, Printers 1919.)

Bowen, Ezra. *Knights of the Air.* (Alexandria, Va.: Time-Life Books, 1980.)

Brewer, Leighton. *Riders in the Sky.* (Boston and New York: Houghton Mifflin Company, 1934.)

Bryan, Julien H. *Ambulance 464: Encore des Blessés.* (New York: The MacMillan Company, 1918.)

Buckley, Harold. *Squadron 95: An Intimate History of the 95th Squadron, First American Flying Squadron to Go to the Front in the War of 1914–1918.* (Paris: The Obelisk Press, 1933.)

Campbell, Christopher. *Aces and Aircraft of World War I.* (Poole Dorset: Blandford Press, 1981.)

Campbell, Douglas. *Let's Go Where the Action Is!* Privately Printed by the author (Cos Cob, Conn.)

Clark, Alan. *The Donkeys.* (New York: William Morrow and Company, 1962.)

Cooke, James J. *The U.S. Air Service in the Great War, 1917–1919.* (Westport, Conn.: Praeger, 1996.)

Cooke, James J. *Billy Mitchell.* (Boulder: Lynne Rienner Publishers, 2002.)

Coolidge, Hamilton, Captain. *Letters of an American Airman, Being the War Record of Captain Hamilton Coolidge, USA 1917–1918.* (Boston: Privately Printed, 1919.)

Cutler, Carl C. *Greyhounds of the Sea: The Story of the American Clipper Ship.* (New York: G.P. Putnam's Sons, 1930.)

*Decorations United States Army—1862–1926.* (Washington: U.S. Government Printing Office, 1927.)

Davies, John. *The Legend of Hobey Baker.* (Boston: Little, Brown, 1966.)

Earhart, Amelia. *20 Hrs. 40 Min.: Our Flight in the Friendship.* (New York: G.P. Putnam's Sons, 1928.)

Editors of the Army Times. *A History of the U.S. Signal Corps.* (New York: G.P. Putnam's Sons, 1961.)

Franks, Norman. *Aircraft Versus Aircraft: The Illustrated History of Fighter Pilot Combat from 1914 to the Present Day.* (New York: Barnes & Noble, 1998.)

Fuess, Claude Moore, ed. *Phillips Academy, Andover in the Great War.* (New Haven: Yale University Press, 1919.)

Fussell, Paul. *The Great War and Modern Memory.* (New York: Oxford University Press, 1975.)

Geller, L. D. *The American Field Service Archives of World War I, 1914–1917.* (New York: Greenwood Publishing Group, 1989.)

Goldstein, Donald M. and Katherine V. Dillon. *Amelia: The Centennial Biography of an Aviation Pioneer.* (Washington: Brassey's, 1997.)

Gorrell, Edward S., Colonel, U.S.A., et al. *History of the U.S. Army Air Service 1917–1919.* (National Archives Record Group 120 A.E.F. [World War I] 1917–1923.)

Hall, James Norman and Charles Bernard Nordhoff, eds. *The Lafayette Flying Corps.* 2 Volumes (Boston and New York: Houghton Mifflin Company, 1920.)

Hansen, Arlen J. *Gentlemen Volunteers: The Story of the American Ambulance Drivers in the Great War, August 1914–September 1918.* (New York: Arcade Publishing, 1996.)

Hartney, Lieut. Col. Harold E. *Up and At 'Em.* (Harrisburg, Pa. Stackpole Sons, 1940.)

*History of the American Field Service in France, Vol. I, II, III.* (Boston: Houghton Mifflin Company, 1920.)

Halpert, Stephen and Brenda Halpert. *Brahmins & Bullyboys: G. Frank Radway's Boston Album.* (Boston: Houghton Mifflin Company, 1973.)

Howe, M. A. DeWolfe. *Memoirs of the Harvard Dead in the War Against Germany.* 5 Volumes. (Cambridge, Mass.: Harvard University Press, 1924.)

Kaplan, Philip. *Fighter Pilots: A History and Celebration.* (New York: Barnes & Noble, 1999.)

Livesey, Anthony. *The Historical Atlas of World War I.* (New York: Henry Holt and Company, 1994.)

Lovell, Mary S. *The Sound of Wings: The Life of Amelia Earhart.* (New York: St. Martin's Press, 1989.)

Massachusetts Institute of Technology. *Courses of Study 1915–1916.* (Boston: MIT, 1915.)

Maurer, Maurer, ed. *The U.S. Air Service in World War I: Volume I, the Final Report and a Tactical History.* (Washington: U.S. Government Printing Office for the Office of Air Force History, Headquarters USAF, 1978.)

Mead, Frederick S. *Harvard's Military Record in the World War.* (Boston: The Harvard Alumni Association, 1921.)

Morrow, Jr. John H. *The Great War in the Air: Military Aviation from 1909 to 1921.* (Washington and London: Smithsonian Institution Press, 1993.)

Nettleton, George Henry, Editor: *Yale in the World War,* 2 Volumes. (New Haven: Yale University Press, 1925.)

Nevin, David. *Architects of Air Power.* (Alexandria, Va.: Time-Life Books, 1981.)

O'Shea, Stephen. *Back to the Front: An Accidental Historian Walks the Trenches of World War I.* (New York: Walker & Company, 1996.)

Reynolds, Quentin. *They Fought for the Sky: The Dramatic Story of the First War in the Air.* (New York: Henry Holt & Company, 1957.)

Rich, Doris L. *Amelia Earhart: A Biography.* (Washington, D.C.: Smithsonian Institution, 1989.)

Richards, Henry Howe (editor) *Groton School in the War.* (Groton, Con.: Printed for Groton School, 1925.)

Rickenbacker, Edwin V. *Fighting the Flying Circus.* (New York, N.Y.: Doubleday, 1919.)

Robertson, Bruce, ed. *Air Aces of the 1914–1918 War.* (Letchworth, Herts: Harleyford Publications Limited, 1959.)

Roosevelt, Kermit, ed. *Quentin Roosevelt: A Sketch with Letters.* (New York: Charles Scribner's Sons, 1921.)

Rockwell, Paul Ayers. *American Fighters in the Foriegn Legion 1914–1918.* (Boston and New York: Houghton Mifflin Company, 1930.)

*St. Paul's School in the Great War 1914–1918.* (Concord, New Hampshire: Published by the Alumni Association, 1926.)

Sherry, Michael S. *The Rise of American Air Power: The Creation of Armageddon.* (New Haven: Yale University Press, 1987.)

Solberg, Carl. *Conquest of the Skies: A History of Commercial Aviation in America.* (Boston: Little, Brown and Company, 1979.)

Spick, Mike. *Fighters at War: The Story of Air-to-Air Combat.* (New York: Barnes & Noble, 1997.)

Springs, Elliot White. *Nocturne Militaire.* (New York: George H. Doran Company, 1927.)

Stokesbury, James L. *A Short History of Air Power.* (New York: William Morrow, 1986.)

Ticknor, Caroline, compiler. *New England Aviators, 1914–1918, 2* Volumes. (Atglen, Penn.: Schiffer Military History, 1997.) Reprint.

Vanderwarker, Peter. *Boston Then and Now: 59 Boston Sites Photographed in the Past and Present.* (New York: Dover Publications, Inc., 1983.)

Weeks, Dr. Raymond, et al. *History of the American Field Service in France,* III Volumes. (Boston and New York: Houghton Mifflin Company, 1920.)

Whitehouse, Arch. *The Years of the Sky Kings.* (New York: Doubleday & Company Inc., 1959.)

Winter, Denis. *First of the Few: Fighter Pilots of the First World War.* (Athens, Georgia: The University of Georgia Press, 1983.)

Wolff, Leon. *In Flanders Field: Passchendaele 1917.* (London: Penguin, 2001.)

Woolley, Charles. *First to the Front: The Aerial Adventures of 1st Lt. Waldo Heinrichs and the 95th Aero Squadron, 1917–1918.* (Atglen, Pa.: Schiffer Publishing, 1999.)

Woolley, Charles. *The Hat in the Ring Gang: The Combat History of the 94th Aero Squadron in World War I.* (Atglen, Pa.: Schiffer Publishing, 2001.)

Young, Brigadier Peter, editor-in-chief. *The Marshall Cavendish Illustrated Encyclopedia of World War I.* (London: Marshall Cavendish, 1984.)

Zieger, Robert H. *America's Great War: World War I and the American Experience.* (Lanham, Md.: Rowman & Littlefield, 2000.)

# Index

# Acknowledgments

Our thanks go first and foremost to the family members of the early flyers who are the heroes of this volume, who have generously shared diaries, notes, photographs, and letters of the period.

Research for *Echoes of Eagles* began over thirty-five years ago, and throughout those years, my wife, Nancy Woolley, was a tough critic, staunch supporter, and tireless scribe. Lori Borden has enthusiastically and closely read the manuscript ensuring that a layperson could understand all that *viraging* and *vrilling* eighty-five years ago over the skies of France.

Thanks also go to Mel Brown for his illustrations; Roger Freeman of the Vintage Aviation Historical Foundation for a rewarding day discussing seat belts, airframe structures, and other technical issues; Eleanora Golobic, archivist at AFS International for generously opening her archives and patiently screening historic film footage of the ambulance drivers in France; and Erik D. Carlson, Department Head, Special Collections, McDermott Library at the University of Texas at Dallas.

Finally, we also appreciate the support and encouragement of our agent, Jim Hornfischer, and our editor, Doug Grad.

# About the Authors

**Charles Woolley,** born in 1930, attended schools in the Washington, D.C., area before serving for four years in the United States Air Force during the Korean Conflict. Attached to the National Security Agency, he performed communications intelligence work during his military service. Since a boy he has been active in collecting militaria and pursuing military history. He was a past editor of the *Cross and Cockade Journal of World War I Aero Historians,* is the curator of the Vermont Veterans and Militia Museum, and serves on the Committee of Management of the Anne S. K. Brown Military Collection, Brown University. He is a member of the Company of Military Historians, the League of World War I Aviation Historians, and numerous other arms and militaria collecting groups. In his retirement from a long career in the financial services industry, he lives in a small village in Vermont where he continues military research and active collecting. With the technical and editorial assistance of his wife, Nancy, he has written several books on military matters. On the non-military side, he enjoys restoring and driving antique British sports cars and gets pleasure from sailing and puttering with classic boats on the coast of Maine. His four children and seven grandchildren live in various sections of the United States and, as yet, have not been taken by the love of military history.

**Bill Crawford** is a Harvard educated writer based in Austin, Texas. A frequent contributor to the *Austin Chronicle*, *Texas Monthly*, and a number of other publications, Crawford is the author or coauthor of a dozen books including *Border Radio: Quacks, Yodelers, Pitchmen, Psychics and Other Amazing Broadcasters of the American Airwaves*; *Stevie Ray Vaughan: Caught in the Crossfire*; *Cerealizing America: The Unsweetened Story of American Breakfast Cereal*; *Rock Stars Do the Dumbest Things*; and *Austin: An Illustrated History*. In addition to writing projects, Crawford is the creator of *The Dad Show*, talk radio for dads and everyone who has a dad, and has appeared as a commentator on Fox News Channel, Fox and Friends, MSNBC and C-SPAN, as well as Westwood 1 radio networks and dozens of other radio stations across the country. Crawford lives in Austin, Texas, with his wife, who is a brilliant attorney, and two athletic, hardworking kids.